THE MELTING-POT

broadview editions
series editor: Martin R. Boyne

Israel and Edith Ayrton Zangwill visiting Florida in 1905; third individual not identified (Central Zionist Archives).

THE MELTING-POT

Israel Zangwill

edited by Meri-Jane Rochelson

broadview editions

BROADVIEW PRESS – www.broadviewpress.com
Peterborough, Ontario, Canada

Founded in 1985, Broadview Press remains a wholly independent publishing house. Broadview's
focus is on academic publishing; our titles are accessible to university and college students as well a
scholars and general readers. With over 600 titles in print, Broadview has become a leading international publisher in the humanities, with world-wide distribution. Broadview is committed to enviror
mentally responsible publishing and fair business practices.

The interior of this book is printed
on 100% recycled paper.

PERMANENT   100%

BIO GAS
E N E R G Y

Ancier
Forest
Friend

Library and Archives Canada Cataloguing in Publication

Zangwill, Israel, 1864-1926, author
    The melting-pot / Israel Zangwill ; edited by Meri-Jane Rochelson.

(Broadview editions)
Includes bibliographical references.
ISBN 978-1-55481-243-1 (softcover)

    I. Title. II. Series: Broadview editions

PR5922.M4 2017   822'.8   C2017-906544-0

Broadview Editions
The Broadview Editions series is an effort to represent the ever-evolving canon of texts in the disci-
plines of literary studies, history, philosophy, and political theory. A distinguishing feature of the
series is the inclusion of primary source documents contemporaneous with the work.

Advisory editor for this volume: Colleen Humbert

Broadview Press handles its own distribution in North America:
PO Box 1243, Peterborough, Ontario K9J 7H5, Canada
555 Riverwalk Parkway, Tonawanda, NY 14150, USA
Tel: (705) 743-8990; Fax: (705) 743-8353
email: customerservice@broadviewpress.com

Distribution is handled by Eurospan Group in the UK, Europe, Central Asia, Middle East, Africa,
India, Southeast Asia, Central America, South America, and the Caribbean. Distribution is handled
by Footprint Books in Australia and New Zealand.

Broadview Press acknowledges the financial support of the Government
of Canada through the Canada Book Fund for our publishing activities.

Canada

Typesetting and assembly: True to Type Inc., Claremont, Canada
Cover Design: Lisa Brawn

PRINTED IN CANADA

Contents

Poster for the very first performance of *The Melting-Pot*, in Little-hampton, England, with Walker Whiteside and members of the Zang-will family in the cast. Billy Rose Theatre Division, New York Public Library.

Acknowledgements

I am grateful to many institutions and individuals who have assisted me in producing this edition. First, I wish to express my deepest gratitude to the librarians and archivists who assisted me in using their resources and in some cases granted me permission to reprint, most especially Rochelle Rubinstein, Deputy Director of the Central Zionist Archives in Jerusalem; Vital Zajka, Information Manager in the Archives, Photo Archives and Library, and Gunnar Berg, Project Archivist, at the YIVO Institute for Jewish Research; Susan Liberator and Marilyn Scott, at the Ohio State University Billy Ireland Cartoon Library & Museum; and Barbara Cohen-Stratyner, formerly Curator of Exhibitions at the Billy Rose Theater Division of the New York Public Library. I am grateful to Ana Cabrera-Luna and Karen Medin of the Interlibrary Loan department at Florida International University, and to the libraries of Swarthmore College and Florida Atlantic University, which generously let me borrow microfilms from the Jane Addams Personal Papers collection. The Microforms Department staff at Butler Library, Columbia University, were extremely helpful as I searched for (and found) newspapers difficult to locate elsewhere.

On the Internet, invaluable resources for *Melting-Pot* era documents were Hathitrust.org and the Internet Archive (archive.org), as well as databases such as the New York Times Historical Database, the (London) Times Digital Archive, the California Digital Newspaper Collection, and Chronicling America: Historical American Newspapers. My access to these databases and to all FIU services was enabled and enhanced by my receiving Emerita status as soon as I retired from active employment, and for that I am sincerely grateful to FIU President Mark Rosenberg, Provost Kenneth Furton, and Dean of the College of Arts, Sciences, and Education Mike Heithaus, as well as my former Chairperson, James M. Sutton, and my colleagues in the English Department. I am grateful, too, to Vice Provost Meredith Newman, Dean Heithaus, and Associate Dean Jeremy Rowan for giving me an office on campus with all the equipment I needed to complete this project the year after I retired. The many students at FIU to whom I taught *The Melting-Pot*, most of them immigrants or children of immigrants themselves, have given me insights over the years that have found their way into this volume and have made it a better book.

Among professional colleagues who have helped me produce this book are, whether they know it or not, the editors of past Broadview Editions whom I have consulted and whose books I have used in the classroom, especially Maria K. Bachman, Susan David Bernstein, Martin Danahay, and Diana Maltz. Thanks belong, as well, to Susan David Bernstein and the other organizers of the Harry and Marjorie Tobias Lecture in November 2008, at the George L. Mosse/Laurence A. Weinstein Center for Jewish Studies, University of Wisconsin-Madison, for which I most fully developed my ideas on connections between *The Melting-Pot* and *The Principle of Nationalities*. In addition to those mentioned, I wish to acknowledge the collegial insights and support, for many years as well as recently, of Eitan Bar-Yosef, Lynne Barrett, Nathaniel Cadle, the late David Cesarani, Bryan Cheyette, Phillip Church, Keith Cushman, Marian Demos, Hasia Diner, Todd Endelman, Lilian Falk, Michael Galchinsky, Naomi Hetherington, Tometro Hopkins, Linda K. Hughes, Heidi Kaufman, the late Philip Kleinberg, Shoshana Milgrim Knapp, Mark Samuels Lasner, Geraldine Maschio, Kathleen McCormack, Edna Nahshon, Judith W. Page, Howard Rock, Marsha L. Rozenblit, Jonathan Sarna, Margaret Diane Stetz, Nadia Valman, the late Harry S. Ward, Donna Aza Weir-Soley, and Linda Gertner Zatlin. I am also grateful to colleagues whose names I may have inadvertently omitted.

Rivka Schiller, an outstanding translator, provided important assistance as I worked with Yiddish materials. For friendship, encouragement, and sometimes a place to stay while I did research, I am grateful to Margaret Blank, Marge Greene, Janet Heettner, Deb Kayman, Lisa Okubo, Sharon Polansky, Susan R. Schneider, Eleanor Wagner, and Joan S. Weber (and spouses and partners), as well as many other friends, too numerous to name but not to be thankful for. Mentors including Harriet S. Turner, Dennis Dalton, Diana Postlethwaite, Martha Vicinus, and the late Wayne C. Booth helped me get to the place where I could produce this edition. Kathryn Wildfong and Arthur Evans of Wayne State University Press have long had faith in my research and have brought much of it to light.

My first contact with Don LePan, founder of Broadview Press, was when I sent him an e-mail thanking him for including a section on British antisemitism[1] in the literature anthology *The Twentieth Century and Beyond*. He replied quickly, letting me

---

1   This usage (antisemitism) is becoming preferred in scholarly writing to represent anti-Jewish feeling. The older spelling (anti-Semitism) is maintained in the works of authors quoted or reprinted in this edition.

know he was pleased that I also had found it an important theme, too often overlooked. Next, we met at a workshop on editions he led at a meeting of the North American Victorian Studies Association—a workshop that helped me enormously as I worked on this book. Tara Lowes and Tara Trueman kept the publication schedule on track, and I am grateful to them as well as to everyone else at Broadview who worked on this project. I am supremely thankful to Marjorie Mather and Martin Boyne, the editors who encouraged me to produce this edition and have given me the best possible support along the way, and to Colleen Franklin Humbert, Broadview's extraordinary copy editor, whose fund of knowledge has aided me with obscure references as well as matters of style.

The family of Israel Zangwill—including Shirley Zangwill, Caroline Zangwill, Patricia Z. Holland-Branch, the late Edith Z. Bohanon, and Kevin Bohanon—have helped me enormously throughout my research. They exemplify Israel Zangwill's melting pot in action, as well as his intellect and wisdom. My own family deserves more thanks than I can give in an acknowledgements section. Joel Mintz, Serafima Mintz, Daniel Mintz, Sarah Allison, Samuel Brian Mintz, Karl David Mintz, Burt Rochelson, Eleanor Mintz, and the late Samuel I. Mintz have supported me with advice, encouragement, great ideas, and enduring love.

To four more people who are no longer here, I must give special thanks. My maternal grandparents, Masha and Max Friedman, were among the great wave of immigrants that Israel Zangwill depicted; they were the first to make my opportunities in the melting pot possible. My father, Dr. Eli G. Rochelson, arrived in New York after the great pogrom of the Holocaust; most of the rest of his family suffered and died as a result of immigration restrictions that Zangwill had hoped to prevent. My late father has always exemplified for me strength and resilience. My mother, Pearl F. Rochelson, was the only child of her parents to be born in the United States. She navigated the many worlds of family and heritage with me, with intelligence and grace—and she, along with my father, gave me the gifts of learning and literature. This book is a tribute to them, and to all who seek in new lands, now and in the future, a life free from suffering, violence, and oppression.

Introduction

Most of us have heard the phrase: "This city is a melting pot." "The school is a melting pot." "The audience was a melting pot." These days, we take it as a kind of shorthand to represent a diverse population, from many countries or ethnic groups, assembled together for some common purpose or simply in some common place. Israel Zangwill's play *The Melting-Pot*, first performed in 1908, popularized this phrase that still has positive connotations in discussions of American culture. Yet associations with assimilation, and the word *melting*, itself, have led to controversy from the time of the play to the present. Indeed, Horace Kallen, just a few years after *The Melting-Pot*'s premiere, suggested a model of "cultural pluralism," and in the identity-conscious, multicultural 1960s and 1970s new metaphors arose of the United States as a salad or a mosaic, with individual ingredients keeping their integrity while contributing to a distinctive whole. In 1908, rates of immigration to the United States were high and many Americans feared that these particular newcomers would unalterably change the nation's character. Politicians and others called for restricted immigration and stringent tests for citizenship. Into such a setting came this play purporting to dramatize an ideal, by a Jewish Englishman whose parents had been immigrants themselves to a country that was now enacting restrictions. Thus the history of *The Melting-Pot* and of its author, Israel Zangwill, not only evokes questions about diversity and national identity but also illuminates an era characterized by those eternal partners, anxiety and social change.

Israel Zangwill

Israel Zangwill was born on 21 January 1864, in the East End of London, to Moses and Ellen Marks Zangwill, immigrants from Latvia and Poland. He was educated at the Jews' Free School in the East End and graduated with honours from the University of London. Israel was the second of five children, and his brothers, too, earned reputations in the arts. Louis Zangwill (1869–1938), known as "Z. Z.," was a novelist. Mark Zangwill (1869–1945) was an artist who illustrated some of his brother's fiction, as well as a good deal of other work.

Israel Zangwill was not strict in his religious observance, but he was educated in Judaism and strongly identified as a Jew, making his name as an interpreter of Jewish life. His novel *Children of the Ghetto* (1892) centred on the lives of newly arrived Jewish immigrants to London as well as their more established predecessors in the West End. Commissioned by the newly formed Jewish Publication Society of America, the novel was published in both the United States and the United Kingdom (as would be most of Zangwill's writings) and was translated into many languages. Collections of stories on Jewish life followed: *Ghetto Tragedies* (1893; expanded in 1899) and *Ghetto Comedies* (1907), as well as *The King of Schnorrers:*[1] *Grotesques and Fantasies* (1894), which combined a humorous short novel of Jews in the eighteenth century with stories not specifically Jewish in content. Indeed, Zangwill aimed to alternate specifically "Jewish" work with writings about more general themes and characters. He had begun his career writing for both the Jewish and the general press, and most of the stories he later collected (and some of his novels), regardless of content, appeared first in general-interest periodicals such as the *Idler*, *Cosmopolitan*, and *Harper's*. Zangwill was a member of the Vagabond, Dramatists', and Playgoers' clubs, and he numbered among his acquaintance the writers Arthur Conan Doyle (1859–1930), George Bernard Shaw (1856–1950), H.G. Wells (1866–1946), and Frances Hodgson Burnett (1849–1924), to name those best remembered today. He served as a mentor and friend to Burnett and others, women and men, well-known figures and struggling immigrants alike.

At the start of the twentieth century, Zangwill published his last completed novel, *The Mantle of Elijah* (1900), which, despite its title, has only one Jewish character. Its major themes are pointless colonial war and the rights of women, issues that signalled Zangwill's turn to political work over the next 25 years. He and his wife, Edith Ayrton Zangwill (1875–1945), and her stepmother, Hertha Marks Ayrton (1854–1923), were activists in the British women's suffrage movement; Israel himself gave talks and wrote essays for the radical Women's Social and Political Union, the Men's League for Women's Suffrage, and the Jewish League for Women's Suffrage. Edith, whom Zangwill married in 1903, came from an intellectually prominent as well as activist family. She was the daughter of W.E. (William Edward) Ayrton (1847–1908), a professor of electrical science at Cambridge, and Matilda Chaplin Ayrton (1846–83), a pioneer in women's medical education and practice, who died during Edith's child-

---

1 Yiddish: beggars.

hood. Hertha Ayrton, Edith's stepmother, was a Jewish woman who had studied mathematics at Girton College, Cambridge, and became a scientist, inventor, and suffragette. (Despite her original name of Phoebe Marks, Hertha does not seem to have been related to Zangwill's mother's family.) Edith and Israel were both close to Hertha, and Edith was also an author, publishing numerous essays and several novels. The protagonist of Edith's *The Call* (1924) is a suffragette and scientist based on Hertha. Israel's ideas on war and peace found expression in a number of his plays, in particular *The War God* (1911), *The Cockpit* (1921), and *The Forcing House* (1922). Away from the stage, Zangwill was an early member of the Union of Democratic Control, an organization founded to protest Britain's entry into World War I without parliamentary approval. *The Melting-Pot*, as I will discuss, is significantly connected to Zangwill's ideas about the wars of Europe.

Zangwill's third major area of activism, however, is also connected to his 1908 play. Zangwill was an early Zionist, committed to establishing a homeland for the Jews in Palestine at least as early as 1895, when Theodor Herzl (1860–1904), founder of the modern Zionist movement, came to London. Zangwill introduced Herzl to the Maccabaeans, a group of Jewish professionals and intellectuals, and attended several Zionist congresses in Switzerland. However, when Britain offered the Zionists the possibility of an autonomous homeland in East Africa in 1903, Herzl considered the idea and Zangwill embraced it even more enthusiastically, even though it would enmesh the Jews in the British colonial system. When Herzl died in 1904, the great majority of Zionists, particularly in Russia, resolved that only Palestine could be a cultural and spiritual home for the Jewish people, and eventually the British government withdrew the offer. Zangwill and Herzl both were well aware of increasing violence against Jews in the Russian Empire; 1903 was also the year of the Kishinev pogrom (see below), which has been viewed as a motivating force behind both men's considerations.[1]

After Herzl's death, Zangwill saw little prospect of the Zionists obtaining Palestine from the Sultan of the Ottoman Empire (nor, later, from the British Crown). Thus he founded the Jewish Territorial Organization (known as the ITO) in 1905 "to procure a territory upon an autonomous basis for those Jews who cannot or

---

1   Monty Noam Penkower, "The Kishinev Pogrom of 1903: A Turning Point in Jewish History," *Modern Judaism* 24.3 (Oct. 2004): 191–92.

will not remain in the lands in which they at present live."[1] He insisted on the voluntary nature of repatriation to such a land, and he viewed the American melting pot as an alternative for those who did not wish to live in a Jewish state. Zangwill sent expeditions to places as far-flung as Cyprus, Cyrenaica (a region of Libya), Angola, Canada, Mexico, and Australia, and while his efforts had some promising moments they were ultimately unsuccessful at creating an autonomous Jewish land.[2] In 1908, when *The Melting-Pot* was first produced, the ITO had been working for two years with Jacob Schiff's Jewish Immigrant Information Bureau to resettle Russian Jews in the United States through the Texas port of Galveston, which had recently experienced a major hurricane and was eager for the shipping business. Galveston was also an attractive port to those Americans who feared an increased number of Jewish immigrants in the cities of the Northeast; to allay anti-Jewish and anti-immigrant fears, Schiff had promised that he would resettle these new immigrants in the West and other areas of small Jewish population.[3] After bringing in approximately 10,000 immigrants, the project ended in 1914. Thus while Zangwill worked on his play promoting America as a welcoming home for Russian Jews, he was also doing all that he could in the practical realm to find actual places of refuge for them in the United States and elsewhere.

The Melting-Pot and Immigration Debates

Israel Zangwill wrote *The Melting-Pot* during the successful theatrical runs of *Merely Mary Ann* (his most financially successful play) and *Nurse Marjorie*. Neither of these plays had any Jewish

---

1   From the ITO manifesto, quoted by Zangwill in "A Land of Refuge" (1907), *Speeches, Articles and Letters of Israel Zangwill*, ed. Maurice Simon (London: Soncino, 1937), 234. ITO was an acronym either for the "official" title, International Territorial Organization (a name that was hardly ever used by the group) or, possibly, for the Yiddish-language title.

2   For discussions of Zangwill's and other Jewish efforts to obtain a state outside of Palestine, see, for instance, Adam Rovner, *In the Shadow of Zion: Promised Lands Before Israel* (New York: New York UP, 2014); Laura Almagor, "Forgotten Alternatives. Jewish Territorialism as a Movement of Political Action and Ideology, 1905–1965" (PhD Dissertation, European University Institute, Florence, 2015); Robert Weisbord, *African Zion* (Philadelphia: Jewish Publication Society of America, 1968).

3   See Meri-Jane Rochelson, *A Jew in the Public Arena: The Career of Israel Zangwill* (Detroit: Wayne State UP, 2008), 152–53.

content, and his previous play on a Jewish theme, *Children of the Ghetto* (1899), had only moderate success in the United States and closed after seven performances in London. The success of his "non-Jewish" dramas may have convinced Zangwill to try his hand at a Jewish subject again, and events in Europe as well as his work for the ITO would have moved him to tackle the subject of immigration. In 1905, the British Parliament had passed the Aliens Act, which restricted immigration of people from outside the British Empire. Since the greatest numbers of aliens entering Britain at the time were Jews from the Russian Empire, it was clearly aimed at them. Jews still entered Britain until 1914 (when World War I started), but in greatly reduced numbers. A much more stringent law adopted in 1919 ended Jewish immigration for years to come. In the United States, the 1890s saw an extremely nationalistic "nativist" movement that first sought to limit citizenship to speakers of English and later sought to restrict immigration itself. What followed upon fears of immigrant radicalism and anti-Catholic feeling in earlier years was, as described by historian John Higham, "the old idea that America belongs particularly to the Anglo-Saxon race."[1] The stereotype of Jews as greedy international capitalists had led to antisemitic[2] violence in the 1880s, especially in the American South; now northeasterners began to distinguish between the good "old" immigrants from northern Europe (regions and nations such as Scandinavia, Britain, and Germany) and the problematic "new" immigrants from southern and eastern Europe (Italians, Jews, Greeks, and Slavs). This distinction is emphasized by those opposed to keeping the doors open, such as Edward A. Ross (Appendix F2), while those who approved immigration, such as Horace Kallen (Appendix G2), placed new and old immigrants on an equal plane with each other.

Ross's arguments were founded in the so-called science of eugenics, developed by the British scholar Sir Francis Galton (1822–1911) in the 1880s. Galton classified the varieties of human populations according to physical characteristics and assigned value to the characteristics and the population groups. His ideas became widely accepted in the scientific community, even among Jewish theorists such as the Anglo-American folklorist Joseph Jacobs (1854–1916) and the Italian criminologist Cesare Lombroso (1835–1909). Eugenicists such as Ross advocated ways to increase the number of members of so-called desir-

---

1 John Higham, *Strangers in the Land: Patterns of American Nativism 1860–1925* (1955; New Brunswick, NJ: Rutgers UP, 1988), 95.
2 See p. 10, n. 1.

able races in the population and to reduce the number of "undesirables." In the United States such ideas informed the Chinese Exclusion Acts of the 1880s, which were not fully repealed until 1943 (see Appendix F). Later, Ross and others encouraged the old immigration from western and northern Europe, while denigrating the newer, larger numbers of immigrants from southern and eastern Europe—Jews, Italians, Greeks, and Slavs. Eugenic classifications thus determined the restrictive quotas in US immigration laws of 1921 and 1924, and to some extent underlay the health inspections and resulting rejections at Ellis Island, established in 1890 as the first federal immigrant inspection station (see Appendix D).

Zangwill saw the debates on both sides of the Atlantic and feared that doors might close in America, too. As he worked with Jews in London's East End to find refuge through the ITO for those suffering in Russia, he saw America as the most likely alternative to a Jewish homeland—a point, indeed, that he makes clear in the play itself, as well as in his debate with Jewish business leader Daniel Guggenheim on "melting-pot" intermarriage (see Appendix B1). Zangwill's clear and immediate practical purpose was furthered by the "melting pot" image itself. If nativists felt that the "old" Anglo-Saxon immigrants were most likely to assimilate, Zangwill's play would show that assimilation need not be limited to that group. As Higham put it, Zangwill "attached a vivid symbol to the old assimilationist ideal of American nationality. America [...] was God's fiery crucible, consuming the dross of Europe and fusing all of its warring peoples into 'the coming superman.'"[1] Although complete assimilation to an "American" norm is no longer generally seen as an ideal—nor is an Anglo-Saxon America the norm—it was the goal promoted by those in power who longed for their old America, and it was indeed embraced by many Jewish immigrants, as Mary Antin's *The Promised Land* demonstrates (see Appendix G1). *The Melting-Pot* was intended to show that the "new" immigrants could be Americans too, and in new ways. The legislative restriction that Zangwill feared was forestalled for a little while in the United States. However, two years before Zangwill's death, the Johnson-Reed Act of 1924 put in place a quota system that favoured the "good" immigrants of northern Europe over the stigmatized "bad" from the south and east, most tragically limiting the immigration of Jews from that time until after the Holocaust.

---

1   Higham 124.

Although his play popularized the phrase, Israel Zangwill did not invent the term "the melting pot." Werner Sollors, in his groundbreaking study *Beyond Ethnicity* (1986), recounted the earliest use of at least half the phrase in Michel Guillaume Jean de Crèvecœur's[1] 1782 *Letters from an American Farmer*: "Here individuals of all nations are melted into a new race of men, whose labours and posterity will one day cause great changes in the world."[2] C.J. Taylor's cartoon "The Mortar of Assimilation" (see Appendix F1) is an 1887 image of America as a cook, possibly melting (although apparently just stirring) Americans of many ethnicities together, except for the Irish—"the One Element that Won't Mix." Philip Gleason cites similar nineteenth-century instances of the metaphor in Ralph Waldo Emerson (1803–82) and Frederick Jackson Turner (1861–1932), but he confirms, as well, "that the melting pot symbol did not go into general usage until the presentation of Zangwill's play."[3]

Zangwill himself envisions the melting pot as a crucible, the kind used by chemists to melt metals together into new substances, or the kind used by alchemists to melt base metals into gold. Indeed, at one point Zangwill had wanted to title his play *The Crucible*, but after considering the possible obscurity of the term and other current works with that name, he came to the title we now know well.[4] The idea of assimilation evoked in the image, as well as the plot device of interreligious romantic love, prompted debates in the Jewish community that are reflected in the excerpts in Appendix B and in Kallen's "Democracy Versus the Melting-Pot," abridged in Appendix G2. Henry Ford (1863–1947), who became known in the 1920s as a virulent anti-semite, used a giant melting pot onstage in 1917 in a pageant for graduates of his English School, showing how its pupils lost all their ethnic distinctiveness and became Americans indistinguishable from one another.[5] This type of enforced conformity, which Ford saw as ideal for his immigrant workforce, was something that many Jews feared. A small minority wherever they had lived, Jews were often persecuted and oppressed. Even in western

---

1 Also known as J. Hector St. John de Crèvecœur (1735–1813).
2 Quoted in Werner Sollors, *Beyond Ethnicity: Consent and Descent in American Culture* (New York: Oxford UP, 1986), 75–76.
3 Philip Gleason, "The Melting Pot: Symbol of Fusion or Confusion?," *American Quarterly* 16.1 (1964): 23.
4 Edna Nahshon, ed., *From the Ghetto to the Melting Pot: Israel Zangwill's Jewish Plays* (Detroit: Wayne State UP, 2006), 213–14.
5 Sollors, *Beyond Ethnicity* 89–91.

European countries, where they may have achieved political rights, they remained quintessential "others." Yet their unique religious and cultural identities (and the two are not always easy to disentangle) have historically been a source of strength and survival for the Jewish people. Thus Zangwill sought to reassure Jewish audiences and readers that becoming part of the melting pot did not require complete assimilation.

In his Afterword to the published version of the play, reprinted as part of his text in this volume, Zangwill explains that "the process of American amalgamation is not assimilation or simple surrender to the dominant type, as is popularly supposed, but an all-round give-and-take by which the final type may be enriched or impoverished" (p. 172). He supports this important statement with evidence from the play: it does not take long, he notes, for the mildly antisemitic Kathleen of Act I to learn Yiddish and celebrate Purim. By referring to (and opposing) "simple surrender to the dominant type," Zangwill rejected the most common understanding of assimilation in his time, the idea that newcomers would adapt to and become part of what Russell Kazal refers to as an "Anglo-American core" and what Milton Gordon, in 1964, terms "Anglo-conformity."[1] In Zangwill's view, immigrants experiencing the melting pot would not conform to a pre-existing Anglo-Saxon type. Indeed, Gordon names "the melting pot" as a second type of American assimilation that retains elements of Zangwill's own definition—although, unlike Zangwill, who believed that "melting" did not require "gamic interaction" (p. 175), Gordon saw the melting pot as "a biological merger of the Anglo-Saxon peoples with other immigrant groups and a blending of their respective cultures into a new indigenous American type."[2]

For Jewish-American philosopher Horace Kallen (1882–1974), even this degree of blending was too much. Asserting that "whatever else [the immigrant] changes, he cannot change his grandfather" (Appendix G2, p. 265), Kallen proposed the idea of "cultural pluralism," a condition in which Americans can retain those aspects of their original cultures that have meaning for them, so that ethnic newspapers, clubs, and languages can flourish even as

---

1   Russell A. Kazal, "Revisiting Assimilation: The Rise, Fall, and Reappraisal of a Concept in American Ethnic History," *The American Historical Review* 100.2 (Apr. 1995): 437; Milton M. Gordon, *Assimilation in American Life: The Role of Race, Religion, and National Origins* (New York: Oxford UP, 1964), 85.

2   Gordon 85.

immigrants become part of American life. In such a situation, Kallen writes, "Americanization has not repressed nationality. Americanization has liberated nationality" (p. 267). Kallen first used the term "cultural pluralism" in 1924, but the concept is central to his 1915 essay, abridged in Appendix G2. Kallen's "cultural pluralism" becomes Gordon's third and final model of immigrant assimilation.[1]

Kallen's essay is framed as a review of a book by Edward A. Ross, a sociologist who approved of "Anglo-conformity" but, influenced by eugenic theory, favoured restricting immigration by those who might not easily conform (see Appendix F2). Thus Kallen posits harmony against what he saw as the "unison" proposed by Ross, as well as by others who favoured a melting pot that would produce cultural blending:

At the present time there is no dominant American mind. Our spirit is inarticulate, not a voice, but a chorus of many voices each singing a rather different tune. How to get order out of this cacophony is the question for all those who are concerned about those things which alone justify wealth and power, concerned about justice, the arts, literature, philosophy, science. What must, what *shall* this cacophony become— a unison or a harmony? (p. 266; emphasis in original)

As the title of his essay indicates, Kallen viewed the repression of ethnic identifications as anti-democratic. In the same spirit, the idea of cultural pluralism took hold in the last half of the twentieth century through ethnic pride movements as against melting-pot ideology, which, as Daniel Greene explains, "became a shorthand description both for complete assimilation and for the blending of various cultures" in one.[2] However, while the extremes of Kallen's and Zangwill's positions may differ, they surely meet in the middle, in the image of a harmonious symphony used by both to represent American multicultural life.

---

1 Randolph Bourne (1886–1918) offered views similar to Kallen's in a 1916 essay titled "Trans-National America." He points out that "the failure of the melting-pot, far from closing the great American democratic experiment, means that it has only just begun. Whatever American nationalism turns out to be, we see already that it will have a color richer and more exciting than our ideal has hitherto encompassed" (*Atlantic Monthly* 118 [July 1916]: 93).

2 Daniel Greene, *The Jewish Origins of Cultural Pluralism: The Menorah Association and American Diversity* (Bloomington: Indiana UP, 2011), 75.

At this point some readers may wonder why "ethnicity" in these early-twentieth-century discussions seems limited to immigrants from other nations, and those predominantly European. In fact, immigration from Asia was a highly contested issue in the years in question, with US policy seeking to accommodate the needs of business for contract workers with, to be blunt, racist fears of Asian immigrants desiring citizenship (see Appendix F). This policy only began to change in 1943. The vast expansion of immigration from Latin America took place mostly after 1960.[1] However, African Americans, considered an ethnic group today, tended to be ignored by immigration theorists, although Zangwill includes blacks, Asians, and immigrants from the tropics in David Quixano's "crucible" speeches. Most theorists of the time tended to dismiss African Americans as a historical anomaly of the South, an omission that W.E.B. Du Bois (1868–1963) sought to redress in his own writings (see Appendix G3). To Kallen, in the American South "the descendants of the native white stock [...] live among nine million negroes, whose own mode of living tends, by its mere massiveness, to standardize the 'mind' of the proletarian South in speech, manner, and the other values of social organization" (pp. 264–65). He writes that Ross ignores both these whites and blacks, and then Kallen himself omits African Americans, at least in this essay, when discussing the pluralistic America he envisions. African Americans, however, understood that a preference for white labour over black could make immigrants a threat to their own well-being. In the Epilogue to his 1990 biography of Israel Zangwill, Joseph Udelson notes many parallels in the lives of Zangwill and Du Bois, each of whom, in Du Bois's term, experienced the "double-consciousness" of the member of a minority group, the "sense of always looking at one's self through the eyes of others, of measuring one's soul by the tape of a world that looks on in amused contempt and pity."[2] Both Zangwill and Du Bois represented their people at the idealistic Universal Races Congress held in London in 1911. However, in American discussions of ethnicity at that time, Jews, as immigrants, came to have the

---

1 David G. Gutierrez, "An Historic Overview of Latino Immigration and the Demographic Transformation of the United States," *American Latino Theme Study: Immigration*, https://www.nps.gov/heritageinitiatives/latino /latinothemestudy/immigration.htm.

2 W.E.B. Du Bois, *The Souls of Black Folk* (1903), ed. Henry Louis Gates Jr. and Terri Hume Oliver (New York: Norton, 1999), 11.

status of other European newcomers, often through the efforts of Jewish writers such as Zangwill and Kallen. The work of Du Bois and others in asserting the rights of black Americans would take longer to complete.

Introducing Du Bois into the discussion, of course, raises the question of differences between ethnicity and race. In his introduction to *Theories of Ethnicity*, Werner Sollors points out that in 1988, sociologist Milton Gordon presented ethnicity as a larger concept that includes race, while indicating that both the physical characteristics used to define race and the cultural phenomena that make up ethnicity rest largely on "perception."[1] More affirmatively, in 1998 the American Anthropological Association issued a statement explaining that race is entirely a social construct, not biological, and that distinctions between one "race" and another have generally been devised by those in power to justify the oppression of groups unlike their own. The term continues to have practical meanings and consequences in a world where racism, if not "race," exists. In 1908, when the Jews and other groups were often described as races, the word tended to imply common ancestry or heritage—in short, ethnicity—but often, too, with a connotation of separateness or otherness. We see such usage frequently in *The Melting-Pot* and in contemporary discussions of the play.

Additional Contemporary Contexts

The Kishinev Pogrom

It is a little odd to use today's standard English spelling of Kishinev. In 1903, the time we are discussing, the standard spelling in Britain and America was Kishineff. Today, those living in the capital of Moldova call their city Chişinău. But regardless of how the name of the town is spelled, its significance today, for many, derives from a major act of violence against its Jewish community on Easter Sunday and Monday in 1903. The literal meaning of the word *pogrom* in Russian is destruction or devastation. However, its meaning since the anti-Jewish riots of 1881 and 1882 has been "an outbreak of mass violence directed against a minority religious, ethnic, or social group"—specifically, in the context of the nineteenth and twen-

---

1 Werner Sollors, ed., *Theories of Ethnicity: A Classical Reader* (New York: New York UP, 1996), xxx.

tieth centuries, an outbreak of such violence against Jews in Russia or elsewhere.[1]

Although many American Jews claim that their ancestors came to the United States to escape pogroms, that answer is only in part accurate. As John Klier points out, pogroms in the Russian Empire prior to 1881 (when they intensified after Jews were falsely blamed for the assassination of Tsar Alexander II) were scattered and relatively few in number, and they destroyed property more often than human lives. Klier and other scholars, such as Lloyd Gartner, have explained that Russia's wars and revolutions of 1905, economic pressures, and occupational and residential restrictions (especially after the May Laws of 1882),[2] combined with open borders in nations such as the United States and United Kingdom, encouraged the major wave of Russian Jewish immigration that peaked around 1906 in both England and the United States.[3] Yet that date also suggests an important psychological effect of the Kishinev pogrom, in particular. The death toll in Kishinev, which has been estimated at between 49 and 51, was unprecedented; 500 people were injured, and one in three buildings was damaged.[4] As word spread to Jewish communities throughout the Pale of Settlement (which included the Baltic areas as well as Bessarabia, where the pogrom took place), fears of violence increased.

In 1903, Jews made up one-third to one-half of the population of Kishinev, and relations between the Jewish and non-Jewish communities had been fairly good. Historians such as Edward Judge,

---

1 John Klier, "Pogroms," *YIVO Encyclopedia of Jews in Eastern Europe*, http://www.yivoencyclopedia.org/article.aspx/Pogroms.

2 The May Laws were a series of restrictions put in place by the government of Tsar Alexander III (1845–94), creating regulations for when and how Jews could transact business and where they could live, followed by other laws that restricted access to education and professions. The restrictions were meant to be temporary, but they lasted until the 1917 Russian Revolution.

3 Lloyd P. Gartner, "The Great Jewish Migration 1881–1914: Myths and Realities," Kaplan Centre Papers (Cape Town: U of Cape Town, 1984), rpt. in Gartner, *American and British Jews in the Age of the Great Migration* (London: Vallentine Mitchell, 2009); Rita James Simon, *In the Golden Land: A Century of Russian and Soviet Jewish Immigration in America* (Westport, CT: Praeger, 1997), 3.

4 J.J. Goldberg, "Kishinev 1903: The Birth of a Century. Reconsidering the 49 Deaths that Galvanized a Generation and Changed Jewish History," *The Forward* (4 April 2003): n.p.; Edward H. Judge, *Easter in Kishinev: Anatomy of a Pogrom* (New York: New York UP, 1992), 76.

Klier, and Monty Noam Penkower confirm the origins of the Kishinev pogrom in an accusation of blood libel when a fourteen-year-old Christian boy went missing in the nearby town of Dubossary. The idea of "blood libel" or "ritual murder" dates to early medieval Europe, when Jews were first accused of killing Christian children to use their blood in religious rituals, specifically in baking matzah for Passover. The accusation has no basis; in fact, Jews are forbidden to consume any human flesh or blood, and the laws of keeping kosher require that as much blood as possible be removed from meat before cooking. Yet many blood libels have been recorded throughout the centuries, resulting in the arrests and murders of innocent Jews. The most famous case of the twentieth century was the charge against Mendel Beilis, a Russian Jew, in 1913. He was acquitted, but, as Zangwill points out in Appendix D of *The Melting-Pot*, Beilis's life remained unsafe in Russia, and ultimately he emigrated to the United States. The Dubossary case took place in February 1903, two months before the Kishinev pogrom. When the boy's body was found it underwent two autopsies—one by a Jewish medical examiner and one by a Christian—and both confirmed that blood had not been drained; eventually, the boy's uncle was found guilty of the murder. However, the nationalistic newspaper *Bessarabets*—which had recently appointed a new and highly anti-semitic editor—circulated all the rumours, and Governor Rudolf von Raaben (1843–1917), urged to take action, did little to quell these rumours or to protect the Jews, a devastating pattern that would continue during the pogrom.[1]

The ritual murder allegation, along with other rumours, fed violence that began in Chuflinskii Square, where a small carnival had been set up and where Christians, many of them drunk, gathered after church services. Young hooligans joined them as they called for attacks on Jewish homes and businesses. Although for a long time it was believed that the tsar and his government were behind all the pogroms, recent scholarship has confirmed that this was not the case; the violence was indigenous in origin and the tsar had no interest in promoting civil unrest.[2] Still, the patterns of attack in Kishinev seemed to be well organized, suggesting that the attacks were not entirely spontaneous and had been planned in advance by the rioters themselves.[3] On the

---

1   Judge 41–47.
2   See Klier.
3   Judge 51.

second day, rape, murder, mutilation, and other physical violence took over, along with continued attacks on property. Von Raaben remained passive, and soldiers who had been called in to stop the violence received no orders; many Jews and Christians believed the soldiers were there to protect Christian property. Other, seemingly more respectable townspeople often encouraged the rioters and murderers, and some attacks even continued into Tuesday, although it was late on Monday when the governor finally ordered the military to stop the riots by force.[1]

Thus Zangwill's portrayal of Baron Revendal's role in the pogrom is not based in fact; the rioters were largely working-class rather than noble, and, although some soldiers may have joined in, most simply did nothing to aid the victims. However, the "von" in von Raaben signifies noble ancestry, and the distance in sound between Revendal and Raaben is small. Zangwill may have chosen the Baron's name to implicate the governor who allowed the pogrom to happen. As to the atrocities of the pogrom, Zangwill's descriptions are close to the facts. For example, he is correct in having David describe feathers filling the air; every Jewish family had at least one featherbed, a feather-filled mattress or mattress topper made by hand and a prized possession, and the marauders slit open featherbeds and pillows. The result appears in contemporary newspaper articles and in the long poem by Chaim Nachman Bialik, "In the City of Slaughter" (see Appendix C4). Bialik, a young Hebrew poet who lived in Odessa, a city in southern Ukraine that had experienced the pogroms of the 1880s, was sent to Kishinev to report on the catastrophe. His poem helped spread news of the horror and energized young Jews in Russia who soon became part of the 1905 revolutionary movements. Worldwide newspaper coverage led to protests and relief committees formed by Jews and their allies in a number of countries. In the United States, President Theodore Roosevelt supported a petition organized by a Jewish group to be sent to the Russian government, which ultimately refused to receive it.[2]

"In the City of Slaughter," however, also reinforced a myth of Jewish passivity that Bialik had internalized from early Zionist manifestos. He overlooked evidence of Jewish resistance that had been reported even at the time, although, as Judge notes, Bialik's graphic and at times unfair depictions "serve[d] to highlight the helplessness of Kishinev Jews."[3] Penkower, analysing the mas-

---

1 Judge 56–69.
2 Penkower 191.
3 Judge 143; see also Goldberg.

sacre as a "turning point" in Jewish history, notes its impact on both the Zionist and Territorialist movements. Bialik's poem energized Russian Jews, who called for both self-defence and the creation of a Jewish state in Palestine. However, it also led Herzl to propose, at the 1903 Sixth Zionist Congress, that the East Africa plan be considered as at least a temporary refuge.[1] When the Congress rejected that idea it became the origin of Zangwill's ITO.

Zangwill's descriptions of the pogrom vividly depict both the helplessness of the victims and the brutality of the perpetrators. Interestingly, the detailed and harrowing account in Act III of *The Melting-Pot* was added in the summer of 1908, at the suggestion of Walker Whiteside (1869–1942), who originated the role of David Quixano. While visiting Zangwill in England to prepare for a trial run of the play in Littlehampton, a seaside town next to where the Zangwills lived, Whiteside mentioned to his host that there seemed to be a "gap" in the third act. When he suggested that what was needed was a "description of the massacre," Zangwill protested that such a scene would be "too revolting." Whiteside's answer: "Not as you would write it, as David Quixano should describe it."[2] The play was performed at Littlehampton with members of Zangwill's family in key roles, Walker Whiteside reciting the harrowing description of the pogrom that would become a permanent part of Act III.

The Settlement House Movement

The unnamed settlement house at which Vera Revendal works plays an important role in *The Melting-Pot*, just as real settlement houses were significant in helping Jews and other immigrants gain a foothold in American life. Zangwill would have been familiar with three of the earliest: Hull-House, in Chicago, founded by Jane Addams (1860–1935) in 1889 on the model of Toynbee Hall in London's East End (which Zangwill would also have known); the Educational Alliance, founded in the same year by a group of Jewish organizations including the Aguilar Free Library, the Young Men's Hebrew Association, and the Hebrew Institute; and

---

1   Penkower 193, 190.
2   Walker Whiteside, "The History of a Zangwill Drama," newspaper clipping date-stamped 16 January 1910, no newspaper title or page number, Walker Whiteside Papers, Manuscripts and Archives Division, Billy Rose Theatre Division, The New York Public Library, MWEZ/x n.c. 13, 787. See also image on p. 8.

the Henry Street Settlement, founded in 1893 by Lillian Wald (1867–1940), a Jewish-American social service and public health pioneer who also founded the Visiting Nurse Service of New York and was among the founders of the National Association for the Advancement of Colored People (NAACP). While Hull-House and the Henry Street Settlement served diverse groups of immigrants in Chicago and the Lower East Side of New York, respectively, the work of the Educational Alliance was at first directed specifically toward Jews. As the demographics of the neighbourhoods they served changed, however, all three adapted to serve new clienteles. Hull-House ended its social service activities in 2012; the Educational Alliance and Henry Street Settlement still offer vibrant and vital community programs.

Jane Addams was the daughter of a wealthy Illinois family. Her father was a member of the Illinois state senate and an early supporter of Abraham Lincoln's presidential campaign. In 1931 she became the first American woman to receive the Nobel Peace Prize; a pacifist and a feminist, she was one of the founders of the American Civil Liberties Union. Visiting Toynbee Hall in London, she was impressed not only with the organization's programs for the poor but also with the fact that university students (in that case, all male) staffed the centre and worked with its clients. She founded Hull-House, in part, as a way to give young women of the middle and upper classes meaningful work to do (see Appendices E1–E2). Thus Vera Revendal's position as an assistant is in keeping with early settlement house organization. Indeed, Zangwill may have met Addams on a visit to Chicago in 1898; he sent her a ticket to attend a performance of *The Melting-Pot* in Chicago, and her calendar for 1908 indicates that she saw or intended to see the play on 23 October and 15 December.[1] That there are no Jews in Vera's settlement (as David Quixano points out in Act I: "If you only had Jews, it would be as good as going to Ellis Island," p. 79) is peculiar, as is the placement of the settlement and the Quixano home in Staten Island. We must assume that the settlement is there, since otherwise Frau Quixano would not have been able to walk to it from her home on the Sabbath, as she does in the play; there was no bridge then

---

1 Jane Addams, Calendars and Correspondence, accessed on microfilm from the Jane Addams Collection, Reel 29/1379, Swarthmore College Peace Collection, DG 001. Addams's praise of the play was quoted in subsequent programs, and Zangwill referred to her suffrage work admiringly in *The War for the World* (London: Heinemann; New York: Macmillan, 1916), 337–38.

to join the Island borough to the rest of the city and she would have had to take a ferry. However, various other hints in the text suggest that Zangwill's model for Vera's settlement house, as well as for the "People's Alliance" that David mentions, was the Educational Alliance, housed in a large, tall building that still stands at 197 East Broadway in Manhattan, the roof garden of which gave immigrant children fresh air and would likely also have provided a view of the Statue of Liberty.[1]

The settlement house movement was part of the larger Progressivism in the United States, a bipartisan umbrella movement in the early years of the twentieth century that, according to Nathaniel Cadle, "sought to address a dizzying array of challenging social conditions that were transforming the realities of everyday life" and was, in fact, "filled with contradictions."[2] The inconsistencies of the era—anti-immigration efforts and racial segregation propounded at the same time as women's suffrage and anti-corruption campaigns—have led scholars to explain why the Progressives might not have been so progressive after all. On the settlement house movement, Rivka Shpak Lissak has criticized Hull-House, in particular, for seeing and acting upon the idea that "the dissolution of immigrant subcommittees and the loosening of ethnic affiliation and identity [are] necessary for the survival of American democracy."[3] Middle-class "home visitors" have been criticized in later eras for trying to impose their own values of hygiene, nutrition, and even home décor on immigrant families.[4] Indeed, the aristocratic antisemitism that Vera Revendal expresses early in *The Melting-Pot* (despite the fact that she left her family to join the Revolution) suggests the kind of class distance that could separate clients from settlement house

---

1 Indeed, the iconic statue would be more easily visible from the Lower East Side than from Staten Island. See Hasia R. Diner, *Lower East Side Memories: A Jewish Place in America* (Princeton, NJ: Princeton UP, 2000), 128.

2 Nathaniel Cadle, *The Mediating Nation: Late American Realism, Globalization, and the Progressive State* (Chapel Hill: U of North Carolina P, 2014), 20.

3 Rivka Shpak Lissak, *Pluralism & Progressives: Hull House and the New Immigrants, 1890–1919* (Chicago: U of Chicago P, 1989), 25; for a more positive recent view, see Susan Roth Breitzer, "Uneasy Alliances: Hull House, the Garment Workers Strikes, and the Jews of Chicago," *Indiana Magazine of History* 106.1 (Mar. 2010): 40–70.

4 Gwendolyn Wright, *Building the Dream: A Social History of Housing in America* (Cambridge, MA: MIT P, 1981), 131–33.

workers. Addams's own writings, however (see Appendices E1–2), indicate that she tried to strike a balance between helping immigrants assimilate and helping them perpetuate their unique cultures. The Labor Museum at Hull-House, where immigrants worked at traditional crafts, came about when Addams saw an elderly Italian woman spinning thread on a rudimentary spindle: "It seemed so difficult to come into genuine relations with the Italian women and [...] they themselves so often lost their hold upon their Americanized children. It seemed to me that Hull-House ought to be able to devise some educational enterprise which should build a bridge between European and American experiences in such wise as to give them both more meaning and a sense of relation."[1]

However, along with efforts to maintain cultural traditions and without desiring to obliterate them, settlement houses rightly focused on helping immigrants adapt to American life. While perhaps in line with the values of those who wished to restrict immigration (and thus politically advantageous), assisting assimilation to American expectations was also an economic necessity. For Jews who wished employment beyond the Jewish-owned sweatshop, learning English was essential. The Educational Alliance, like other settlements, offered evening classes in English, as well as lectures on American history and current events "in simple English." David Quixano's concert would have fit right in at the Educational Alliance, which frequently offered concerts of patriotic music as well as classical standards, inculcating a love for America while also providing the European music that immigrants may have enjoyed at home. Lectures by physicians and public health workers taught tenement-dwellers how to prevent communicable diseases such as tuberculosis; announcements of such events and programs, from the YIVO archive of the Educational Alliance, are reprinted in Appendix E4. The description of youngsters reciting the pledge "Flag of Our Great Republic" depicts actual events reported in New York and London newspapers, and in H.G. Wells's recollections of a visit to New York (see Appendix E3), a scene noted approvingly and indeed with emotion by contemporary observers. Still, what Zangwill meant by assimilation became highly contested in reviews and periodical debates of the time (as evident in Appendices B and G), and debates over the idea of assimilation continue. Yet David's symphony of a multitude of American voices represented America of

---

1 Jane Addams, *Twenty Years at Hull-House with Autobiographical Notes* (New York: Macmillan, 1910), 235–36; see also Appendix E2.

the melting-pot just as much as Horace Kallen's "symphony of civilization" could figure cultural pluralism.

The Play

Early Production History, Contemporary Reviews, and Major Contemporary Themes

The Melting-Pot had its first production in Washington, DC, on 5 October 1908. President Theodore Roosevelt, who was in the audience, is said to have exclaimed at the end of the opening night performance, "That's a great play, Mr. Zangwill."[1] Reviews and other accounts report various versions of the president's words, but his enthusiasm was clear. Zangwill dedicated the published version of the play to him and even made a change in wording at his request in Act III (footnoted in this edition, p. 126). Edna Nahshon records that, after a less than warm reception of Zangwill's Jewish-themed play *Children of the Ghetto* in New York in 1899, his producer George Tyler postponed *The Melting-Pot*'s New York opening until December 1909, taking the play to Chicago from Washington and then to a number of other American cities before bringing it to Broadway.[2] Zangwill kept careful track of the responses to his plays, employing a clipping service to send him copies of all the reviews, which he carefully placed in scrapbooks now held in the Central Zionist Archives, Jerusalem. Some plays received so few reviews that their clippings shared scrapbooks. *The Melting-Pot*, however, received more reviews than any other of Zangwill's theatrical productions, and they fill three large archival files.[3] It is hard to do justice to such vast and mixed commentary, but I have tried to include in Appendix A representative samplings from each of the play's major venues.

To some extent the American reviews support Tyler's trepidation about New York. In Washington and Chicago, for example, approval or disapproval often rested on how critics felt about the

---

1 Maurice Wohlgelernter, *Israel Zangwill: A Study* (New York: Columbia UP, 1964), 176.

2 Nahshon 243–44.

3 These three files, held in the Central Zionist Archives (CZA) in Jerusalem, have two file numbers, A120/164a and 164b for reviews mainly of British productions, A120/165 for reviews mainly of American and other productions. I omit the distinction between the two British files in my references.

ideas of the play, while New York critics focused on aesthetic concerns, more often pointing out occasions of melodrama or bombast. For the Washington *Evening Star* reviewer, the play was "a sociological drama; one in which hard, solid thought takes the place of sentimentality; a work of great artistic value and of philosophic suggestion" (see Appendix A1, p. 183). For the critic in the *Washington Post*, the disappearance of the Jewish people, on the one hand, and the encouragement of undesirable immigration, on the other, were both reasons for finding fault with *The Melting-Pot*'s theme (see Appendix A2). Burns Mantle, in Chicago, approved "the ardor of [David Quixano's] plea and the magnificent sincerity with which it was presented" (see Appendix A3, p. 186), and Constance Skinner called *The Melting-Pot* "the great American play" (see Appendix A4, p. 187). Yet Amy Leslie, another Chicago reviewer, pointed out with unmistakable prejudice that "Jews do not want to be melted up, however, and Americans are not anxious to be melted up with them or the Irish or the Dutch or the Hottentots[1] and the rest any more than any other nation is, so 'The Melting Pot' fails of its mission" (see Appendix A5, p. 188). Yet this geographic dichotomy between message and method is too simple. Like Adolph Klauber, who in the *New York Times* called the play "cheap and tawdry" (see Appendix A8, p. 190), with its "obvious spread-eagleism and appeal to claptrap patriotism" (see Appendix A9, p. 190), Leslie also decries "an avalanche of brilliant arguments steeped in red, white and blue, with a kind of mongrel spread-eagle screaming liberty, fraternity and great inequality" (see Appendix A5, p. 187). A.B. Walkley, who reviewed the New York and London performances for the London *Times*, agreed with Klauber's assessment that the plot is poorly developed and the character of David Quixano excessive (or, in Klauber's words, David is a "neurotic sentimentalist" [see Appendix A9, p. 191]). But, like Leslie, Walkley also questioned the wisdom of pouring "the beauty of Jewish character and tradition" into the melting pot (see Appendix A12, p. 195).

The Melting-Pot opened in London for a few performances, at the end of January 1914 at the Court Theatre, by the non-profit Play Actors Company. When it was produced commercially by Gaston Mayer at the Queen's Theatre, beginning on 7 February, it maintained most of the cast of the Court production except for

---

1   The Khoikhoi people of South Africa, formerly called Hottentots by the Dutch settlers. The term is now considered offensive.

the role of David Quixano, now played again by Walker White-side. Nahshon writes that Whiteside was brought in from America to take over the role he had created.[1] Whiteside himself, in comments printed in several papers, insisted that he had simply been visiting on other business when he discovered that the play was being performed: "Nothing was further from my thoughts than to remain in England, and I should have been already on the Atlantic had not negotiations begun to induce me to stay."[2] Whiteside may have been engaging in a bit of press-agentry to promote interest in his performance while preserving the dignity of the Play Actors' David, Harold Chapin. The reader is free to decide.

London reviewers, like others, could combine dismay at a "melodramatic" story with praise for "a palpitating human document" (see Appendix A13, p. 196). J.T. Grein, an Englishman, a Jew, and the founder of the Independent Theatre, questioned Zangwill's omission of some of the disheartening elements of American life and asserted that England was a truer and more welcoming melting pot (see Appendix A15). "As a plea," wrote Grein, "Zangwill's work, despite its inordinate length and radical faults, is as eloquent as it is thoughtful and often cogent. As a dramatic work it interests, but it fails to grip. It is a play to be read, to be digested, to be discussed, but on the stage it sounds unreal."[3] Yet the following week Grein "rejoice[d] that a play of such earnest purpose and depth of thought has been made accessible to a wider public" by the commercial run at the Queen's Theatre (see Appendix A15, p. 199). And so it was with many reviews. In the Jewish press, in particular, efforts were made to find something good to say about the drama even when debating issues of assimilation and intermarriage. The London *Jewish Chronicle*, while arguing against ideas of assimilation it saw as implicit in the play, pointed out that, like the words of the prophets of Israel, "the message which Mr. Zangwill felt impelled to deliver it was his business to deliver without qualification and without equivocation" (see Appendix A14, p. 198). One American reviewer for the Jewish press was entirely laudatory, while also realistic; Leon Zolotkoff wrote in a Yiddish paper that in *The Melting-Pot* Zangwill "is more than an artist, for there he is also a

---

1 Nahshon 256.

2 "Mr. Walker Whiteside Engaged Yesterday in London for 'The Melting Pot,'" *The Referee* (1 Feb. 1914): n.p. CZA A120/164.

3 J.T. Grein, "The Week's Premieres, (1) Court: 'The Melting-Pot,'" *Sunday Times* [London] 1 Feb. 1914: 6.

Walker Whiteside, who originated the role of David Quixano. Billy Rose Theatre Division, New York Public Library.

philosopher, a poet, and a prophet, with a deep insight into the future [...]. [On intermarriage and assimilation] Zangwill does not preach but merely points out what is going on in the melting pot, and we know that it is true" (see Appendix A7, p. 189).

To understand why the issue was so controversial in 1908 and why, to an extent, it still is, one needs to understand why Jewish people have opposed marriage to those outside the faith. This traditional concern has roots not in Jewish prejudice but in a history of persecution against Jews and their tenuous status as a minority group, which led to well-founded fears of "the other." Moreover, Jews have long desired to see Jewish religion and traditions carried on in future generations. The argument for this last consideration appears clearly in the debate between David and Mendel toward the end of Act II of *The Melting-Pot*, when Mendel asserts that Jewish distinctiveness in lands where they have been accepted, reinforced by marriage to other Jews, has allowed the Jewish people and religion to continue. David replies that in countries like England and Holland, with established nationalities, this may have been true, but that in America, with its crucible, everyone would join in a new American ethnicity. Such loss of Jewish distinctiveness, then and now, would be troubling to Jews who value Judaism and Jewish culture, and for most of the twentieth century marriage to people of the majority religion often meant loss of Jewishness. Yet Zolotkoff and others who accepted the growing reality of such marriages might have been heartened as well as justified by recent developments. In twenty-first-century America, being Jewish is not necessarily the disadvantage it was in previous times. In fact, so many American Jews form interfaith families today that the term "intermarriage"—which has always had pejorative connotations—may even recede from use in favour of more welcoming expressions,[1] and many families with parents of two religious backgrounds decide to bring up their children as Jews or with respect for their Jewish heritage. It is unclear what the situation will be decades from now, but it is worth noting that the melting pot still boils, perhaps in ways that Israel Zangwill could not imagine and as reflected in recent discussions of American ethnicity (see below).

Certain details in *The Melting-Pot* suggest Zangwill's awareness of potential controversy as well as anti-Jewish feeling and his desire to combat or forestall antisemitic responses. His setting of the Quixano family home in Staten Island (known as the

---

1 See, for example, Susan Katz Miller, "Drop the Word 'Intermarriage' from Your Vocabulary for Good," *Forward* (9 Dec. 2016): 16–17.

Borough of Richmond in 1908) is odd, since that part of New York City was home to very few Jews at the time. As a report on Jewish demography points out, "[a]bout 5,000 Jews called the little-settled, isolated borough of Richmond (Staten Island) home in 1918," very few compared to the nearly 700,000 who lived in Manhattan at the same time.[1] Zangwill may not have wanted to present a large Jewish community, given the negative reviews of extended community scenes in the London production of *Children of the Ghetto*.[2] But he may also have sought to isolate his central characters from widespread poverty and a group looked down upon even by more established Jews. As David Biale and others point out, Quixano is a Sephardic name, and while the family's migration from Spain to Bessarabia is "historically possible, if improbable,"[3] Zangwill gives them a name that in Britain and America would be associated with the aristocratic connotations of Sephardic Jews, among the first Jewish immigrants to both nations and by 1908 leaders of their Jewish communities. Quixano was in fact the name of a prominent, wealthy Sephardic family in England, among those who tried to assist the embarrassingly foreign Russian Jews to assimilate quickly.

Finally, as even some reviewers noted, Zangwill transcribes the Yiddish of Frau Quixano and others as if it were German. Yiddish, the language developed by Ashkenazi Jews[4] in Europe, is written in Hebrew characters, so it must be transliterated into Latin characters for an English play. Today there is a standard system of transliteration, developed by the YIVO Institute for Jewish Research. Zangwill wrote before this system was established, but he might still have transliterated with more accuracy

---

1 "New York City," *Encyclopedia Judaica*, Gale Group, 2008, accessed online via *Jewish Virtual Library*, http://www.jewishvirtuallibrary.org/jsource/judaica/ejud_0002_0015_0_1 4806.html#DEMOGRAPHY_1. Large numbers of immigrant Jews lived in Brooklyn and the Bronx by then as well, although, as Diner points out, the Lower East Side has become emblematic of Jewish immigrant settlement in Zangwill's era (Diner 49 and 188n68).

2 Nahshon 87–88.

3 David Biale, "The Melting Pot and Beyond: Jews and the Politics of American Identity," *Insider/Outsider: American Jews and Multiculturalism*, ed. David Biale, Michael Galchinsky, and Susannah Heschel (Berkeley: U of California P, 1998), 20.

4 Jews of eastern and central European origin, as opposed to Sephardic, Jews originating in the Iberian peninsula, and Mizrahi, Jews of the Middle East.

rather than using, as he often does, German cognates (i.e., words of the same linguistic origin) of Yiddish words. Although Yiddish originates in an early form of German (and adds vocabulary from the languages of regions where its speakers live), it is not identical to it, and at the time Zangwill wrote, it was often considered an embarrassing "jargon" by assimilated English-speaking Jews. When Zangwill wrote the novel *Children of the Ghetto* (1892), he found that readers objected to his rendering of Yiddish speech, and each edition of the published novel contained less Yiddish than in his typescript draft.[1] When he was prevailed upon to include a glossary of Yiddish terms, he often included their sources in other European languages, as well as Hebrew, to underscore their linguistic and historical respectability.[2] Zangwill's approach to Yiddish onstage, then, might best be considered ambivalent. By having Yiddish in *The Melting-Pot* read and sound like German, he may have been attempting to achieve the effect of etymologies in *Children of the Ghetto*'s glossary, to include Yiddish speech in his writing and onstage while at the same time trying to "normalize" it and make it respectable for his non-Jewish audience. His attempt ultimately seems less than successful, although the various German, French, and Irish accents in the play (the last not without its detractors in the press) demonstrate the diversity of speech in America.[3]

Regardless of reviews or controversy, *The Melting-Pot* had 136 performances in New York[4] and was presented throughout the United States for three years after its initial opening. Similarly, when the London run ended, it was performed throughout the provinces of Britain. In both countries, especially in cities with large Jewish populations, audiences were large and enthusiastic. Zangwill's scrapbooks include reviews from productions during his lifetime from all over the world. In Britain, however, with the

1 The draft, in the archives of Hebrew Union College-Jewish Institute of Religion, is incomplete, but there is more representation of Yiddish words in it than in the comparable published passages.
2 See Meri-Jane Rochelson, "Introduction," *Children of the Ghetto: A Study of a Peculiar People*, by Israel Zangwill (Detroit: Wayne State UP, 2008), 23–24; and Jessica R. Valdez, "How to Write Yiddish in English, or Israel Zangwill and Multilingualism in *Children of the Ghetto*," *Studies in the Novel* 46.3 (2014): 315–34.
3 Hana Wirth-Nesher has a different, intriguing explanation for Frau Quixano's lapses into German and faulty Yiddish. See "Recent Critical Evaluations," below.
4 Gleason 24.

onset of World War I, a proposed Edinburgh production in June 1915 was withdrawn at the request of the Foreign Office, which did not want to offend Russia, a wartime ally. This began what was in effect a ban on UK productions of the play until 1917.[1] In 1915, William Cort produced a black-and-white film version of the play; its opening in May of that year filled New York's largest movie theatre. Although prints of the film no longer exist, Nahshon refers to reports of the "thrilling, gripping and horrifying" representation of the Kishinev pogrom and notes that "extras were recruited from New York's Lower East Side." Although this film received critical as well as popular praise, the Cort Company failed, and Zangwill ultimately had to sue (successfully) for royalties and film negatives.[2]

Recent Critical Evaluations

Some scholarly appraisals of *The Melting-Pot* have worked to demonstrate that both the play and the concept suggest something more nuanced than an ideal of complete assimilation, while more recent analyses of American multiculturalism suggest limitations and competing models. In a survey of the symbol, Philip Gleason points out that while the melting pot engages all immigrants, in this play Zangwill is specifically concerned with the situation of Jews in America, which in turn reflects "his overriding preoccupation with the destiny of the Jews in the modern world."[3] Throughout his writings (and, I will add, directly within the play itself), Zangwill offers Jews the alternatives of life in a Jewish homeland or assimilation into the life of another country in which they choose to live. Of course, what assimilation means was contested at the time of the play and is still a subject of debate. Gleason writes that "*The Melting-Pot* seemed clearly to preach the doctrine of complete assimilation" and thus led to complaints not only by many American Jews but also by Germans, Norwegians, and Slavs who had set up strong cultural institutions in the United States and also rejected the metaphor.[4] Neil Larry Shumsky suggests that "Zangwill envisioned a melted America in which Judaism survived."[5] He points to several places

---

1 Nahshon 262.
2 Nahshon 254.
3 Gleason 23.
4 Gleason 27–28.
5 Neil Larry Shumsky, "Zangwill's The Melting Pot: Ethnic Tensions on Stage," *American Quarterly* 27 (1975): 31.

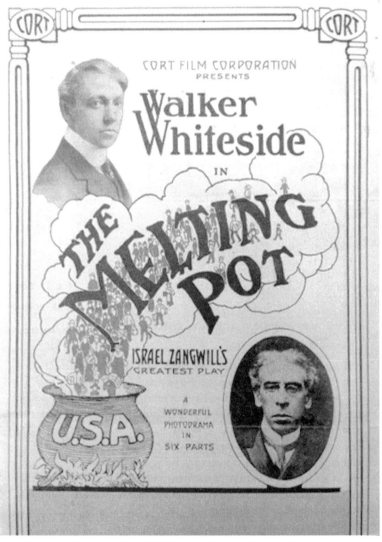

Program for a film presentation by the Cort Company; Billy Rose
Theatre Division, New York Public Library.

in the play where David is seen to value his Jewish heritage, especially as represented by his grandmother, Frau Quixano, and
shows how Kathleen O'Reilly changes so much over the course
of the drama that as early as the Purim scene of Act II she refers
to herself as a "Hebrew" and in Act IV laments, "we Jews never

An evening with a cheerful Jewish family at Hampstead (Everyman Theatre).

Cartoon from a review of the Everyman Theatre production, London, 1920, no newspaper title, page, or date; Billy Rose Theatre Division, New York Public Library.

know our way" (pp. 148–49).[1] Zangwill, too, had referred to this give-and-take of assimilation in his Afterword, but Shumsky goes further when he discusses the play's theme in relation to Zangwill's universalism. Shumsky sees *The Melting-Pot* as affirming Zangwill's view that the United States was based in Hebrew concepts of law and justice, and he suggests that Zangwill separated Jewish "race" and Jewish religion, a still vexed question in considerations of Jewish identity. Thus Shumsky posits "that Judaism will survive in the melting pot of America and will be accepted there when its racial aspects, those which keep Jews apart, have been abandoned. The play may be seen as advocating the conjunction of Judaism's spiritual message with the [universal] sectarian message of America. [...] The melting pot and Judaism could exist in America at the same time."[2]

---

1 Shumsky 35–36.
2 Shumsky 40.

Hana Wirth-Nesher, in "Hebrew in the Crucible," takes Shum-sky's view even further by documenting the significance of the Hebrew language in Zangwill's play. Wirth-Nesher views *The Melting-Pot* as a multilingual play in which Hebrew "not only with-stands being melted but also serves as the common element of Jewish and American identity."[1] She analyses the surprisingly numerous ways in which Hebrew appears, from Frau Quixano's Sabbath blessings to the Hebrew writing visible on the books in the stage set, all rendered with accuracy. But regarding Frau Quixano's lapses into German rather than Yiddish, and her failure to distin-guish between the Yiddish words for sacred and profane books, "Zangwill does not seem too concerned about authenticity when it comes to Yiddish." While Yiddish will go into the melting pot with other immigrant languages, writes Wirth-Nesher, "for Zangwill, Hebrew must remain unmeltable."[2] She argues persuasively that, for Zangwill, Hebrew is the language of Judaism, as opposed to Jewishness, and thus it will eternally distinguish the Jews, wherever they may live. At the same time, Wirth-Nesher sees Zangwill's use of music in *The Melting-Pot* as a sign of the author's engagement in European high culture and "the crucial role of music in discussions of the Jews' eligibility to participate in Western high culture."[3] She alludes to Sander Gilman's essay "Are Jews Musical?," which, in part, views the emphasis on music in the play as a rebuke against antisemitic stereotypes of Jews as unmusical and unable to appre-ciate European musical traditions.[4]

Zangwill's universalist values in conjunction with his ideas on Judaism cast light, as well, on the intermarriage plot. In many of his writings Zangwill looks at the ethics of Judaism as the founda-tion for a universal faith; indeed, he views the teachings of Jesus as an extension of Jewish scripture.[5] Of his non-Jewish wife, Edith Ayrton Zangwill, Israel Zangwill said that her "religious outlook was nearer to his own than that of any Jewess he had met."[6] Vera

---

1 Hana Wirth-Nesher, "Hebrew in the Crucible: Multilingual Voices in Israel Zangwill's The Melting Pot," *Languages of Modern Jewish Cultures: Comparative Perspectives*, ed. Joshua L. Miller and Anita Norich (Ann Arbor: U of Michigan P, 2016), 154.

2 Wirth-Nesher 162.

3 Wirth-Nesher 154.

4 Sander L. Gilman, "Are Jews Musical? Historical Notes on the Question of Jewish Musical Modernism and Nationalism," *Modern Judaism* 28.3 (2008): 239–56.

5 See Rochelson, *Jew in the Public Arena* 103–05.

6 Joseph Leftwich, *Israel Zangwill* (London: James Clarke, 1957), 52.

Revendal reiterates that sentiment in the play when she tells the Baron that she has no more become a Jew than David has become a Christian: "We were already at one—all honest people are" (p. 126). Vera and David are not in fact married by the end of the play, although they have lovingly reconciled and marriage appears to be in their future. But although Vera uses the words of Ruth—"thy people shall be my people and thy God my God!" (p. 141)—her earlier statement makes clear that she will not need to formally convert. Thus the prospective union of Vera and David figures one important action of the melting pot as it creates understanding and even love between people who see the world in similar ways.

Werner Sollors explores this idea as he takes *The Melting-Pot* as a key text for understanding how "consent"—the role of individual agreement to ideals or nationhood—replaces "descent"—ancestry or hereditary privilege—in the making of American identity. Sollors's exemplary close reading of the play demonstrates the multiple ways in which it contrasts hardness and melting, the past and the future, QUIncy DAVenport and DAVid QUIxano (the latter evoking quixotic idealism). He points out that the hypocritical "gondola-guzzler" Quincy is "the only white Anglo-Saxon Protestant" in the play;[1] as others, too, have noted, Davenport is also the only non-immigrant American. As Zangwill states in his Afterword, amalgamation as an American does not require intermarriage. But in the play, as Sollors makes clear, the love between ethnic opposites serves an important symbolic function: "In the world of Zangwill's *Melting-Pot*, descent is secular and temporal, consent is sacred and eternal."[2] Lori Harrison-Kahan returns to the metaphoric role of interfaith love, suggesting a possible source for *The Melting-Pot*'s romance in San Franciscan Emma Wolf's *Other Things Being Equal* (1892), which centres on an intermarriage, and *Heirs of Yesterday* (1900), in which Jewish lovers differ over the role Judaism will have in their lives. Zangwill and Wolf corresponded, and Wolf sent Zangwill her work to read. Harrison-Kahan proposes that the mentorship may have been mutual, and that Emma Wolf's fiction, depicting better-off and more acculturated Jews in the American West, may have contributed to Vera and David's pioneering relationship.[3]

---

1 Sollors, *Beyond Ethnicity* 70.
2 Sollors, *Beyond Ethnicity* 74.
3 Lori Harrison-Kahan, "'A Grave Experiment': Emma Wolf's Marriage Plots and the Deghettoization of American Jewish Fiction," *American Jewish History* 101.1 (2017): 5–34.

Both the metaphor of the melting pot and the play itself have figured in studies of American ethnic groups. David Biale looks at *The Melting-Pot* in the context of the current position of Jews in American multicultural society. Using Du Bois's term to express a different kind of "double consciousness," Biale describes how, unlike most other immigrants who were ethnically part of the majority in the countries they left, Jews came to the United States in the hope of "liberation" and success while also continuing to see themselves as a vulnerable minority group. Thus, in Biale's view, *The Melting-Pot* and even Horace Kallen's cultural pluralism, far from being "paradigmatic statements" applicable to all immigrant groups, are in fact "pregnant with ambiguity and tension, reflecting the very ambiguities of Jewish self-consciousness."[1] Jonathan Freedman points out that Jewishness unsettles ethnic and racial categories in ways discussed above, but also that the Jewish example has led to the "model minority" narrative that challenges and unfairly critiques other American groups. Although Freedman does not specifically mention the play, he locates the concept of the melting pot "at the crossroads of the discourses of ethnicity and assimilation."[2]

Thus, recent theorists have used Zangwill's image of the crucible to suggest alternative models for immigrant enculturation, as well as to return to issues of descent, heredity, and the terminology of race. The authors of "Heritage in Melting Pot Models" conclude that melting pots, which "result in a new single core that is not the same as any of its constituents [...] either fail, in which case they [...] evolve into other models which can accommodate greater pluralism; or they succeed, in which case they are likely to become indistinguishable from the assimilation model."[3] In "From Melting Pot to Simmering Stew," Paul Smokowski and Martica Bacallao develop "alternation theory," a model in which an individual easily "navigate[s] within and between two different cultures" as against the "unidirectional" model of assimilation.[4] Focusing specifically

---

1 Biale 19.
2 Jonathan Freedman, *Klezmer America: Jewishness, Ethnicity, Modernity* (New York: Columbia UP, 2008), 12.
3 G.J. Ashworth, Brian Graham, and J.E. Tunbridge, "Heritage in Melting Pot Models," *Pluralising Pasts: Heritage, Identity and Place in Multicultural Societies* (London: Pluto P, 2007), 117, 128.
4 Paul R. Smokowski and Martica Bacallao, "From Melting Pot to Simmering Stew: Acculturation, Enculturation, Assimilation, and Biculturalism in American Racial Dynamics," *Becoming Bicultural: Risk, Resilience, and Latino Youth* (New York: New York UP, 2011), 21.

on Latino and Asian youth, they see these groups today as having less opportunity to enter an American ethnic mainstream than European immigrants of the early 1900s, and intermarriage today as producing the positive result of a bicultural generation. Similarly, Asian American theorist David Leiwei Li critiques Werner Sollors's formulations by insisting that consent does not erase descent, and that racial "particularities"—of biology, culture, and performance—not only have meaning as social signifiers but also help to develop a "culture of democracy that cherishes difference in identity."[1]

The title of Aviva Taubenfeld's "Mendel's Melting Pot" puns on David Quixano's uncle Mendel—who deplores the idea of Jews marrying non-Jews—and Gregor Mendel (1822–84), the early influential genetic theorist. Taubenfeld sees the play as a dramatic working-out of Theodore Roosevelt's ideas on "true Americanism," although while "Zangwill believed that race mixture in the melting pot would produce an entirely new race, superior to its component parts," Roosevelt envisioned immigrants blending into an existing American type.[2] Despite the many examples of cultural, non-biological exchange within the play, Taubenfeld sees the potential marriage of Vera and David—and the biological children it will produce—as central to Zangwill's image of American melting.[3] Citing Zangwill's 1911 address at the Universal Races Congress, Taubenfeld illustrates his view that, both because Jews are diverse and because they can mingle easily with other cultures, "Zangwill ultimately rests his case for the unity of the human species on the racial intermixture of the Jew."[4] However, like other scholars, Taubenfeld writes, "though Jewish features may disappear, Zangwill believes that Jewish ethos will dominate,"[5] in part because American principles of ethics and justice are based in Hebrew scripture.

---

1 David Leiwei Li, "On Ascriptive and Acquisitional Americanness: *The Accidental Asian* and the Illogic of Assimilation," *Culture, Identity, Commodity: Diasporic Chinese Literatures in English*, ed. Tseen Khoo and Kam Louie (Montreal: McGill-Queen's UP, 2005), 260, 267.

2 Aviva F. Taubenfeld, "Mendel's Melting Pot: Israel Zangwill and the Science of the Crucible," *Rough Writing: Ethnic Authorship in Theodore Roosevelt's America* (New York: New York UP, 2008), 17. "True Americanism" is the title of an essay Roosevelt published in *The Forum* in 1894. Also unlike Zangwill, Roosevelt believed that non-whites, including Asians and blacks, could not blend into American culture.

3 Taubenfeld 22–23.

4 Taubenfeld 29. I discuss a similar passage in another context, below.

5 Taubenfeld 33.

While most critical accounts focus on how to interpret Zang-will's views on immigration, assimilation, and intermarriage, and what they mean for Jews and other ethnic groups, several allude to the "feuds and vendettas" (p. 81) that David scorns as European detritus to be discarded in the new America. As Biale states, "Europe is the land of persecution and oppression [...] and is rife with ancient hatreds between peoples. America represents redemption through the effacing of all hostile differences."[1] Biale's statement points to another important theme of *The Melting-Pot*, one that explains the significance of Act IV, unfortunately maligned by critics in 1908 and later. Burns Mantle, reviewing the play in Chicago, called it "a master work, for three of its four acts at least" (see Appendix A3, p. 186). Shumsky finds Act IV anticlimactic, calling the reunion between Vera and David "contrived" as it "appears to contradict much of the play's development."[2] In fact, however, the "three kisses of peace" that Vera bestows on David are more than simply an interreligious gesture. They allow him to love her and to forget the violent past, and according to the logic of the play such peace between peoples can occur only in a melting pot. Once again, Zangwill was concerned not only with the situation of the Jews but also with the ethnic rivalries he saw throughout Europe that ultimately led to World War I. He frequently referred to Europe as a "cockpit," and when he wrote a play by that name, about international antagonism and war, he thought of it as a "pendant to 'The Melting Pot.'"[3] Bringing people together in America would create not only a state in which immigrants could find equality, but also one in which they might live without constant battle.

Gleason points out that ideas such as these, "presented dramatically in *The Melting Pot*[,] are restated in more systematic fashion" in *The Principle of Nationalities*, an essay by Zangwill published in 1917 and originally a lecture he presented in memory of a leading ethical humanist, Moncure D. Conway.[4] In this essay Zangwill emphasizes how slippery the idea of "nation-

---

1 Biale 21.

2 Shumsky 35.

3 The quotation is from a letter to Zangwill's friend Nina Salaman, 14 Aug. 1920, Cambridge University Library Add. Ms. 8171/Box 24. See Rochelson, *Jew in the Public Arena*, 187.

4 Gleason 25; Conway (1832–1907) was an American abolitionist who went to London during the Civil War and stayed to become a leader of the South Place Religious Society in London, later renamed the South Place Ethical Society.

ality" can be, at times crossing boundaries of race, religion or peoplehood, or being defined, at other times, strictly along those lines. He contrasted nationality—"a state of mind corresponding to a political fact"[1]—with nationalism, the too often oppressive and divisive result of adding power or force to national feeling. The title phrase refers to an idea that took hold in Europe in the latter half of the nineteenth century, affirming the rights of nations to form themselves into states. In 1917 Zangwill hoped that this principle would be applied in guaranteeing national and minority rights after World War I, which was being fought as he spoke. Certainly he saw in this principle the hope of a Jewish state. But Zangwill also classified different kinds of nationhood according to what today might be considered their embodiment or lack of diversity. A "simple" nationality appears when the "same language, race, religion, culture, and territory are common to all the group."[2] But when he points out that, in the midst of war, "the production of [... simple nationalities] everywhere is precisely the process history is engaged upon,"[3] Zangwill insists, first of all, that even apparently homogeneous nations are formed through the blending of varied national identities, and, second, that this process of amalgamation is still going on. As he moves to oppose the oppressiveness of forced nationalism and despotic nation-states, Zangwill alludes to the inevitability of national feeling to project a new kind of universalism: the melting pot.

Zangwill argues that nationality types are not fixed but rather are living, changing entities, and that melting pots are more easily formed by love and tolerance than by persecution—which, he writes, tends to intensify minority self-identification.[4] In his view, America formed a model for human unity, and the Jews were the exemplar of universal nationhood:

> If America can make Americans out of Serbians and Bulgarians and Greeks and any old nationality, it is because Bulgarians *are* Serbians and both of them Greeks: at any rate the

---

1   Israel Zangwill, *The Principle of Nationalities*, Conway Memorial Lecture, delivered at South Place Institute on 8 March 1917 (London: Watts & Co., 1917), 39.

2   Zangwill, *Principle of Nationalities* 39–40.

3   Zangwill, *Principle of Nationalities* 43.

4   Zangwill refers here, as elsewhere, to Aesop's fable of the beggar "who only hugged his cloak the closer when the wind raged its wildest, [but] threw it off when the sun came out" (55).

traits of their common humanity exceed their differences. [...] and if [t]he people who do not exist on the map [i.e., the Jews] have lived with every other, from Babylonians, to New Zealanders, from Abyssinians to Mormons— [...] I draw the Euclidean conclusion that those to whom the Jews can be brothers are brothers to one another and that it is not any racial obstacle that impedes the Nationality of Man.[1]

Yet Zangwill realized the world was nowhere close to this spirit of perfection. He points out that civil rights were being cut back both for Jews in Russia and for "the coloured population" of the United States, giving both states the characteristics of despotism.[2] In Europe, he proclaims, combatants had become new incarnations of empire, "created for disruption of the planet, not integration."[3]

Toward the end of "The Principle of Nationalities," Zangwill acknowledges that the goods of a united world need not be purchased at the expense of more localized loyalties; in a larger sense he sees the universalist goal as both "the problem and the ideal— how to maintain the virtues of tribalism without losing the wider vision; how to preserve the brotherhood of Israel without losing the brotherhood of man; how to secure that, though there *shall* be both Jew and Greek, there shall yet be neither."[4] In the end, Zangwill's lecture suggests that such a world—in which differences are recognized in a context of equality and unity—is the most important ideal to strive for, against which the assimilationist ethos of the melting pot remains a necessary starting point. It is only in the melting pot that David can find spiritual peace through his love for Vera, and he can commit himself to that love only when he is able to experience that sense of peace. In the last spoken words of the play, he extends the melting pot's vision of peace to humankind: "Peace, peace, to all ye unborn millions, fated to fill this giant continent—the God of our *children* give you Peace" (p. 156; italics in original). *The Melting-Pot* remains about hopes for the future.

One hundred years and more after *The Melting-Pot* first appeared, its debates and its vision take on considerable urgency,

---

1 Zangwill, *Principle of Nationalities* 59–60.

2 Zangwill, *Principle of Nationalities* 41.

3 Zangwill, *Principle of Nationalities* 62.

4 Zangwill, *Principle of Nationalities* 89; emphasis in original. The mention of "Jew and Greek" alludes to Galatians 3:28.

and the play is still occasionally performed.[1] Apart from questions of how immigrants will or should adapt to their new environments remains the question that inspired Zangwill in the first place: Why is it important to admit immigrants to nations where they will be free to live and pursue their aspirations? Looking at early responses to the play, Joe Kraus determined that, regardless of flaws in technique or plot in *The Melting-Pot*, the play provided "a valid label" for what its immigrant consumers were experiencing in their lives: "the real show was happening in the audience."[2] In an era when refugees plead for admittance while governments propose grave restrictions and deportations, *The Melting-Pot* and its core ideas remain as significant, if also as controversial, as ever.

---

1 Reviewing the Metropolitan Playhouse of New York's production in 2006, Martin Denton wrote, "The story is as timely and resonant as ever" ("Reviews: The Melting Pot," *Metropolitan Playhouse: The American Legacy*, nytheatre.com, 12 Mar. 2006). Some years ago an Orthodox Jewish student of mine lent me a video of a production that was staged at his Jewish summer camp. In 2014, under the direction of Phillip Church, students and faculty of the Florida International University Theatre Program presented several scenes to a fascinated audience as part of a day-long conference on Zangwill.

2 Joe Kraus, "How *The Melting Pot* Stirred America: The Reception of Zangwill's Play and Theater's Role in the American Assimilation Experience," *MELUS* 24.3 (1999): 14, 15.

Israel Zangwill: A Brief Chronology

1864   Israel Zangwill is born in London's East End on 21
            January to immigrant parents, Moses and Ellen (or
            Helen) Zangwill. Israel is the second of five children
            in the Zangwill family, along with brothers Mark
            and Louis and sisters Leah and Dinah.

1872   Is enrolled at the Jews' Free School in East London's
            Bell Lane. Becomes the first recipient of the Roth-
            schild Medal, and in 1877 and 1878 earns the Rev.
            A.L. Green Prize for Hebrew.

1881   Wins £5 in a magazine competition for his story
            "Professor Grimmer."

1882   Publishes a satirical story, "Motso Kleis, or the
            Green Chinee," which gets him into trouble with
            authorities at the Jews' Free School, where he
            teaches.

c. 1883–85 Edits and contributes to *Purim*, a Jewish magazine
            of humour and fiction.

1884   Receives a degree from the University of London,
            with honours in French, English, and Mental and
            Moral Science.

1888   After resigning his position at the Jews' Free
            School, publishes two stories in the *Jewish Calen-
            dar, Manual, and Diary*, using the pseudonym
            "Baroness von S." Begins to work as a sub-editor
            and columnist for *The Jewish Standard*. His first
            novel, *The Premier and the Painter*, is written collab-
            oratively with Louis Cowen and published under
            the pseudonym of "J. Freeman Bell."

1889   The essay "English Judaism: A Criticism and a
            Classification" is published in the first volume of
            the *Jewish Quarterly Review*.

1890   From 1890 to 1892, writes for and edits a humour
            paper, titled *Puck* and then *Ariel, or the London
            Puck*.

1891   *The Bachelors' Club* is published. *The Big Bow
            Mystery* is serialized in the London *Star*. Zangwill
            and Eleanor Marx Aveling publish "A Doll's House
            Repaired" in *Time*.

1892   Begins writing stories for the *Idler*. *The Old Maids'
            Club* is published and his short play *The Great*

	Demonstration (written with Louis Cowen) is produced in London. His novel *Children of the Ghetto* is published to great acclaim late in the year.
1893	Begins his column, "Without Prejudice," in the *Pall Mall Magazine*. Publishes *The King of Schnorrers* as a serial in the *Idler*, and publishes the short novel *Merely Mary Ann* and the collection of stories *Ghetto Tragedies*. Writes and oversees production of the short play "Aladdin at Sea," and another of his short plays, *Six Persons*, is produced in London.
1894	His column "Men, Women and Books," drawn largely from "Without Prejudice," begins to appear in the New York *Critic*. *The King of Schnorrers: Grotesques and Fantasies* is published in volume form. *The Master*, a novel, is serialized in *Harper's Weekly* (New York) and *To-Day* (London).
1895	*The Master* is published in volume form, and his farce *Threepenny Bits* is produced in London. Max Nordau introduces Zangwill to Theodor Herzl, founder of the modern Zionist movement. Zangwill sponsors Herzl's first address in England. Zangwill and Edith Ayrton meet at the home of a mutual friend.
1896	*Without Prejudice*, a selection of essays from his column, is published in volume form.
1897	Travels to France, Switzerland, Italy, Egypt, Palestine, Syria, Lebanon, Turkey, and Greece. Attends the First Zionist Congress at Basel in August. Continues to write and to publish stories that will comprise *Dreamers of the Ghetto*.
1898	Embarks on an extensive lecture tour of the United States to promote *Dreamers*.
1899	*"They That Walk in Darkness": Ghetto Tragedies* (an expanded version of the 1893 collection) is published. His play *Children of the Ghetto* is performed in the US and London.
1900	The novel *The Mantle of Elijah* is serialized in *Harper's* and then published in volume form. His short play *The Moment of Death* (also called *The Moment Before*) is performed in New York.
1901	*The Revolted Daughter* is performed in London. Joins the English Zionist Federation and represents it at the Fifth World Zionist Congress at Basel.

1902	The *Sketch* calls "S. Cohn & Son: or 'Anglicisation'" (published in the *Pall Mall Magazine* in February) the best story of the month.
1903	*The Grey Wig: Stories and Novelettes* is published, as is *Blind Children*, a collection of poetry. Essays that will become part of *Italian Fantasies* are serialized in *Harper's*. At the Sixth Zionist Congress, Zangwill supports the offer of land in East Africa extended by the British government, beginning his move away from mainstream Zionism. On 26 November, he marries Edith Ayrton, a writer and suffragette. A massive act of violence against Jews takes place in Kishinev, Easter Sunday and Monday. Forty-nine Jews are killed, and approximately 500 injured.
1904	Theatrical adaptations of his short novels *The Serio-Comic Governess* and *Merely Mary Ann* are produced in New York and published in New York and London. *Merely Mary Ann* is performed in London. A Yiddish production of *Children of the Ghetto* opens in New York. Zangwill continues to speak on behalf of the East Africa Offer.
1905	Attends the opening of his play *Jinny the Carrier* in Boston. When the Seventh Zionist Congress rejects the East Africa option, Zangwill forms the Jewish Territorial Organization (ITO) to find a land for the Jewish people wherever one might be found. The Aliens Act is passed by the British Parliament, severely restricting Jewish immigration into the United Kingdom.
1906	Ayrton Israel Zangwill is born in August, in Haslemere, Surrey, not far the from the home that the Zangwills buy for their newly enlarged family: Far End, East Preston, Sussex. Zangwill's play *Nurse Marjorie* is produced in New York. Zangwill and the ITO work with Jacob Schiff in the Galveston Plan, bringing Jews to the United States through that Texas port. The new English *Maḥzor* (Jewish prayerbook for Rosh Hashanah and Yom Kippur) appears, edited by Arthur Davis, with translations of Hebrew poetry by Zangwill.
1907	*Ghetto Comedies*, a collection of short stories, is published. *Merely Mary Ann* and *Nurse Marjorie* are performed outside of London. Continues to work

	for the ITO and the Galveston Plan. Campaigns for women's suffrage through the Women's Social and Political Union and the Men's League for Women's Suffrage, of which he is a founding member.
1908	On 21 August, *The Melting-Pot* has its first performance before an audience, at the Terminus Hall in Littlehampton, near Far End. The cast includes Israel and Edith Zangwill and members of their family and friends along with Walker Whiteside, the original David in commercial productions, and his wife. *The Melting-Pot* has its first US performance on 5 October, in Washington DC, and then continues to Toledo, Chicago, and other North American cities. Israel and Edith arrive in the United States on 24 September. Israel supervises rehearsals of the play and meets with Jacob Schiff regarding the ITO.
1909	On 6 September *The Melting-Pot* opens in New York, the first play to be performed at the new Comedy Theatre.
1910	Margaret Ayrton Zangwill (Peggy) is born in April, while Israel is in Italy working on *Italian Fantasies*. The collection, which expands his *Harper's* series, is published later in the year. Becomes a member of the Dramatists' Club, London.
1911	Early in the year, is in Essex caring for his health. In July he is a delegate to the Universal Races Congress, in London, representing the Jewish people. *The War God* is produced in London.
1912	The Yiddish People's Theatre in London produces *The Melting-Pot* (in Yiddish). *The Next Religion*, his play about a humanistic pastor, is banned by the censor for treating a religious theme. *Six Persons* has one performance in London. Writes *The Marriage of To-morrow*, which criticizes the sexual double standard. It is never published. Joins the Jewish League for Women's Suffrage.
1913	Oliver Louis Zangwill, the Zangwills' third and last child, is born in October.
1914	*The Melting-Pot* opens in London at the Court Theatre, on 25 January, performed by the non-profit

Play Actors. Soon after, on 7 February, it begins a commercial run at the Queen's Theatre, with Walker Whiteside, from the American production, in the leading role of David Quixano. The play is published with Zangwill's appendices and Afterword. *Plaster Saints* and *Six Persons* are performed in London. The Galveston immigration program ends. When the Great War begins in August 1914, joins the Union of Democratic Control, which protests Britain's entry into the war without parliamentary approval.

1915   The Cort Film Company releases a film of *The Melting-Pot*, starring Walker Whiteside and Henry Bergman, who created the role of Mendel in the United States. The William Fox Company releases a film of *Children of the Ghetto*. The British Foreign Office bans UK performances of *The Melting-Pot* because of its portrayal of Russia, now a wartime ally. *Plaster Saints* is published. Joins the effort to admit women to the Dramatists' Club. Supports the Jewish brigades formed to fight on behalf of Britain in Palestine, against the Ottoman Empire.

1916   Publishes *The War for the World*, a collection of essays on current affairs. The film *Merely Mary Ann* is produced by the Fox Film Corporation. The Dramatists' Club resolves to admit women, but without full voting rights.

1917   Presents *The Principle of Nationalities* as the annual Conway Memorial Lecture of the South Place Ethical Society. The British ban on performing *The Melting-Pot* is rescinded. Arranges for the production of plays by other authors for wounded soldiers at military hospitals near Far End. Initially supports both the Russian Revolution and the Balfour Declaration (in which Britain "views with favour" the establishment of a Jewish homeland in Palestine), but later becomes disillusioned with both.

1918   *Too Much Money* is performed in Glasgow and London. Presents the Arthur Davis Memorial Lecture, *Chosen Peoples*, for the Jewish Historical Society of England.

1919   His novel *Jinny the Carrier* is published; it is based on his earlier play of that name.

1920	*The Voice of Jerusalem*, a collection of essays, is published in London. The film *Nurse Marjorie* is released in the United States.
1921	His play *The Cockpit* is published; *The Voice of Jerusalem* is published in New York.
1922	His play *The Forcing House* is published.
1923	In October, delivers his address "Watchman, What of the Night?" to the American Jewish Congress at Carnegie Hall; in the controversial speech, he declares political Zionism dead. *Selected Religious Poems of Solomon Ibn Gabirol*, a dual-language edition with translations from the Hebrew by Zangwill, is published. *The Forcing House* is produced in London. Begins writing "The Baron of Offenbach," a novel that remains unfinished.
1924	His play *We Moderns* opens on Broadway with Helen Hayes in the ingenue role. The Johnson-Reed Act is passed by the United States Congress, severely restricting immigration by national groups that did not have a large presence in the US in 1890. Its effects are felt harshly by Jews from Russia and Eastern Europe.
1925	The production of *We Moderns* in London fails, although a film version is produced by First National Pictures late in the year. Successfully sues the Cort company, which had withheld ten years of royalties for the film of *The Melting-Pot* and falsely claimed ownership of the rights. Ill health leads him to resign the leadership of the ITO, which is then dissolved.
1926	Suffers a nervous collapse and enters a nursing home at Midhurst, Sussex. Dies there, of pneumonia, on 1 August.
1945	Edith Ayrton Zangwill dies of cancer on 8 May. She had published six novels between 1904 and 1928 and remained active in the pacifist and Zionist causes after her husband's death.

A Note on the Text

The text of *The Melting-Pot* (which includes Israel Zangwill's Appendices and Afterword from the 1914 first printed edition) is from the Project Gutenberg electronic text, which uses the 1921 Macmillan printing. I have checked this line by line against the 1932 Macmillan printing, used in the photo-reprint edition by Ayer Publishing (1999). Where discrepancies appear, I have gone to the 1914 edition in the Cornell University Library, available via Hathitrust.com, which is the final arbiter. I have silently corrected only the most obvious typographical errors. Significant differences between texts are indicated in the footnotes.

I have maintained Zangwill's British English spellings, as well as his italicization of words such as *Purim* and *pogrom*, which are now naturalized into American English.

THE MELTING-POT

DRAMA IN FOUR ACTS

BY

ISRAEL ZANGWILL

AUTHOR OF "CHILDREN OF THE GHETTO,"
"MERELY MARY ANN," ETC., ETC.

NEW AND REVISED EDITION

New York
THE MACMILLAN COMPANY
1914
All Rights Reserved

TO

THEODORE ROOSEVELT

IN RESPECTFUL RECOGNITION OF
HIS STRENUOUS STRUGGLE AGAINST
THE FORCES THAT THREATEN TO
SHIPWRECK THE GREAT REPUBLIC
WHICH CARRIES MANKIND AND
ITS FORTUNES, THIS PLAY IS, BY
HIS KIND PERMISSION, CORDIALLY
DEDICATED

The rights of performing or publishing this play in any country or language are strictly reserved by the author.[1]

---

1 In the 1932 Macmillan edition, this passage continues as follows: *Application for stock or amateur dramatic production rights should be made to Messrs. Samuel French, 25 West 45th Street, New York. Application for all other rights should be made to Mrs. Zangwill, care of The Macmillan Company. (The film rights are already sold in perpetuity.)* The play was released as a silent film in 1915, starring Walker Whiteside and Henry Bergman in the roles they originated in the first US production. It was produced and distributed by the Centaur Film Company and directed by Oliver D. Bailey and James Vincent.

THE CAST

[As first produced at the Columbia Theatre, Washington, on the fifth of October 1908]

David Quixano	WALKER WHITESIDE
Mendel Quixano	HENRY BERGMAN
Baron Revendal	JOHN BLAIR
Quincy Davenport, Jr.	GRANT STEWART
Herr Pappelmeister	HENRY VOGEL
Vera Revendal	CHRYSTAL HERNE
Baroness Revendal	LEONORA VON OTTINGER
Frau Quixano	LOUISE MULDENER
Kathleen O'Reilly	MOLLIE REVEL
Settlement Servant	ANNIE HARRIS

Produced by HUGH FORD

[As first produced by the Play Actors at the Court Theatre, London on the twenty-fifth of January 1914]

David Quixano	HAROLD CHAPIN
Mendel Quixano	HUGH TABBERER
Baron Revendal	H. LAWRENCE LEYTON
Quincy Davenport, Jr.	P. PERCEVAL CLARK
Herr Pappelmeister	CLIFTON ALDERSON
Vera Revendal	PHYLLIS RELPH
Baroness Revendal	GILLIAN SCAIFE
Frau Quixano	INEZ BENSUSAN
Kathleen O'Reilly	E. NOLAN O'CONNOR
Settlement Servant	RUTH PARROTT

Produced by NORMAN PAGE

Act I

The scene is laid in the living-room of the small home of the
QUIXANOS *in the Richmond or non-Jewish borough of New York,*
about five o'clock of a February afternoon. At centre back is a
double street-door giving on a columned veranda in the Colonial
style. Nailed on the right-hand door-post gleams a Mezuzah, *a tiny*
metal case, containing a Biblical passage. On the right of the door is
a small hat-stand holding MENDEL'S *overcoat, umbrella, etc.*
There are two windows, one on either side of the door, and three
exits, one down-stage on the left leading to the stairs and family bed-
rooms, and two on the right, the upper leading to KATHLEEN'S
bedroom and the lower to the kitchen. Over the street door is pinned
the Stars-and-Stripes. On the left wall, in the upper corner of which
is a music-stand, are bookshelves of large mouldering Hebrew books,
and over them is hung a Mizrach, *or Hebrew picture, to show it is*
the East Wall.[1] *Other pictures round the room include Wagner,*
Columbus, Lincoln, and "Jews at the Wailing place."[2] *Down-stage,*
about a yard from the left wall, stands DAVID'S *roll-desk, open*
and displaying a medley of music, a quill pen, etc. On the wall
behind the desk hangs a book-rack with brightly bound English
books. A grand piano stands at left centre back, holding a pile of
music and one huge Hebrew tome. There is a table in the middle of
the room covered with a red cloth and a litter of objects, music, and
newspapers. The fireplace, in which a fire is burning, occupies the
centre of the right wall, and by it stands an armchair on which lies
another heavy mouldy Hebrew tome. The mantel holds a clock, two
silver candlesticks, etc. A chiffonier stands against the back wall on
the right. There are a few cheap chairs. The whole effect is a curious
blend of shabbiness, Americanism, Jewishness, and music, all four
being combined in the figure of MENDEL QUIXANO, *who, in a*
black skull-cap, a seedy velvet jacket, and red carpet-slippers, is dis-

---

1   Devout Jews recite certain Hebrew prayers daily, facing east, and a
    Mizrach (meaning "East") placed on the wall would indicate that
    direction.

2   Richard Wagner (1813–83), German composer, best known for his
    operas, considered avant-garde in his time; Christopher Columbus
    (c. 1451–1506), explorer long considered the European discoverer of
    the Americas; Abraham Lincoln (1809–65), sixteenth president of
    the United States; the Western Wall, or remnant of a retaining wall of
    the Second Temple in Jerusalem, destroyed in 70 CE. There were
    numerous images with this title in the nineteenth and early twentieth
    centuries.

covered standing at the open street-door. He is an elderly music master with a fine Jewish face, pathetically furrowed by misfortunes, and a short grizzled beard.

MENDEL. Good-bye, Johnny! ... And don't forget to practise your scales. [*Shutting door, shivers.*] Ugh! It'll snow again, I guess. [*He yawns, heaves a great sigh of relief, walks toward the table, and perceives a music-roll.*] The chump! He's forgotten his music! [*He picks it up and runs toward the window on the left, muttering furiously.*] Brainless, earless, thumb-fingered Gentile! [*Throwing open the window.*] Here, Johnny! You can't practise your scales if you leave 'em here! [*He throws out the music-roll and shivers again at the cold as he shuts the window.*] Ugh! And I must go out to that miserable dancing class to scrape the rent together. [*He goes to the fire and warms his hands.*] Ach Gott![1] What a life! What a life! [*He drops dejectedly into the armchair. Finding himself sitting uncomfortably on the big book, he half rises and pushes it to the side of the seat. After an instant an irate Irish voice is heard from behind the kitchen door.*]

KATHLEEN [*Without*]. Divil take the butther![2] I wouldn't put up with ye, not for a hundred dollars a week.

MENDEL [*Raising himself to listen, heaves great sigh*]. Ach! Mother and Kathleen again!

KATHLEEN [*Still louder*]. Pots and pans and plates and knives! Sure 'tis enough to make a saint chrazy.

FRAU QUIXANO [*Equally loudly from kitchen*]. *Wos schreist du? Gott in Himmel, dieses Amerika!*[3]

KATHLEEN [*Opening door of kitchen toward the end of* FRAU QUIXANO'S *speech, but turning back, with her hand visible on the door*]. What's that ye're afther jabberin' about America? If ye don't like God's own counthry, sure ye can go back to your own Jerusalem, so ye can.

---

1 Yiddish: Oh, God! This expression and others like it in the speech of Jewish characters are Zangwill's transcription of Yiddish. Zangwill uses an idiosyncratic, currently non-standard, system of transliteration for Yiddish, often based on the German that is the source of many Yiddish words.
2 Kathleen's speech reflects Irish-accented English.
3 Yiddish: Why are you shouting? God in Heaven, this is America!

MENDEL. One's very servants are anti-Semites.

KATHLEEN [*Bangs her door as she enters excitedly, carrying a folded white table-cloth. She is a young and pretty Irish maid-of-all-work*]. Bad luck to me, if iver I take sarvice again with haythen Jews. [*She perceives* MENDEL *huddled up in the armchair, gives a little scream, and drops the cloth.*] Och, I thought ye was out!

MENDEL [*Rising*]. And so you dared to be rude to my mother.

KATHLEEN [*Angrily, as she picks up the cloth*]. She said I put mate on a butther-plate.[1]

MENDEL. Well, you know that's against her religion.

KATHLEEN. But I didn't do nothing of the soort. I ounly put butther on a mate-plate.

MENDEL. That's just as bad. What the Bible forbids——[2]

KATHLEEN [*Lays the cloth on a chair and vigorously clears off the litter of things on the table*]. Sure, the Pope himself couldn't remimber it all. Why don't ye have a sinsible religion?

MENDEL. You are impertinent. Attend to your work. [*He seats himself at the piano.*]

KATHLEEN. And isn't it laying the Sabbath cloth I am? [*She bangs down articles from the table into their right places.*]

MENDEL. Don't answer me back. [*He begins to play softly.*]

KATHLEEN. Faith, I must answer *somebody* back—and sorra a word of English *she* understands. I might as well talk to a tree.

MENDEL. You are not paid to talk, but to work. [*Playing on softly.*]

KATHLEEN. And who *can* work wid an ould woman nagglin' and grizzlin' and faultin' me? [*She removes the red table-cloth.*] Mate-plates, butther-plates, *kosher*, *trepha*, sure I've smashed up folks' crockery and they makin' less fuss ouver it.

---

1 Putting meat on a butter plate, or vice versa—i.e., mixing meat with dairy—would violate one of the laws of *kashrut* (keeping kosher) that are followed by observant Jews such as Frau Quixano.

2 The prohibition against mixing meat and dairy is based on Exodus 23:19, 34:26, and Deuteronomy 14:21. Further on, the word *kosher* indicates foods that are acceptable to eat, and *trepha* (or *treif*) means not kosher, or prohibited.

MENDEL [*Stops playing*]. Breaking crockery is one thing, and breaking a religion another. Didn't you tell me when I engaged you that you had lived in other Jewish families?

KATHLEEN [*Angrily*]. And is it a liar ye'd make me out now? I've lived wid clothiers and pawnbrokers and Vaudeville actors, but I niver shtruck a house where mate and butther couldn't be as paceable on the same plate as eggs and bacon—the most was that some wouldn't ate the bacon onless 'twas killed *kosher*.[1]

MENDEL [*Tickled*]. Ha! Ha! Ha! Ha! Ha!

KATHLEEN [*Furious, pauses with the white table-cloth half on*]. And who's ye laughin' at? I give ye a week's notice. I won't be the joke of Jews, no, begorra, that I won't. [*She pulls the cloth on viciously.*]

MENDEL [*Sobered, rising from the piano*]. Don't talk nonsense, Kathleen. Nobody is making a joke of you. Have a little patience—you'll soon learn our ways.

KATHLEEN [*More mildly*]. Whose ways, yours or the ould lady's or Mr. David's? To-night being yer Sabbath, *you'll* be blowing out yer bedroom candle, though ye won't light it; Mr. David'll light his and blow it out too; and the misthress won't even touch the candleshtick.[2] There's three religions in this house, not wan.[3]

MENDEL [*Coughs uneasily*]. Hem! Well, you learn the mistress's ways—that will be enough.

KATHLEEN [*Going to mantelpiece*]. But what way can I understand her jabberin' and jibberin'?—I'm not a monkey! [*She takes up a silver candlestick.*] Why doesn't she talk English like a Christian?

---

1 The laws of *kashrut* require that permitted animals be slaughtered in a specific way. However, bacon and all other pork products are prohibited. The other Jewish families Kathleen had worked for (described with stereotypical Jewish occupations) were not as observant as Frau Quixano.

2 Lighting a fire is considered work prohibited on the Jewish Sabbath, the day of rest, which begins at sundown Friday night. Kathleen indicates the different degrees of observance in the household.

3 It's important to recognize that Kathleen is referring to generational fallings-off in observance, something that was common to Jewish immigrants at this time. The differences in degrees of observance do not coincide with any specific denominational differences in Judaism.

MENDEL [*Irritated*]. If you are going on like that, perhaps you had better *not* remain here.

KATHLEEN [*Blazing up, forgetting to take the second candlestick*]. And who's axin' ye to remain here? Faith, I'll quit off this blissid minit!

MENDEL [*Taken aback*]. No, you can't do that.

KATHLEEN. And why can't I? Ye can keep yer dirthy wages. [*She dumps down the candlestick violently on the table, and exit hysterically into her bedroom.*]

MENDEL [*Sighing heavily*]. She might have put on the other candlestick. [*He goes to mantel and takes it. A rat-tat-tat at street-door.*] Who can that be? [*Running to* KATHLEEN'S *door, holding candlestick forgetfully low.*] Kathleen! There's a visitor!

KATHLEEN [*Angrily from within*]. I'm not here!

MENDEL. So long as you're in this house, you must do your work. [KATHLEEN'S *head emerges sulkily.*]

KATHLEEN. I tould ye I was lavin' at wanst. Let you open the door yerself.

MENDEL. I'm not dressed to receive visitors—it may be a new pupil. [*He goes toward staircase, automatically carrying off the candlestick which* KATHLEEN *has not caught sight of. Exit on the left.*]

KATHLEEN [*Moving toward the street-door*]. The divil fly away wid me if ivir from this 'our I set foot again among haythen furriners—— [*She throws open the door angrily and then the outer door.* VERA REVENDAL, *a beautiful girl in furs and muff, with a touch of the exotic in her appearance, steps into the little vestibule.*]

VERA. Is Mr. Quixano at home?

KATHLEEN [*Sulkily*]. Which Mr. Quixano?

VERA [*Surprised*]. Are there two Mr. Quixanos?

KATHLEEN [*Tartly*]. Didn't I say there was?

VERA. Then I want the one who plays.

KATHLEEN. There isn't a one who plays.

VERA. Oh, surely!

KATHLEEN. Ye're wrong entirely. They both plays.

VERA [*Smiling*]. Oh, dear! And I suppose they both play the violin.

KATHLEEN. Ye're wrong again. One plays the piano—ounly the young ginthleman plays the fiddle—Mr. David!

VERA [*Eagerly*]. Ah, Mr. David—that's the one I want to see.

KATHLEEN. He's out. [*She abruptly shuts the door.*]

VERA [*Stopping its closing*]. Don't shut the door!

KATHLEEN [*Snappily*]. More chanst of seeing him out there than in here!

VERA. But I want to leave a message.

KATHLEEN. Then why don't ye come inside? It's freezin' me to the bone. [*She sneezes.*] Atchoo!

VERA. I'm sorry. [*She comes in and closes the door.*] Will you please say Miss Revendal called from the Settlement,[1] and we are anxiously awaiting his answer to the letter asking him to play for us on——

KATHLEEN. What way will I be tellin' him all that? I'm not here.

VERA. Eh?

KATHLEEN. I'm lavin'—just as soon as I've me thrunk packed.

VERA. Then I must *write* the message—can I write at this desk?

KATHLEEN. If the ould woman don't come in and shpy you.

VERA. What old woman?

KATHLEEN. Ould Mr. Quixano's mother—she wears a black wig,[2] she's that houly.

---

1 Settlement houses were established in the 1880s and 1890s by progressive philanthropists such as Jane Addams (1860–1935) and Lillian Wald (1867–1940). Located in major cities and serving largely immigrant populations, these community educational and training institutions were staffed by women of the middle and upper classes. See Introduction, pp. 27–31, and Appendix E.
2 Observant Jewish women who are married or widowed keep their hair covered, particularly those who are Orthodox.

VERA [*Bewildered*]. What? ... But why should she mind my writing?

KATHLEEN. Look at the clock. [VERA *looks at the clock, more puzzled than ever.*] If ye're not quick, it'll be *Shabbos.*[1]

VERA. Be what?

KATHLEEN [*Holds up hands of horror*]. Ye don't know what *Shabbos* is! A Jewess not know her own Sunday!

VERA [*Outraged*]. I, a Jewess! How dare you?

KATHLEEN [*Flustered*]. Axin' your pardon, miss, but ye looked a bit furrin and I——

VERA [*Frozen*]. I am a Russian. [*Slowly and dazedly.*] Do I understand that Mr. Quixano is a Jew?

KATHLEEN. Two Jews, miss. Both of 'em.

VERA. Oh, but it is impossible. [*Dazedly to herself.*] He had such charming manners. [*Aloud again.*] You seem to think everybody Jewish. Are you sure Mr. Quixano is not Spanish?— the name sounds Spanish.

KATHLEEN. Shpanish! [*She picks up the old Hebrew book on the armchair.*] Look at the ould lady's book. Is that Shpanish? [*She points to the Mizrach.*] And that houly picture the ould lady says her pater-noster[2] to! Is that Shpanish? And that houly table-cloth with the houly silver candle—— [*Cry of sudden astonishment.*] Why, I've ounly put—— [*She looks toward mantel and utters a great cry of alarm as she drops the Hebrew book on the floor.*] Why, where's the other candleshtick! Mother in hivin, they'll say I shtole the candleshtick! [*Perceiving that* VERA *is dazedly moving toward door.*] Beggin' your pardon, miss—— [*She is about to move a chair toward the desk.*]

VERA. Thank you, I've changed my mind.

KATHLEEN. That's more than I'll do.

VERA [*Hand on door*]. Don't say I called at all.

KATHLEEN. Plaze yerself. What name did ye say? [MENDEL *enters hastily from his bedroom, completely transmogrified, minus the*

---

1 Yiddish: Jewish Sabbath.
2 Latin: Our Father; that is, the Christian Lord's Prayer. Kathleen uses a term familiar to her from her own Catholic tradition.

skull-cap, with a Prince Albert coat,[1] *and boots instead of slippers, so that his appearance is gentlemanly.* KATHLEEN *begins to search quietly and unostentatiously in the table-drawers, the chiffonier, etc., etc., for the candlestick.*]

MENDEL. I am sorry if I have kept you waiting—— [*He rubs his hands importantly.*] You see I have so many pupils already. Won't you sit down? [*He indicates a chair.*]

VERA [*Flushing, embarrassed, releasing her hold of the door handle*]. Thank you—I—I—I didn't come about pianoforte lessons.

MENDEL [*Sighing in disappointment*]. *Ach!*

VERA. In fact I—er—it wasn't you I wanted at all—I was just going.

MENDEL [*Politely*]. Perhaps I can direct you to the house you are looking for.

VERA. Thank you, I won't trouble you. [*She turns toward the door again.*]

MENDEL. Allow me! [*He opens the door for her.*]

VERA [*Hesitating, struck by his manners, struggling with her anti-Jewish prejudice*]. It—it—was your son I wanted.

MENDEL [*His face lighting up*]. You mean my nephew, David. Yes, *he* gives violin lessons. [*He closes the door.*]

VERA. Oh, is he your nephew?

MENDEL. I am sorry he is out—he, too, has so many pupils, though at the moment he is only at the Crippled Children's Home—playing to them.

VERA. How lovely of him! [*Touched and deciding to conquer her prejudice.*] But that's just what *I* came about—I mean we'd like him to play again at our Settlement. Please ask him why he hasn't answered Miss Andrews's letter.

MENDEL [*Astonished*]. He hasn't answered your letter?

VERA. Oh, I'm not Miss Andrews; I'm only her assistant.

---

1   A double-breasted knee-length man's coat popular in the Victorian era and at the time of the play. It was named after Prince Albert (1819–61), spouse of Queen Victoria (r. 1837–1901).

MENDEL. I see—Kathleen, whatever are you doing under the table? [KATHLEEN, *in her hunting around for the candlestick, is now stooping and lifting up the table-cloth.*]

KATHLEEN. Sure the fiend's after witching away the candle-shtick.

MENDEL [*Embarrassed*]. The candlestick? Oh—I—I think you'll find it in my bedroom.

KATHLEEN. Wisha, now! [*She goes into his bedroom.*]

MENDEL [*Turning apologetically to* VERA]. I beg your pardon, Miss Andrews, I mean Miss—er——

VERA. Revendal.

MENDEL [*Slightly more interested*]. Revendal? Then you must be the Miss Revendal David told me about!

VERA [*Blushing*]. Why, he has only seen me once—the time he played at our Roof-Garden Concert.[1]

MENDEL. Yes, but he was so impressed by the way you handled those new immigrants—the Spirit of the Settlement, he called you.

VERA [*Modestly*]. Ah, no—Miss Andrews is that. And you will tell him to answer her letter at once, won't you, because there's only a week now to our Concert. [*A gust of wind shakes the windows. She smiles.*] Naturally it will *not* be on the Roof Garden.

MENDEL [*Half to himself*]. Fancy David not saying a word about it to me! Are you sure the letter was mailed?

VERA. I mailed it myself—a week ago. And even in New York—— [*She smiles. Re-enter* KATHLEEN *with the recovered candlestick.*]

KATHLEEN. Bedad, ye're as great a shleep-walker as Mr. David! [*She places the candlestick on the table and moves toward her bedroom.*]

MENDEL. Kathleen!

KATHLEEN [*Pursuing her walk without turning*]. I'm not here!

---

1 Roof gardens were common in settlement houses, providing fresh-air environments in crowded city neighbourhoods. The Educational Alliance on New York's Lower East Side (an apparent model for the settlement house in *The Melting-Pot*) had a roof garden.

MENDEL. Did you take in a letter for Mr. David about a week ago? [*Smiling at* MISS REVENDAL.] He doesn't get many, you see.

KATHLEEN [*Turning*]. A letter? Sure, I took in ounly a post-card from Miss Johnson, an' that ounly sayin'——

VERA. And you don't remember a letter—a large letter—last Saturday—with the seal of our Settlement?

KATHLEEN. Last Saturday wid a seal, is it? Sure, how could I forgit it?

MENDEL. Then you *did* take it in?

KATHLEEN. Ye're wrong entirely. 'Twas the misthress took it in.

MENDEL [*To* VERA]. I am sorry the boy has been so rude.

KATHLEEN. But the misthress didn't give it him at wanst—she hid it away bekaz it was *Shabbos*.

MENDEL. Oh, dear—and she has forgotten to give it to him. Excuse me. [*He makes a hurried exit to the kitchen.*]

KATHLEEN. And excuse *me*—I've me thrunk to pack. [*She goes toward her bedroom, pauses at the door.*] And ye'll witness I don't pack the candleshtick. [*Emphatic exit.*]

VERA [*Still dazed*]. A Jew! That wonderful boy a Jew! ... But then so was David the shepherd youth with his harp and his psalms, the sweet singer in Israel. [*She surveys the room and its contents with interest. The windows rattle once or twice in the rising wind. The light gets gradually less. She picks up the huge Hebrew tome on the piano and puts it down with a slight smile as if over-whelmed by the weight of alien antiquity. Then she goes over to the desk and picks up the printed music.*] Mendelssohn's Concerto, Tartini's Sonata in G Minor, Bach's Chaconne ...[1] [*She looks up at the book-rack.*] "History of the American Commonwealth," "Cyclopædia of History," "History of the Jews"—he seems very fond of history. Ah, there's Shelley and Tennyson.[2] [*With sur-*

---

1   Giuseppe Tartini (1692–1779) and Johann Sebastian Bach (1685–1750), Italian and German composers in the Baroque mode of the eighteenth century; Felix Mendelssohn (1809–47), who had Jewish ancestry, a nineteenth-century German Romantic composer.
2   Percy Bysshe Shelley (1792–1822) and Alfred, Lord Tennyson (1809–92), nineteenth-century English poets.

prise.] Nietzsche[1] next to the Bible? No Russian books apparently—— [*Re-enter* MENDEL *triumphantly with a large sealed letter.*]

MENDEL. Here it is! As it came on Saturday, my mother was afraid David would open it!

VERA [*Smiling*]. But what *can* you do with a letter except open it? Any more than with an oyster?

MENDEL [*Smiling as he puts the letter on* DAVID'S *desk*]. To a pious Jew letters and oysters are alike forbidden—at least letters may not be opened on our day of rest.[2]

VERA. I'm sure I couldn't rest till I'd opened mine. [*Enter from the kitchen* FRAU QUIXANO, *defending herself with excited gesticulation. She is an old lady with a black wig, but her appearance is dignified, venerable even, in no way comic. She speaks Yiddish exclusively, that being largely the language of the Russian Pale.*[3]]

FRAU QUIXANO. *Obber ich hob gesogt zu Kathleen*——[4]

MENDEL [*Turning and going to her*]. Yes, yes, mother, that's all right now.

FRAU QUIXANO [*In horror, perceiving her Hebrew book on the floor, where* KATHLEEN *has dropped it*]. *Mein Buch!*[5] [*She picks it up and kisses it piously.*]

MENDEL [*Presses her into her fireside chair*]. *Ruhig, ruhig, Mutter!*[6] [*To* VERA.] She understands barely a word of English—she won't disturb us.

---

1   Friedrich Nietzsche (1844–1900), German philosopher and cultural critic. He is best known for his critique of religion and his concepts of the *Übermensch* (the "great man" or "superman") and the power of the individual will.
2   Oysters, as all shellfish, are prohibited by the laws of *kashrut*. Opening a letter would be considered prohibited work on the Sabbath.
3   The "Pale of Settlement," area in the western Russian Empire to which Tsarist regulations restricted most Jews during the nineteenth and early twentieth centuries, until the Russian Revolution of 1917. It included regions now part of Belarus, Lithuania, Poland, and Ukraine. Yiddish was the main language of Jews in this region as well as in central Europe.
4   Yiddish: But I have said to Kathleen.
5   Yiddish: My book!
6   Yiddish: Calm, calm, Mother!

VERA. Oh, but I must be going—I was so long finding the house, and look! It has begun to snow! [*They both turn their heads and look at the falling snow.*]

MENDEL. All the more reason to wait for David—it may leave off. He can't be long now. Do sit down. [*He offers a chair.*]

FRAU QUIXANO [*Looking round suspiciously*]. *Wos will die Shikseh?*[1]

VERA. What does your mother say?

MENDEL [*Half-smiling*]. Oh, only asking what your heathen ladyship desires.

VERA. Tell her I hope she is well.

MENDEL. *Das Fräulein hofft dass es geht gut——*[2]

FRAU QUIXANO [*Shrugging her shoulders in despairing astonishment*]. *Gut? Un' wie soll es gut gehen—in Amerika!*[3] [*She takes out her spectacles, and begins slowly polishing and adjusting them.*]

VERA [*Smiling*]. I understood that last word.

MENDEL. She asks how can anything possibly go well in America!

VERA. Ah, she doesn't like America.

MENDEL [*Half-smiling*]. Her favourite exclamation is "*A Klog zu Columbessen!*"

VERA. What does that mean?

MENDEL. Cursed be Columbus!

VERA [*Laughingly*]. Poor Columbus! I suppose she's just come over.

MENDEL. Oh, no, it must be ten years since I sent for her.

VERA. Really! But your nephew was born here?

MENDEL. No, he's Russian too. But please sit down, you had better get his answer at once. [VERA *sits.*]

---

1 Yiddish: What does the gentile (or heathen) woman want? *Shikseh* is a derogatory term for a non-Jewish woman.
2 Yiddish: The young lady hopes you are well.
3 Yiddish: Well? And how can it go well—in America!

VERA. I suppose *you* taught him music.

MENDEL. I? I can't play the violin. He is self-taught. In the Russian Pale he was a wonder-child. Poor David! He always looked forward to coming to America; he imagined I was a famous musician over here. He found me conductor in a cheap theatre—a converted beer-hall.

VERA. Was he very disappointed?

MENDEL. Disappointed? He was enchanted! He is crazy about America.

VERA [*Smiling*]. Ah, *he* doesn't curse Columbus.

MENDEL. My mother came with her life behind her: David with his life before him. Poor boy!

VERA. Why do you say poor boy?

MENDEL. What is there before him here but a terrible struggle for life? If he doesn't curse Columbus, he'll curse fate. Music-lessons and dance-halls, beer-halls and weddings—every hope and ambition will be ground out of him, and he will die obscure and unknown. [*His head sinks on his breast,* FRAU QUIXANO *is heard faintly sobbing over her book. The sobbing continues throughout the scene.*]

VERA [*Half rising*]. You have made your mother cry.

MENDEL. Oh, no—she understood nothing. She always cries on the eve of the Sabbath.

VERA [*Mystified, sinking back into her chair*]. Always cries? Why?

MENDEL [*Embarrassed*]. Oh, well, a Christian wouldn't understand——

VERA. Yes I could—do tell me!

MENDEL. She knows that in this great grinding America, David and I must go out to earn our bread on Sabbath as on week-days. She never says a word to us, but her heart is full of tears.

VERA. Poor old woman. It was wrong of us to ask your nephew to play at the Settlement for nothing.

MENDEL [*Rising fiercely*]. If you offer him a fee, he shall not play. Did you think I was begging of you?

VERA. I beg your pardon—— [*She smiles.*] There, *I* am begging of *you*. Sit down, please.

MENDEL [*Walking away to piano*]. I ought not to have burdened you with our troubles—you are too young.

VERA [*Pathetically*]. I young? If you only knew how old I am!

MENDEL. You?

VERA. I left my youth in Russia—eternities ago.

MENDEL. You know our Russia! [*He goes over to her and sits down.*]

VERA. Can't you see I'm a Russian, too? [*With a faint tremulous smile.*] I might even have been a Siberian had I stayed. But I escaped from my gaolers.[1]

MENDEL. You were a Revolutionist!

VERA. Who can live in Russia and not be? So you see trouble and I are not such strangers.

MENDEL. Who would have thought it to look at you? Siberia, gaolers, revolutions! [*Rising.*] What terrible things life holds!

VERA. Yes, even in free America. [FRAU QUIXANO'S *sobbing grows slightly louder.*]

MENDEL. That Settlement work must be full of tragedies.

VERA. Sometimes one sees nothing but the tragedy of things. [*Looking toward the window.*] The snow is getting thicker. How pitilessly it falls—like fate.

MENDEL [*Following her gaze*]. Yes, icy and inexorable. [*The faint sobbing of* FRAU QUIXANO *over her book, which has been heard throughout the scene as a sort of musical accompaniment, has combined to work it up to a mood of intense sadness, intensified by the growing dusk, so that as the two now gaze at the falling snow, the atmosphere seems overbrooded with melancholy. There is a moment or two without dialogue, given over to the sobbing of* FRAU QUIXANO, *the roar of the wind shaking the windows, the quick*

---

1   Jailers. Opponents of the Tsarist regime often suffered harsh imprisonment in Siberia.

falling of the snow. Suddenly a happy voice singing "My Country 'tis of Thee"[1] is heard from without.]

FRAU QUIXANO [*Pricking up her ears, joyously*]. *Do ist Dovidel!*[2]

MENDEL. That's David! [*He springs up.*]

VERA [*Murmurs in relief*]. Ah! [*The whole atmosphere is changed to one of joyous expectation. DAVID is seen and heard passing the left window, still singing the national hymn, but it breaks off abruptly as he throws open the door and appears on the threshold, a buoyant snow-covered figure in a cloak and a broad-brimmed hat, carrying a violin case. He is a sunny, handsome youth of the finest Russo-Jewish type. He speaks with a slight German accent.*[3]]

DAVID. Isn't it a beautiful world, uncle? [*He closes the inner door.*] Snow, the divine white snow—— [*Perceiving the visitor with amaze.*] Miss Revendal here! [*He removes his hat and looks at her with boyish reverence and wonder.*]

VERA [*Smiling*]. Don't look so surprised—I haven't fallen from heaven like the snow. Take off your wet things.

DAVID. Oh, it's nothing; it's dry snow. [*He lays down his violin case and brushes off the snow from his cloak, which MENDEL takes from him and hangs on the rack, all without interrupting the dialogue.*] If I had only known you were waiting——

VERA. I am glad you didn't—I wouldn't have had those poor little cripples cheated out of a moment of your music.

DAVID. Uncle has told you? Ah, it was bully![4] You should have seen the cripples waltzing with their crutches! [*He has moved toward the old woman, and while he holds one hand to the blaze now*

---

1 This song, also known as "America," was written in 1831 by Samuel Francis Smith (1808–95) and sung to the tune of the British national anthem, "God Save the King" (or "Queen"). It served as an unofficial anthem of the United States until "The Star-Spangled Banner" was adopted in 1931, and it was very well known.
2 Yiddish: Here is little David; Frau Quixano uses an affectionate form of David's name.
3 David would be more likely to speak with a Yiddish accent. However, at that time Yiddish was frequently considered a substandard version of German or, as Zangwill often called it, "jargon." See Introduction.
4 Slang: Fine, excellent!

pats her cheek with the other in greeting, to which she responds with a loving smile ere she settles contentedly to slumber over her book.] *Es war grossartig,*[1] Granny. Even the paralysed danced.

MENDEL. Don't exaggerate, David.

DAVID. Exaggerate, uncle! Why, if they hadn't the use of their legs, their arms danced on the counterpane; if their arms couldn't dance, their hands danced from the wrist; and if their hands couldn't dance, they danced with their fingers; and if their fingers couldn't dance, their heads danced; and if their heads were paralysed, why, their eyes danced—God never curses so utterly but you've *something* left to dance with! [*He moves toward his desk.*]

VERA [*Infected with his gaiety*]. You'll tell us next the beds danced.

DAVID. So they did—they shook their legs like mad!

VERA Oh, why wasn't I there? [*His eyes meet hers at the thought of her presence.*]

DAVID. Dear little cripples, I felt as if I could play them all straight again with the love and joy jumping out of this old fiddle. [*He lays his hand caressingly on the violin.*]

MENDEL [*Gloomily*]. But in reality you left them as crooked as ever.

DAVID. No, I didn't. [*He caresses the back of his uncle's head in affectionate rebuke.*] I couldn't play their bones straight, but I played their brains straight. And hunch-*brains* are worse than hunch-*backs.*... [*Suddenly perceiving his letter on the desk.*] A letter for *me!* [*He takes it with boyish eagerness, then hesitates to open it.*]

VERA [*Smiling*]. Oh, you may open it!

DAVID [*Wistfully*]. May I?

VERA [*Smiling*]. Yes, and quick—or it'll be *Shabbos!* [DAVID *looks up at her in wonder.*]

MENDEL [*Smiling*]. You read your letter!

DAVID [*Opens it eagerly, then smiles broadly with pleasure*]. Oh,

---

1 German: It was great, wonderful. However, David would more likely have been using the Yiddish expression, *es iz geven groys* (or *groyserdik*).

Miss Revendal! Isn't that great! To play again at your Settlement. I *am* getting famous.

VERA. But we can't offer you a fee.

MENDEL [*Quickly sotto voce*[1] *to* VERA]. Thank you!

DAVID. A fee! I'd pay a fee to see all those happy immigrants you gather together—Dutchmen and Greeks, Poles and Norwegians, Welsh and Armenians. If you only had Jews, it would be as good as going to Ellis Island.[2]

VERA [*Smiling*]. What a strange taste! Who on earth wants to go to Ellis Island?

DAVID. Oh, I love going to Ellis Island to watch the ships coming in from Europe, and to think that all those weary, sea-tossed wanderers are feeling what *I* felt when America first stretched out her great mother-hand to *me*![3]

VERA [*Softly*]. Were you very happy?

DAVID. It was heaven. You must remember that all my life I had heard of America—everybody in our town had friends there or was going there or got money orders from there. The earliest game I played at was selling off my toy furniture and setting up in America. All my life America was waiting, beckoning, shining—the place where God would wipe away tears from off all faces. [*He ends in a half-sob.*]

MENDEL [*Rises, as in terror*]. Now, now, David, don't get excited. [*Approaches him.*]

---

1 Italian: with a soft voice; quietly.
2 Site of the largest immigration inspection station in the United States from 1892 to 1954. The vast majority of immigrants in the "great wave" of 1892–1920 came in through its facilities. It was also the location where many were sent back due to illness, particularly illnesses of the eyes (see Appendix D3). Some of the Ellis Island buildings and grounds have been restored and are now part of the Statue of Liberty, Ellis Island, and Liberty Island national monument. The absence of Jews from the Settlement house may be explained by its location in Richmond (Staten Island). However, later details suggest a model in the Educational Alliance, a Lower East Side settlement that served a large immigrant Jewish population.
3 David's imagery echoes that of Emma Lazarus's poem about the Statue of Liberty, "The New Colossus" (1883); see Appendix D1.

DAVID. To think that the same great torch of liberty which threw its light across all the broad seas and lands into my little garret in Russia, is shining also for all those other weeping millions of Europe, shining wherever men hunger and are oppressed——

MENDEL [*Soothingly*]. Yes, yes, David. [*Laying hand on his shoulder.*] Now sit down and—

DAVID [*Unheeding*]. Shining over the starving villages of Italy and Ireland, over the swarming stony cities of Poland and Galicia,[1] over the ruined farms of Roumania, over the shambles[2] of Russia——

MENDEL [*Pleadingly*]. David!

DAVID. Oh, Miss Revendal, when I look at our Statue of Liberty, I just seem to hear the voice of America crying: "Come unto me all ye that labour and are heavy laden and I will give you rest—rest——"[3] [*He is now almost sobbing.*]

MENDEL. Don't talk any more—you know it is bad for you.

DAVID. But Miss Revendal asked—and I want to explain to her what America means to me.

MENDEL. You can explain it in your American symphony.

VERA [*Eagerly—to* DAVID]. You compose?

DAVID [*Embarrassed*]. Oh, uncle, why did you talk of—? Uncle always—my music is so thin and tinkling. When I am *writing* my American symphony, it seems like thunder crashing through a forest full of bird songs. But next day—oh, next day! [*He laughs dolefully and turns away.*]

VERA. So your music finds inspiration in America?

DAVID. Yes—in the seething of the Crucible.[4]

VERA. The Crucible? I don't understand!

DAVID. Not understand! You, the Spirit of the Settlement! [*He rises and crosses to her and leans over the table, facing her.*] Not

---

1　Region of Russia-Poland, at that time inhabited by many Jews.
2　Slaughterhouse. The word appears again at the end of Act III (p. 143).
3　See Matthew 11:28.
4　A container in which metals or other substances may be heated to melt or fuse together: a melting-pot.

understand that America is God's Crucible, the great Melting-Pot where all the races of Europe are melting and re-forming! Here you stand, good folk, think I, when I see them at Ellis Island, here you stand [*Graphically illustrating it on the table*] in your fifty groups, with your fifty languages and histories, and your fifty blood hatreds and rivalries. But you won't be long like that, brothers, for these are the fires of God you've come to— these are the fires of God. A fig for your feuds and vendettas! Germans and Frenchmen, Irishmen and Englishmen, Jews and Russians—into the Crucible with you all! God is making the American.

MENDEL. I should have thought the American was made already—eighty millions of him.

DAVID. Eighty millions! [*He smiles toward* VERA *in good-humoured derision.*] Eighty millions! Over a continent! Why, that cockleshell of a Britain has forty millions! No, uncle, the real American has not yet arrived. He is only in the Crucible, I tell you—he will be the fusion of all races, perhaps the coming superman. Ah, what a glorious Finale for my symphony—if I can only write it.

VERA. But you have written some of it already! May I not see it?

DAVID [*Relapsing into boyish shyness*]. No, if you please, don't ask—— [*He moves over to his desk and nervously shuts it down and turns the keys of drawers as though protecting his MS.*]

VERA. Won't you give a bit of it at our Concert?

DAVID. Oh, it needs an orchestra.

VERA. But you at the violin and I at the piano——

MENDEL. You didn't tell me you played, Miss Revendal!

VERA. I told you less commonplace things.

DAVID. Miss Revendal plays quite like a professional.

VERA [*Smiling*]. I don't feel so complimented as you expect. You see I did have a professional training.

MENDEL [*Smiling*]. And I thought you came to *me* for lessons! [DAVID *laughs.*]

VERA [*Smiling*]. No, I went to Petersburg——

DAVID [*Dazed*]. To Petersburg——?

VERA [*Smiling*]. Naturally. To the Conservatoire. There wasn't much music to be had at Kishineff, a town where——

DAVID. Kishineff! [*He begins to tremble.*]

VERA [*Still smiling*]. My birthplace.

MENDEL [*Coming toward him, protectingly*]. Calm yourself, David.

DAVID. Yes, yes—so you are a Russian! [*He shudders violently, staggers.*]

VERA [*Alarmed*]. You are ill!

DAVID. It is nothing, I—not much music at Kishineff! No, only the Death-March! ... Mother! Father! Ah—cowards, murderers! And you! [*He shakes his fist at the air.*] You, looking on with your cold butcher's face! O God! O God! [*He bursts into hysterical sobs and runs, shamefacedly, through the door to his room.*]

VERA [*Wildly*]. What have I said? What have I done?

MENDEL. Oh, I was afraid of this, I was afraid of this.

FRAU QUIXANO [*Who has fallen asleep over her book, wakes as if with a sense of the horror and gazes dazedly around, adding to the thrillingness of the moment*]. Dovidel! Wu is' Dovidel! Mir dacht sach[1]——

MENDEL [*Pressing her back to her slumbers*]. Du träumst, Mutter! Schlaf![2] [*She sinks back to sleep.*]

VERA [*In hoarse whisper*]. His father and mother were massacred?

MENDEL [*In same tense tone*]. Before his eyes—father, mother, sisters, down to the youngest babe, whose skull was battered in by a hooligan's heel.

VERA. How did *he* escape?

MENDEL. He was shot in the shoulder, and fell unconscious.

---

1 Yiddish: David! Where is David! We must——
2 Yiddish: You're dreaming, Mother! Sleep! [spelled as German].

As he wasn't a girl, the hooligans left him for dead and hurried to fresh sport.[1]

VERA. Terrible! Terrible! [*Almost in tears.*]

MENDEL [*Shrugging shoulders, hopelessly*]. It is only Jewish history! ... David belongs to the species of *pogrom* orphan—they arrive in the States by almost every ship.

VERA. Poor boy! Poor boy! And he looked so happy! [*She half sobs.*]

MENDEL. So he is, most of the time—a sunbeam took human shape when he was born. But naturally that dreadful scene left a scar on his brain, as the bullet left a scar on his shoulder, and he is always liable to see red when Kishineff is mentioned.

VERA. I will never mention my miserable birthplace to him again.

MENDEL. But you see every few months the newspapers tell us of another *pogrom*, and then he screams out against what he calls that butcher's face, so that I tremble for his reason. I tremble even when I see him writing that crazy music about America, for it only means he is brooding over the difference between America and Russia.

VERA. But perhaps—perhaps—all the terrible memory will pass peacefully away in his music.

MENDEL. There will always be the scar on his shoulder to remind him—whenever the wound twinges, it brings up these terrible faces and visions.

VERA. Is it on his right shoulder?

MENDEL. No—on his left. For a violinist that is even worse.

---

1 Girls and women would have been subject to rape. Kishineff (or Kishinev), now Chişinău, in Moldova, was the site of a horrific two-day action of violence against Jews on Easter Sunday and Monday, 1903. It resulted in 49 deaths and massive amounts of injury and property damage. *Pogrom* is a Russian word derived from a verb that means "to destroy by violence"; today it is used to describe the organized massacre of an ethnic group, in particular those that occurred against the Jews in the early twentieth century. The Kishinev Pogrom is said to have "shocked the world and changed the course of Jewish history" (Goldberg n.p.). See Introduction, pp. 23–27, and Appendix C.

VERA. Ah, of course—the weight and the fingering. [*Subconsciously placing and fingering an imaginary violin.*]

MENDEL. That is why I fear so for his future—he will never be strong enough for the feats of bravura that the public demands.

VERA. The wild beasts! I feel more ashamed of my country than ever. But there's his symphony.

MENDEL. And who will look at that amateurish stuff? He knows so little of harmony and counterpoint—he breaks all the rules. I've tried to give him a few pointers—but he ought to have gone to Germany.

VERA. Perhaps it's not too late.

MENDEL [*Passionately*]. Ah, if you and your friends could help him! See—I'm begging after all. But it's not for myself.

VERA. My father loves music. Perhaps *he*—but no! he lives in Kishineff. But I will think—there are people here—I will write to you.

MENDEL [*Fervently*]. Thank you! Thank you!

VERA. Now you must go to him. Good-bye. Tell him I count upon him for the Concert.

MENDEL. How good you are! [*He follows her to the street-door.*]

VERA [*At door*]. Say good-bye for me to your mother—she seems asleep.

MENDEL [*Opening outer door*]. I am sorry it is snowing so.

VERA. We Russians are used to it. [*Smiling, at exit.*] Good-bye—let us hope your David will turn out a Rubinstein.[1]

MENDEL [*Closing the doors softly*]. I never thought a Russian Christian could be so human. [*He looks at the clock.*] *Gott in Himmel*[2]—my dancing class! [*He hurries into the overcoat hanging on the hat-rack. Re-enter DAVID, having composed himself, but still somewhat dazed.*]

---

1   Russian pianist and composer Anton Rubinstein (1829–94), born to Jewish parents although the family converted to Christianity. The identification is confirmed in Act III.

2   Yiddish: God in Heaven! [spelled as German].

DAVID. She is gone? Oh, but I have driven her away by my craziness. Is she very angry?

MENDEL. Quite the contrary—she expects you at the Concert, and what is more——

DAVID [*Ecstatically*]. And she understood! She understood my Crucible of God! Oh, uncle, you don't know what it means to me to have somebody who understands me. Even you have never understood——

MENDEL [*Wounded*]. Nonsense! How can Miss Revendal understand you better than your own uncle?

DAVID [*Mystically exalted*]. I can't explain—I feel it.

MENDEL. Of course she's interested in your music, thank Heaven. But what true understanding can there be between a Russian Jew and a Russian Christian?

DAVID. What understanding? Aren't we both Americans?

MENDEL. Well, I haven't time to discuss it now. [*He winds his muffler round his throat.*]

DAVID. Why, where are you going?

MENDEL [*Ironically*]. Where *should* I be going—in the snow—on the eve of the Sabbath? Suppose we say to synagogue!

DAVID. Oh, uncle—how you always seem to hanker after those old things!

MENDEL [*Tartly*]. Nonsense! [*He takes his umbrella from the stand.*] I don't like to see our people going to pieces, that's all.

DAVID. Then why did you come to America? Why didn't you work for a Jewish land? You're not even a Zionist.[1]

---

1   The modern Zionist movement was founded by Theodor Herzl (1860–1904) in 1897, with the purpose of re-establishing the Jewish homeland and Jewish autonomy in the land of Israel; the idea of return had existed much earlier and the Zionist movement brought together a number of organizations in Europe and America. Israel Zangwill was an early proponent of Herzl's Zionism, but by 1908 he headed the Jewish Territorial Organization (ITO), a group whose goal was a Jewish state, with Jewish autonomy, wherever one might be obtained. See Introduction, pp. 15–16.

MENDEL. I can't argue now. There's a pack of giggling school-girls waiting to waltz.

DAVID. The fresh romping young things! Think of their happiness! I should love to play for them.

MENDEL [*Sarcastically*]. I can see you are yourself again. [*He opens the street-door—turns back.*] What about your own lesson? Can't we go together?

DAVID. I must first write down what is singing in my soul—oh, uncle, it seems as if I knew suddenly what was wanting in my music!

MENDEL [*Drily*]. Well, don't forget what is wanting in the house! The rent isn't paid yet. [*Exit through street-door. As he goes out, he touches and kisses the* Mezuzah[1] *on the door-post, with a subconsciously antagonistic revival of religious impulse.* DAVID *opens his desk, takes out a pile of musical manuscript, sprawls over his chair and, humming to himself, scribbles feverishly with the quill. After a few moments* FRAU QUIXANO *yawns, wakes, and stretches herself. Then she looks at the clock.*]

FRAU QUIXANO. *Shabbos!* [*She rises and goes to the table and sees there are no candles, walks to the chiffonier and gets them and places them in the candlesticks, then lights the candles, muttering a ceremonial Hebrew benediction.*] *Boruch atto haddoshem ellôheinu melech hôôlam assher kiddishonu bemitzvôsov vettzivonu lehadlik neir shel shabbos.*[2] [*She pulls down the blinds of the two windows, then she goes to the rapt composer and touches him, remindingly, on the shoulder. He does not move, but continues writing.*] *Dovidel!* [*He looks up dazedly. She points to the candles.*] *Shabbos!* [*A sweet smile*

---

1   Small parchment scroll contained in a case that enables it to be affixed to a doorpost. The scroll contains verses from the Torah (Deuteronomy 6:4–9 and 11:13–21), which remind Jews to follow God's commandments (Deuteronomy 6:9: "And thou shalt write them upon the doorposts of thy house, and upon thy gates"). Many Jews affix a *mezuzah* to the door of each room as well as to the outer door.

2   Hebrew: "Blessed are you, Lord our God, King of the Universe, who sanctifies us with your commandments and commands us to light the Sabbath candles." This is the blessing over the Sabbath candles, traditionally recited by women. As with his Yiddish transliteration, Zangwill's Hebrew transliteration is idiosyncratic. *Adoshem* is substituted in the play for *Adonai* (the name of God), since this is a performance and not an actual blessing.

comes over his face, he throws the quill resignedly away and submits his head to her hands and her muttered Hebrew blessing.] *Yesimcho elôhim ke-efrayim vechimnasseh—yevorechecho haddoshem veyish-merecho, yoer hadoshem ponov eilecho vechunecho, yisso hadoshem ponov eilecho veyosem lecho sholôm.*[1] [*Then she goes toward the kitchen. As she turns at the door, he is again writing. She shakes her finger at him, repeating.*] *Gut Shabbos!*[2]

DAVID. *Gut Shabbos!* [*Puts down the pen and smiles after her till the door closes, then with a deep sigh takes his cape from the peg and his violin-case, pauses, still humming, to take up his pen and write down a fresh phrase, finally puts on his hat and is just about to open the street-door when* KATHLEEN *enters from her bedroom fully dressed to go, and laden with a large brown paper parcel and an umbrella. He turns at the sound of her footsteps and remains at the door, holding his violin-case during the ensuing dialogue.*]

DAVID. You're not going out this bitter weather?

KATHLEEN [*Sharply fending him off with her umbrella*]. And who's to shtay me?

DAVID. Oh, but you mustn't—*I'll* do your errand—what is it?

KATHLEEN [*Indignantly*]. Errand, is it, indeed! I'm not here!

DAVID. Not here?

KATHLEEN. I'm lavin', they'll come for me thrunk—and ye'll witness I don't take the candleshtick.

DAVID. But who's sending you away?

KATHLEEN. It's sending meself away I am—yer houly grand-mother has me disthroyed intirely.

DAVID. Why, what has the poor old la——?

KATHLEEN. I don't be saltin' the mate and I do be mixin' the crockery and——![3]

---

1   This is the blessing given to children on the Sabbath eve: "May God make you like Ephraim and Manasseh [for girls: 'like Sarah, Rebecca, Rachel, and Leah']. May God bless you and keep you; may God shine God's face upon you and be gracious to you; may God shine God's face upon you and grant you peace."

2   Yiddish: Good Sabbath!

3   Kathleen here refers to two more elements of *kashrut* (keeping kosher): salting meat before cooking to remove as much blood as possible and keeping separate dishes for meat and dairy foods.

DAVID [*Gently*]. I know, I know—but, Kathleen, remember she was brought up to these things from childhood. And her father was a Rabbi.

KATHLEEN. What's that? A priest?

DAVID. A sort of priest. In Russia he was a great man. Her husband, too, was a mighty scholar, and to give him time to study the holy books she had to do chores all day for him and the children.

KATHLEEN. Oh, those priests!

DAVID [*Smiling*]. No, *he* wasn't a priest. But he took sick and died and the children left her—went to America or heaven or other far-off places—and she was left all penniless and alone.

KATHLEEN. Poor ould lady.

DAVID. Not so old yet, for she was married at fifteen.

KATHLEEN Poor young crathur!

DAVID. But she was still the good angel of the congregation— sat up with the sick and watched over the dead.

KATHLEEN. Saints alive! And not scared?

DAVID. No, nothing scared her—except me. I got a broken-down fiddle and used to play it even on *Shabbos*—I was very naughty. But she was so lovely to me. I still remember the heavenly taste of a piece of *Motso* she gave me dipped in raisin wine! Passover cake, you know.[1]

KATHLEEN [*Proudly*]. Oh, I know *Motso*.

DAVID [*Smacks his lips, repeats*]. Heavenly!

---

1 *Motso*, more commonly known today as *matzah*, is the unleavened, cracker-like product eaten by Jews on Passover and available now throughout the year. In the nineteenth century and at the time of this play, wine made of raisins (fermented but non-alcoholic) was commonly used on Passover in Britain and the United States. Jonathan Sarna has suggested that the custom originated because the wine was easy to make when there was no kosher-certified wine available, or that it was a vestige of older practice ("Passover Raisin Wine, The American Temperance Movement, and Mordecai Noah: The Origins, Meaning, and Wider Significance of A Nineteenth-Century American Jewish Religious Practice," *Hebrew Union College Annual* 59 [1988]: 269–88). It would also have been the wine of choice to give to children.

KATHLEEN. Sure, I must tashte it.

DAVID [*Shaking his head, mysteriously*]. Only little boys get that tashte.

KATHLEEN. That's quare.

DAVID [*Smiling*]. Very quare. And then one day my uncle sent the old lady a ticket to come to America. But it is not so happy for her here because you see my uncle has to be near his theatre and can't live in the Jewish quarter, and so nobody understands her, and she sits all the livelong day alone—alone with her book and her religion and her memories——

KATHLEEN [*Breaking down*]. Oh, Mr. David!

DAVID. And now all this long, cold, snowy evening she'll sit by the fire alone, thinking of her dead, and the fire will sink lower and lower, and she won't be able to touch it, because it's the holy Sabbath, and there'll be no kind Kathleen to brighten up the grey ashes, and then at last, sad and shivering, she'll creep up to her room without a candlestick, and there in the dark and the cold——

KATHLEEN [*Hysterically bursting into tears, dropping her parcel, and untying her bonnet-strings*]. Oh, Mr. David, I won't mix the crockery, I won't——

DAVID [*Heartily*]. Of course you won't. Good night. [*He slips out hurriedly through the street-door as* KATHLEEN *throws off her bonnet, and the curtain falls quickly. As it rises again, she is seen strenuously poking the fire, illumined by its red glow.*]

Act II

The same scene on an afternoon a month later. DAVID *is discovered at his desk, scribbling music in a fever of enthusiasm.* MENDEL, *dressed in his best, is playing softly on the piano, watching* DAVID. *After an instant or two of indecision, he puts down the piano-lid with a bang and rises decisively.*

MENDEL. David!

DAVID [*Putting up his left hand*]. Please, please—— [*He writes feverishly.*]

MENDEL. But I want to talk to you seriously—at once.

DAVID. I'm just re-writing the Finale. Oh, such a splendid inspiration! [*He writes on.*]

MENDEL [*Shrugs his shoulders and reseats himself at piano. He plays a bar or two. Looks at watch impatiently. Resolutely*]. David, I've got wonderful news for you. Miss Revendal is bringing somebody to see you, and we have hopes of getting you sent to Germany to study composition. [DAVID *does not reply, but writes rapidly on.*] Why, he hasn't heard a word! [*He shouts.*] David!

DAVID [*Writing on*]. I can't, uncle. I *must* put it down while that glorious impression is fresh.

MENDEL. What impression? You only went to the People's Alliance.

DAVID. Yes, and there I saw the Jewish children—a thousand of 'em—saluting the Flag. [*He writes on.*]

MENDEL. Well, what of that?

DAVID. What of that? [*He throws down his quill and jumps up.*] But just fancy it, uncle. The Stars and Stripes unfurled, and a thousand childish voices, piping and foreign, fresh from the lands of oppression, hailing its fluttering folds. I cried like a baby.

MENDEL. I'm afraid you *are* one.

DAVID. Ah, but if you had heard them—"Flag of our Great Republic"—the words have gone singing at my heart ever since—[*He turns to the flag over the door.*] "Flag of our Great Republic, guardian of our homes, whose stars and stripes stand for Bravery, Purity, Truth, and Union, we salute thee. We, the natives of distant lands, who find [*Half-sobbing*] rest under thy folds, do pledge our hearts, our lives, our sacred honour to love and protect thee, our Country, and the liberty of the American people for ever."[1] [*He ends almost hysterically.*]

---

1 "Flag of the Great Republic" seems to be an early version of the Pledge of Allegiance. Zangwill very likely based this incident on an event that took place at the Educational Alliance, a major New York settlement house serving Jewish immigrants of the Lower East Side, in celebration of the 250th anniversary of the municipal administration of New York City. The ceremony, which took place on 26 May 1903, was reported in the London *Times* as well as in the *New York Times*; the London paper quoted the pledge in words nearly identical to David's. See Appendix E3a.

MENDEL [*Soothingly*]. Quite right. But you needn't get so excited over it.

DAVID. Not when one hears the roaring of the fires of God? Not when one sees the souls melting in the Crucible? Uncle, all those little Jews will grow up Americans!

MENDEL [*Putting a pacifying hand on his shoulder and forcing him into a chair*]. Sit down. I want to talk to you about your affairs.

DAVID [*Sitting*]. *My* affairs! But I've been talking about them all the time!

MENDEL. Nonsense, David. [*He sits beside him.*] Don't you think it's time you got into a wider world?

DAVID. Eh? This planet's wide enough for me.

MENDEL. Do be serious. You don't want to live all your life in this room.

DAVID [*Looks round*]. What's the matter with this room? It's princely.

MENDEL [*Raising his hands in horror*]. Princely!

DAVID. Imperial. Remember when I first saw it—after pigging a week in the rocking steerage,[1] swinging in a berth as wide as my fiddle-case, hung near the cooking-engines; imagine the hot rancid smell of the food, the oil of the machinery, the odours of all that close-packed, sea-sick——

MENDEL [*Putting his hand over* DAVID'S *mouth*]. Don't! You make me ill! How could you ever bear it?

DAVID [*Smiling*]. I was quite happy—I only had to fancy I'd been shipwrecked, and that after clinging to a plank five days without food or water on the great lonely Atlantic, my frozen, sodden form had been picked up by this great safe steamer and given this delightful dry berth, regular meals, and the spectacle

---

1 Area of a passenger ship for those with the cheapest tickets, usually the lowest level of the ship. Impoverished immigrants, including most of the Jewish immigrants from Russia, travelled in steerage. "Pigging," in this case, means crowding together in dirty conditions. Mendel's response suggests that he left Russia significantly earlier, prior to the "great wave" of Jewish immigration (1880–1920).

of all these friendly faces.... Do you know who was on board that boat? Quincy Davenport.

MENDEL. The lord of corn and oil?

DAVID [*Smiling*]. Yes, even we wretches in the steerage felt safe to think the lord was up above, we believed the company would never dare drown *him*. But could even Quincy Davenport command a cabin like this? [*Waving his arm round the room.*] Why, uncle, we have a cabin worth a thousand dollars—a thousand dollars a *week*—and what's more, it doesn't wobble! [*He plants his feet voluptuously upon the floor.*]

MENDEL. Come, come, David, I asked you to be serious. Surely, some day you'd like your music produced?

DAVID [*Jumps up*]. Wouldn't it be glorious? To hear it all actually coming out of violins and 'cellos, drums and trumpets.

MENDEL. And you'd like it to go all over the world?

DAVID. All over the world and all down the ages.

MENDEL. But don't you see that unless you go and study seriously in Germany——? [*Enter KATHLEEN from kitchen, carrying a furnished tea-tray with ear-shaped cakes, bread and butter, etc., and wearing a grotesque false nose.*[1] *MENDEL cries out in amaze.*] Kathleen!

DAVID [*Roaring with boyish laughter*]. Ha! Ha! Ha! Ha! Ha!

KATHLEEN [*Standing still with her tray*]. Sure, what's the matter?

DAVID. Look in the glass!

---

1   The "ear-shaped cakes" are generally known as *hamantaschen* (German: Haman's pockets), and they are now widely available in places with Jewish populations, especially around the Purim holiday. They are triangular shaped pastries with a sweet jam-like filling. The "false nose" refers to the custom of dressing in costume during Purim festivities. As indicated later in this scene, the holiday celebrates the story told in the biblical book of Esther, in which the Jews of ancient Persia are saved from Haman's plans to destroy them. The holiday is in some ways a kind of Jewish Mardi Gras (or Carnival), with costume parties; joyful, often raucous celebrations; and the sharing of gifts of food and candy— all just four weeks before the more serious and abstemious holiday of Passover.

KATHLEEN [*Going to the mantel*]. Houly Moses! [*She drops the tray, which* MENDEL *catches, and snatches off the nose.*] Och, I forgot to take it off—'twas the misthress gave it me—I put it on to cheer her up.

DAVID. Is she so miserable, then?

KATHLEEN. Terrible low, Mr. David, to-day being *Purim*.

MENDEL. *Purim!* Is to-day *Purim*? [*Gives her the tea-tray back.* KATHLEEN, *to take it, drops her nose and forgets to pick it up.*]

DAVID. But *Purim* is a merry time, Kathleen, like your Carnival. Haven't you read the book of Esther—how the Jews of Persia escaped massacre?

KATHLEEN. That's what the misthress is so miserable about. Ye don't *keep* the Carnival.[1] There's noses for both of ye in the kitchen—didn't I go with her to Hester Street to buy 'em? — but ye don't be axin' for 'em. And to see your noses layin' around so solemn and neglected, faith, it nearly makes me chry meself.

MENDEL [*Bitterly to himself*]. Who can remember about *Purim* in America?

DAVID [*Half-smiling*]. Poor granny, tell her to come in and I'll play her *Purim* jig.

MENDEL [*Hastily*]. No, no, David, not here—the visitors!

DAVID. Visitors? What visitors?

MENDEL [*Impatiently*]. That's just what I've been trying to explain.

DAVID. Well, I can play in the kitchen. [*He takes his violin. Exit to kitchen.* MENDEL *sighs and shrugs his shoulders hopelessly at the boy's perversity, then fingers the cups and saucers.*]

MENDEL [*Anxiously*]. Is that the *best* tea-set?

KATHLEEN. Can't you see it's the Passover set![2] [*Ruefully.*] And shpiled intirely it'll be now for our Passover.... And the

---

1   The falling off of Purim observance, especially by the young, was a concern among Jews in Britain and America at the start of the twentieth century.

2   Observant Jews use separate sets of dishes for Passover, which are not used during the rest of the year.

misthress thought the visitors might like to thry some of her *Purim* cakes. [*Indicates ear-shaped cakes on tray.*]

MENDEL [*Bitterly*]. *Purim* cakes! [*He turns his back on her and stares moodily out of the window.*]

KATHLEEN [*Mutters contemptuously*]. Call yerself a Jew and you forgettin' to keep *Purim*! [*She is going back to the kitchen when a merry Slavic dance breaks out, softened by the door; her feet unconsciously get more and more into dance step, and at last she jigs out. As she opens and passes through the door, the music sounds louder.*]

FRAU QUIXANO [*Heard from kitchen*]. Ha! Ha! Ha! Ha! Ha! Kathleen!! [MENDEL'S *feet, too, begin to take the swing of the music, and his feet dance as he stares out of the window. Suddenly the hoot of an automobile is heard, followed by the rattling up of the car.*]

MENDEL. Ah, she has brought somebody swell![1] [*He throws open the doors and goes out eagerly to meet the visitors. The dance music goes on softly throughout the scene.*]

QUINCY DAVENPORT [*Outside*]. Oh, thank you—I leave the coats in the car. [*Enter an instant later* QUINCY DAVENPORT *and* VERA REVENDAL, MENDEL *in the rear.* VERA *is dressed much as before, but with a motor veil, which she takes off during the scene.* DAVENPORT *is a dude,[2] aping the air of a European sporting clubman. Aged about thirty-five and well set-up, he wears an orchid and an intermittent eyeglass, and gives the impression of a coarse-fibred and patronisingly facetious but not bad-hearted man, spoiled by prosperity.*]

MENDEL. Won't you be seated?

VERA. First let me introduce my friend, who is good enough to interest himself in your nephew—Mr. Quincy Davenport.

MENDEL [*Struck of a heap*].[3] Mr. Quincy Davenport! How strange!

VERA. What is strange?

---

1   Slang: A person of high social position.
2   A dandy or fop.
3   Astonished, disconcerted.

MENDEL. David just mentioned Mr. Davenport's name—said they travelled to New York on the same boat.

QUINCY. Impossible! Always travel on my own yacht. Slow but select. Must have been another man of the same name—my dad. Ha! Ha! Ha!

MENDEL. Ah, of course. I thought you were too young.

QUINCY. My dad, Miss Revendal, is one of those antiquated Americans who are always in a hurry!

VERA. He burns coal and you burn time.

QUINCY. Precisely! Ha! Ha! Ha!

MENDEL. Won't you sit down—I'll go and prepare David.

VERA [*Sitting*]. You've not prepared him yet?

MENDEL. I've tried to more than once—but I never really got to—— [*He smiles.*] to Germany. [QUINCY *sits.*]

VERA. Then prepare him for *three* visitors.

MENDEL. Three?

VERA. You see Mr. Davenport himself is no judge of music.

QUINCY [*Jumps up*]. I beg your pardon.

VERA. In manuscript.

QUINCY. Ah, of course not. Music should be heard, not seen—like that jolly jig. Is that your David?

MENDEL. Oh, you mustn't judge him by that. He's just fooling.

QUINCY. Oh, he'd better not fool with Poppy. Poppy's awful severe.

MENDEL. Poppy?

QUINCY. Pappelmeister—my private orchestra conductor.

MENDEL. Is it *your* orchestra Pappelmeister conducts?

QUINCY. Well, I pay the piper—and the drummer too! [*He chuckles.*]

MENDEL [*Sadly*]. *I* wanted to play in it, but he turned me down.

QUINCY. I told you he was awful severe. [*To* VERA.] He only allows me comic opera once a week. My wife calls him the Bismarck[1] of the baton.

MENDEL [*Reverently*]. A great conductor!

QUINCY. Would he have a twenty-thousand-dollar job with me if he wasn't? Not that he'd get half that in the open market— only I have to stick it on to keep him for my guests exclusively. [*Looks at watch.*] But he ought to be here, confound him. A conductor should keep time, eh, Miss Revendal? [*He sniggers.*]

MENDEL. I'll bring David. Won't you help yourselves to tea? [*To* VERA.] You see there's lemon for you—as in Russia. [*Exit to kitchen—a moment afterwards the merry music stops in the middle of a bar.*]

VERA. Thank you. [*Taking a cup.*] Do *you* like lemon, Mr. Davenport?

QUINCY [*Flirtatiously*]. That depends. The last I had was in Russia itself—from the fair hands of your mother, the Baroness.

VERA [*Pained*]. Please don't say my mother, my mother is dead.

QUINCY [*Fatuously*[2] *misunderstanding*]. Oh, you have no call to be ashamed of your step-mother—she's a stunning creature; all the points of a tip-top Russian aristocrat, or Quincy Davenport's no judge of breed! Doesn't speak English like your father—but then the Baron is a wonder.

VERA [*Takes up teapot*]. Father once hoped to be British Ambassador—that's why *I* had an English governess. But you never told me you met him in *Russia*.

QUINCY. Surely! When I gave you all those love messages——

VERA [*Pouring tea quickly*]. You said you met him at Wiesbaden.[3]

QUINCY. Yes, but we grew such pals I motored him and the Baroness back to St. Petersburg. Jolly country, Russia—they know how to live.

---

1 Otto von Bismarck (1815–98), powerful Prussian leader who united the German Empire and dominated European politics in the nineteenth century, earning the epithet "Iron Chancellor."
2 With complacent foolishness.
3 Spa town in Germany.

VERA [*Coldly*]. I saw more of those who know how to die.... Milk and sugar?

QUINCY [*Sentimentally*]. Oh, Miss Revendal! Have you forgotten?

VERA [*Politely snubbing*]. How should I remember?

QUINCY. You don't remember our first meeting? At the Settlement Bazaar? When I paid you a hundred dollars for every piece of sugar you put in?

VERA. Did you? Then I hope you drank syrup.

QUINCY. Ugh! I hate sugar—I sacrificed myself.

VERA. To the Settlement? How heroic of you!

QUINCY. No, not to the Settlement. To you!

VERA. Then I'll only put milk in.

QUINCY. I hate milk. But from you——

VERA. Then we *must* fall back on the lemon.

QUINCY. I loathe lemon. But from——

VERA. Then you shall have your tea neat.

QUINCY. I detest tea, and here it would be particularly cheap and nasty. But——

VERA. Then you shall have a cake! [*She offers plate.*]

QUINCY [*Taking one*]. Would they be eatable? [*Tasting it.*] Humph! Not bad. [*Sentimentally.*] A little cake was all you would eat the only time you came to one of my private concerts. Don't you remember? We went down to supper together.

VERA [*Taking his tea for herself and putting in lemon*]. I shall always remember the delicious music Herr Pappelmeister gave us.

QUINCY. How unkind of you!

VERA. Unkind? [*She sips the tea and puts down the cup.*] To be grateful for the music?

QUINCY. You know what I mean—to forget *me*! [*He tries to take her hand.*]

VERA [*Rising*]. Aren't you forgetting yourself?

QUINCY. You mean because I'm married to that patched-and-painted creature? She's hankering for the stage again, the old witch.

VERA. Hush! Marriages with comic opera stars are not usually domestic idylls.[1]

QUINCY. I fell a victim to my love of music.

VERA [Murmurs, smiling]. Music!

QUINCY. And I hadn't yet met the right breed—the true blue blood of Europe. I'll get a divorce. [Approaching her.] Vera!

VERA [Retreating]. You will make me sorry I came to you.

QUINCY. No, don't say that—promised the Baron I'd always do all I could for——

VERA. You promised? You dared discuss my affairs?

QUINCY. It was your father began it. When he found I knew you, he almost wept with emotion. He asked a hundred questions about your life in America.

VERA. His life and mine are for ever separate. He is a Reactionary, I a Radical.

QUINCY. But he loves you dreadfully—he can't understand why you should go slaving away summer and winter in a Settlement—you a member of the Russian nobility!

VERA [With faint smile]. I might say, noblesse oblige.[2] But the truth is, I earn my living that way. It would do you good to slave there too!

QUINCY [Eagerly]. Would they chain us together? I'd come tomorrow. [He moves nearer her. There is a double knock at the door.]

VERA [Relieved]. Here's Pappelmeister!

QUINCY. Bother Poppy—why is he so darned punctual? [Enter KATHLEEN from the kitchen.]

VERA [Smiling]. Ah, you're still here.

---

1 Extremely happy, often pastoral, idealized scenes.
2 French: nobility obliges. It refers to the responsibility of the wealthy or high-ranking to care about the conditions of those less fortunate. It is often used with irony to refer to those who do so in a condescending way.

KATHLEEN. And why would I not be here? [*She goes to open the door.*]

PAPPELMEISTER. Mr. Quixano?

KATHLEEN. Yes, come in. [*Enter* HERR PAPPELMEISTER, *a burly German figure with a leonine[1] head, spectacles, and a mane of white hair—a figure that makes his employer look even coarser. He carries an umbrella, which he never lets go. He is at first grave and silent, which makes any burst of emotion the more striking. He and* QUINCY DAVENPORT *suggest a picture of "Dignity and Impudence."[2] His English, as roughly indicated in the text, is extremely Teutonic.[3]*]

QUINCY. You're late, Poppy! [PAPPELMEISTER *silently bows to* VERA.]

VERA [*Smilingly goes and offers her hand*]. Proud to meet you, Herr Pappelmeister!

QUINCY. Excuse me—— [*Introducing.*] Miss Revendal! —I forgot you and Poppy hadn't been introduced—curiously enough it was at Wiesbaden I picked him up too—he was conducting the opera—your folks were in my box. I don't think I ever met anyone so mad on music as the Baron. And the Baroness told me he had retired from active service in the Army because of the torture of listening to the average military band. Ha! Ha! Ha!

VERA. Yes, my father once hoped *my* music would comfort him. [*She smiles sadly.*] Poor father! But a soldier must bear defeat. Herr Pappelmeister, may I not give you some tea? [*She sits again at the table.*]

QUINCY. Tea! Lager's more in Poppy's line. [*He chuckles.*]

PAPPELMEISTER [*Gravely*]. Bitte.[4] Tea. [*She pours out, he sits.*] Lemon. Four lumps.... *Nun,*[5] five! ... Or six! [*She hands him the cup.*] *Danke.*[6] [*As he receives the cup, he utters an exclamation, for*

---

1 Lion-like.
2 Reference to the popular 1839 painting of two dogs, a bloodhound and a terrier, by British artist Sir Edwin Henry Landseer (1802–73).
3 Germanic.
4 German: Please.
5 German: Now.
6 German: Thank you.

KATHLEEN *after opening the door has lingered on, hunting around everywhere, and having finally crawled under the table has now brushed against his leg.*]

VERA. What are you looking for?

KATHLEEN [*Her head emerging*]. My nose! [*They are all startled and amused.*]

VERA. Your nose?

KATHLEEN. I forgot me nose!

QUINCY. Well, follow your nose—and you'll find it. Ha! Ha! Ha!

KATHLEEN [*Pouncing on it*]. Here it is! [*Picks it up near the armchair.*]

OMNES.[1] Oh!

KATHLEEN. Sure, it's gotten all dirthy. [*She takes out a handkerchief and wipes the nose carefully.*]

QUINCY. But why do you want a nose like that?

KATHLEEN [*Proudly*]. Bekaz we're Hebrews!

QUINCY. What!

VERA. What *do* you mean?

KATHLEEN. It's our Carnival to-day! *Purim.* [*She carries her nose carefully and piously toward the kitchen.*]

VERA. Oh! I see. [*Exit* KATHLEEN.]

QUINCY [*In horror*]. Miss Revendal, you don't mean to say you've brought me to a Jew!

VERA. I'm afraid I have. I was thinking only of his genius, not his race. And you see, so many musicians are Jews.

QUINCY. Not *my* musicians. No Jew's harp[2] in my orchestra, eh? [*He sniggers.*] I wouldn't have a Jew if he paid *me*.

VERA. I daresay you have some, all the same.

QUINCY. Impossible. Poppy! Are there any Jews in my orchestra?

---

1 Latin: All, everybody.
2 A small musical instrument, held in the mouth and strummed with a finger. Quincy is making a not very funny pun.

PAPPELMEISTER [*Removing the cup from his mouth and speaking with sepulchral[1] solemnity*]. Do you mean are dere any Christians?

QUINCY [*In horror*]. Gee-rusalem! Perhaps *you're* a Jew!

PAPPELMEISTER [*Gravely*]. I haf not de honour. But, if you brefer, I will gut out from my brogrammes all de Chewish composers. *Was?*[2]

QUINCY. Why, of course. Fire 'em out, every mother's son of 'em.

PAPPELMEISTER [*Unsmiling*]. *Also*[3]—no more comic operas!

QUINCY. What!!!

PAPPELMEISTER. Dey write all de comic operas!

QUINCY. Brute! [PAPPELMEISTER'S *chuckle is heard gurgling in his cup. Re-enter* MENDEL *from kitchen.*]

MENDEL [*To* VERA]. I'm so sorry—I can't get him to come in—he's terrible shy.

QUINCY. Won't face the music, eh? [*He sniggers.*]

VERA. Did you tell him *I* was here?

MENDEL. Of course.

VERA [*Disappointed*]. Oh!

MENDEL. But I've persuaded him to let me show his MS.[4]

VERA [*With forced satisfaction*]. Oh, well, that's all we want. [MENDEL *goes to the desk, opens it, and gets the MS. and offers it to* QUINCY DAVENPORT.]

QUINCY. Not for me—Poppy! [MENDEL *offers it to* PAPPELMEISTER, *who takes it solemnly.*]

MENDEL [*Anxiously to* PAPPELMEISTER]. Of course you must remember his youth and his lack of musical education——

---

1 Tomb-like, sombre. Beginning with his speech here, Zangwill's representation of Pappelmeister's English is meant to reflect his heavy German accent.
2 German: What?
3 German: So, therefore.
4 Manuscript.

PAPPELMEISTER. *Bitte, das Pult!*[1] [MENDEL *moves* DAVID'S *music-stand from the corner to the centre of the room.* PAPPELMEISTER *puts MS. on it.*] *So!*[2] [*All eyes centre on him eagerly,* MENDEL *standing uneasily, the others sitting.* PAPPEL-MEISTER *polishes his glasses with irritating elaborateness and weary "achs," then reads in absolute silence. A pause.*]

QUINCY [*Bored by the silence*]. But won't you play it to us?

PAPPELMEISTER. Blay it? Am I an orchestra? I blay it in my brain. [*He goes on reading, his brow gets wrinkled. He ruffles his hair unconsciously. All watch him anxiously—he turns the page.*] *So!*

VERA [*Anxiously*]. You don't seem to like it!

PAPPELMEISTER. I do not comprehend it.

MENDEL. I knew it was crazy—it is supposed to be about America or a Crucible or something. And of course there are heaps of mistakes.

VERA. That is why I am suggesting to Mr. Davenport to send him to Germany.

QUINCY. I'll send as many Jews as you like to Germany. Ha! Ha! Ha![3]

PAPPELMEISTER [*Absorbed, turning pages*]. *Ach!—ach!—So!*[4]

QUINCY. I'd even lend my own yacht to take 'em back. Ha! Ha! Ha!

VERA. Sh! We're disturbing Herr Pappelmeister.

QUINCY. Oh, Poppy's all right.

PAPPELMEISTER [*Sublimely unconscious*]. *Ach so—so—SO! Das ist etwas neues!*[5] [*His umbrella begins to beat time, moving more and more vigorously, till at last he is conducting elaborately, stretching out his left palm for pianissimo passages, and raising it vigorously for*

---

1 German: The desk.
2 German: All right!
3 In the post-Holocaust era, this statement seems particularly insidious and horrifying. However, in 1908 Quincy Davenport, an antisemite, is making an offensive joke about deporting Jews from the United States, to Germany or to anywhere else.
4 German: Aha! I see!
5 German: That is something new.

forte, with every now and then an exclamation.] *Wunderschön! ...*
pianissimo!—now the flutes! Clarinets! *Ach, ergötzlich ...* bassoons and drums! ... *Fortissimo! ... Kolossal! Kolossal!*[1] [*Conducting in a fury of enthusiasm.*]

VERA [*Clapping her hands*]. Bravo! Bravo! I'm so excited!

QUINCY [*Yawning*]. Then it isn't bad, Poppy?

PAPPELMEISTER [*Not listening, never ceasing to conduct*]. *Und* de harp solo ... *ach, reizend!*[2] ... Second violins——!

QUINCY. But Poppy! We can't be here all day.

PAPPELMEISTER [*Not listening, continuing pantomime action*]. Sh! Sh! *Piano.*

QUINCY [*Outraged*]. Sh to *me!* [*Rises.*]

VERA. He doesn't know it's you.

QUINCY. But look here, Poppy—— [*He seizes the wildly-moving umbrella. Blank stare of* PAPPELMEISTER *gradually returning to consciousness.*]

PAPPELMEISTER. *Was giebt's ...?*[3]

QUINCY. We've had enough.

PAPPELMEISTER [*Indignant*]. Enough? Enough? Of such a beaudiful symphony?

QUINCY. It may be beautiful to you, but to us it's damn dull. See here, Poppy, if you're satisfied that the young fellow has sufficient talent to be sent to study in Germany——

PAPPELMEISTER. In Germany! Germany has nodings to teach him, he has to teach Germany.

VERA. Bravo! [*She springs up.*]

MENDEL. I always said he was a genius!

QUINCY. Well, at that rate you could put this stuff of his in one of my programmes. *Sinfonia Americana,*[4] eh?

---

1   Italian: *Pianissimo:* play softly; *forte* and *fortissimo:* play loudly and very loudly. German: *Wunderschön:* wonderful; *ergötzlich:* delightful; *kolossal:* colossal, tremendous.
2   German: And the harp solo ... oh, charming!
3   German: What's the matter?
4   Italian: *American Symphony.*

VERA. Oh, that *is* good of you.

PAPPELMEISTER. I should be broud to indroduce it to de vorld.

VERA. And will it be played in that wonderful marble music-room overlooking the Hudson?

QUINCY. Sure. Before five hundred of the smartest[1] folk in America.

MENDEL. Oh, thank you, thank you. That will mean fame!

QUINCY. And dollars. Don't forget the dollars.

MENDEL. I'll run and tell him. [*He hastens into the kitchen,* PAPPELMEISTER *is re-absorbed in the MS., but no longer conducting.*]

QUINCY. You see, I'll help even a Jew for your sake.

VERA. Hush! [*Indicating* PAPPELMEISTER.]

QUINCY. Oh, Poppy's in the moon.

VERA. You must help him for his own sake, for art's sake.

QUINCY. And why not for heart's sake—for my sake? [*He comes nearer.*]

VERA [*Crossing to* PAPPELMEISTER]. Herr Pappelmeister! When do you think you can produce it?

PAPPELMEISTER. *Wunderbar!*[2] ... [*Becoming half-conscious of* VERA.] Four lumps.... [*Waking up.*] *Bitte?*

VERA. How soon can you produce it?

PAPPELMEISTER. How soon can he finish it?

VERA. Isn't it finished?

PAPPELMEISTER. I see von Finale scratched out and anoder not quite completed. But anyhow, ve couldn't broduce it before Saturday fortnight.

QUINCY. Saturday fortnight! Not time to get my crowd.

PAPPELMEISTER. Den ve say Saturday dree veeks. Yes?

---

1 Most fashionable.

2 German: Wonderful!

QUINCY. Yes. Stop a minute! Did you say Saturday? That's my comic opera night! You thief!

PAPPELMEISTER. Somedings must be sagrificed.

MENDEL [*Outside*]. But you *must* come, David. [*The kitchen door opens, and* MENDEL *drags in the boyishly shrinking* DAVID. PAPPELMEISTER *thumps with his umbrella*, VERA *claps her hands*, QUINCY DAVENPORT *produces his eyeglass and surveys* DAVID *curiously*.]

VERA. Oh, Mr. Quixano, I am so glad! Mr. Davenport is going to produce your symphony in his wonderful music-room.

QUINCY. Yes, young man, I'm going to give you the smartest audience in America. And if Poppy is right, you're just going to rake in the dollars. America wants a composer.

PAPPELMEISTER [*Raises hands emphatically*]. Ach Gott, ja![1]

VERA [*To* DAVID]. Why don't you speak? You're not angry with me for interfering——?

DAVID. I can never be grateful enough to you——

VERA. Oh, not to me. It is to Mr. Davenport you——

DAVID. And I can never be grateful enough to Herr Pappelmeister. It is an honour even to meet him. [*Bows.*]

PAPPELMEISTER [*Choking with emotion, goes and pats him on the back*]. Mein braver Junge![2]

VERA [*Anxiously*]. But it is Mr. Davenport——

DAVID. Before I accept Mr. Davenport's kindness, I must know to whom I am indebted—and if Mr. Davenport is the man who——

QUINCY. Who travelled with you to New York? Ha! Ha! Ha! No, *I'm* only the junior.

DAVID. Oh, I know, sir, you don't make the money you spend.

QUINCY. Eh?

VERA [*Anxiously*]. He means he knows you're not in business.

DAVID. Yes, sir; but is it true you are in pleasure?

---

1 German: Oh God, yes!
2 German: My brave young (man)!

QUINCY [*Puzzled*]. I beg your pardon?

DAVID. Are all the stories the papers print about you true?

QUINCY. *All* the stories. That's a tall order. Ha! Ha! Ha!

DAVID. Well, anyhow, is it true that——?

VERA. Mr. Quixano! What *are* you driving at?

QUINCY. Oh, it's rather fun to hear what the masses read about me. Fire ahead. Is what true?

DAVID. That you were married in a balloon?

QUINCY. Ho! Ha! Ha! That's true enough. Marriage in high life, they said, didn't they? Ha! Ha! Ha!

DAVID. And is it true you live in America only two months in the year, and then only to entertain Europeans who wander to these wild parts?

QUINCY. Lucky for you, young man. You'll have an Italian prince and a British duke to hear your scribblings.

DAVID. And the palace where they will hear my scribblings—is it true that——?

VERA [*Who has been on pins and needles*]. Mr. Quixano, what possible——?

DAVID [*Entreatingly holds up a hand*]. Miss Revendal! [*To QUINCY DAVENPORT.*] Is this palace the same whose grounds were turned into Venetian canals where the guests ate in gondolas—gondolas that were draped with the most wonderful trailing silks in imitation of the Venetian nobility in the great water fêtes?[1]

QUINCY [*Turns to* VERA]. Ah, Miss Revendal—what a pity you refused that invitation! It was a fairy scene of twinkling lights and delicious darkness—each couple had their own gondola to sup in, and their own side-canal to slip down. Eh? Ha! Ha! Ha!

DAVID. And the same night, women and children died of hunger in New York!

QUINCY [*Startled, drops eyeglass*]. Eh?

---

1 In the 1932 and subsequent printings, the words after the dash are given to Quincy Davenport.

DAVID [*Furiously*]. And this is the sort of people you would invite to hear my symphony—these gondola-guzzlers!

VERA. Mr. Quixano!

MENDEL. David!

DAVID. These magnificent animals who went into the gondolas two by two, to feed and flirt!

QUINCY [*Dazed*]. Sir!

DAVID. I should be a new freak for you for a new freak evening—I and my dreams and my music!

QUINCY. You low-down, ungrateful——

DAVID. Not for you and such as you have I sat here writing and dreaming; not for you who are killing my America!

QUINCY. *Your* America, forsooth, you Jew-immigrant!

VERA. Mr. Davenport!

DAVID. Yes—Jew-immigrant! But a Jew who knows that your Pilgrim Fathers came straight out of his Old Testament,[1] and that our Jew-immigrants are a greater factor in the glory of this great commonwealth than some of you sons of the soil. It is you, freak-fashionables, who are undoing the work of Washington and Lincoln,[2] vulgarising your high heritage, and turning the last and noblest hope of humanity into a caricature.

QUINCY [*Rocking with laughter*]. Ha! Ha! Ha! Ho! Ho! Ho! [*To* VERA.] You never told me your Jew-scribbler was a socialist!

DAVID. I am nothing but a simple artist, but I come from Europe, one of her victims, and I know that she is a failure; that her palaces and peerages are outworn toys of the human spirit, and that the only hope of mankind lies in a new world. And here—in the land of to-morrow—you are trying to bring back Europe——

---

1 The English Pilgrims and Puritans who came to America to escape religious persecution identified with the Israelites fleeing from Egypt, seeking a new promised land.

2 George Washington (1732–99), first president of the United States; Abraham Lincoln (1809–65), sixteenth president of the United States, who served during the Civil War and ended slavery with the Emancipation Proclamation (1863).

QUINCY [*Interjecting*]. I wish we could!——

DAVID. Europe with her comic-opera coronets and her worm-eaten stage decorations, and her pomp and chivalry built on a morass of crime and misery——

QUINCY [*With sneering laugh*]. Morass!

DAVID [*With prophetic passion*]. But you shall not kill my dream! There shall come a fire round the Crucible that will melt you and your breed like wax in a blowpipe[1]——

QUINCY [*Furiously, with clenched fist*]. You——

DAVID. America *shall* make good ...!

PAPPELMEISTER [*Who has sat down and remained imperturbably seated throughout all this scene, springs up and waves his umbrella hysterically*]. *Hoch Quixano! Hoch! Hoch! Es lebe Quixano! Hoch!*[2]

QUINCY. Poppy! You're dismissed!

PAPPELMEISTER [*Goes to DAVID with outstretched hand*]. *Danke.* [*They grip hands. PAPPELMEISTER turns to QUINCY DAVENPORT.*] Comic Opera! Ouf!

QUINCY [*Goes to street-door, at white heat*]. Are you coming, Miss Revendal? [*He opens the door.*]

VERA [*To QUINCY, but not moving*]. Pray, pray, accept my apologies—believe me, if I had known——

QUINCY [*Furiously*]. Then stop with your Jew! [*Exit.*]

MENDEL [*Frantically*]. But, Mr. Davenport—don't go! He is only a boy. [*Exit after QUINCY DAVENPORT.*] You must consider——

DAVID. Oh, Herr Pappelmeister, you have lost your place!

PAPPELMEISTER. And saved my soul. Dollars are de devil. Now I must to an appointment. *Auf baldiges Wiedersehen.*[3] [*He shakes DAVID'S hand.*] Fräulein Revendal! [*He takes her hand and kisses it. Exit. DAVID and VERA stand gazing at each other.*]

VERA. What have you done? What have you done?

---

1 A tube used in fusing metals. Wax would have been used as a fuel.
2 German: Up with Quixano! High! High! Long live Quixano! High!
3 German: See you soon!

DAVID. What else could I do?

VERA. I hate the smart set as much as you—but as your ladder and your trumpet[1]——

DAVID. I would not stand indebted to them. I know you meant it for my good, but what would these Europe-apers have understood of *my* America—the America of my music? They look back on Europe as a pleasure ground, a palace of art—but I know [*Getting hysterical*] it is sodden with blood, red with bestial massacres——

VERA [*Alarmed, anxious*]. Let us talk no more about it. [*She holds out her hand.*] Good-bye.

DAVID [*Frozen, taking it, holding it*]. Ah, you are offended by my ingratitude—I shall never see you again.

VERA. No, I am not offended. But I have failed to help you. We have nothing else to meet for. [*She disengages her hand.*]

DAVID. Why will you punish me so? I have only hurt myself.

VERA. It is not a *punishment*.

DAVID. What else? When you are with me, all the air seems to tremble with fairy music played by some unseen fairy orchestra.

VERA [*Tremulous*]. And yet you wouldn't come in just now when I——

DAVID. I was too frightened of the others ...

VERA [*Smiling*]. Frightened indeed!

DAVID. Yes, I know I became overbold—but to take all that magic sweetness out of my life for ever—you don't call that a punishment?

VERA [*Blushing*]. How could I wish to punish you? I was proud of you! [*Drops her eyes, murmurs*]. Besides it would be punishing *myself*.

DAVID [*In passionate amaze*]. Miss Revendal! ... But no, it cannot be. It is too impossible.

VERA [*Frightened*]. Yes, too impossible. Good-bye. [*She turns.*]

---

1   The metaphor of ladder and trumpet suggests that the "smart set" would help David rise and would publicize his achievements.

DAVID. But not for always? [VERA *hangs her head. He comes nearer. Passionately.*] Promise me that you—that I—— [*He takes her hand again.*]

VERA [*Melting at his touch, breathes*]. Yes, yes, David.

DAVID. Miss Revendal! [*She falls into his arms.*]

VERA. My dear! my dear!

DAVID. It is a dream. You cannot care for me—you so far above me.

VERA. Above you, you simple boy? Your genius lifts you to the stars.

DAVID. No, no; it is you who lift me there——

VERA [*Smoothing his hair*]. Oh, David. And to think that I was brought up to despise your race.

DAVID [*Sadly*]. Yes, all Russians are.

VERA. But we of the nobility in particular.

DAVID [*Amazed, half-releasing her*]. You are noble?

VERA. My father is Baron Revendal, but I have long since carved out a life of my own.

DAVID. Then he will not separate us?

VERA. No. [*Re-embracing him.*] Nothing can separate us. [*A knock at the street-door. They separate. The automobile is heard clattering off.*]

DAVID. It is my uncle coming back.

VERA [*In low, tense tones*]. Then I shall slip out. I could not bear a third. I will write. [*She goes to the door.*]

DAVID. Yes, yes ... Vera. [*He follows her to the door. He opens it and she slips out.*]

MENDEL [*Half-seen at the door, expostulating*]. You, too, Miss Revendal——? [*Re-enters.*] Oh, David, you have driven away all your friends.

DAVID [*Going to window and looking after* VERA]. Not all, uncle. Not all. [*He throws his arms boyishly round his uncle.*] I am so happy.

MENDEL. Happy?

DAVID. She loves me—Vera loves me.

MENDEL. Vera?

DAVID. Miss Revendal.

MENDEL. Have you lost your wits? [*He throws* DAVID *off.*]

DAVID. I don't wonder you're amazed. Maybe you think *I* wasn't. It is as if an angel should stoop down——

MENDEL [*Hoarsely*]. This is true? This is not some stupid *Purim* joke?

DAVID. True and sacred as the sunrise.

MENDEL. But you are a Jew!

DAVID. Yes, and just think! She was bred up to despise Jews—her father was a Russian baron——

MENDEL. If she was the daughter of fifty barons, you cannot marry her.

DAVID [*In pained amaze*]. Uncle! [*Slowly.*] Then your hankering after the synagogue was serious after all.

MENDEL. It is not so much the synagogue—it is the call of our blood through immemorial generations.

DAVID. *You* say that! You who have come to the heart of the Crucible, where the roaring fires of God are fusing our race with all the others.

MENDEL [*Passionately*]. Not *our* race, not your race and mine.

DAVID. What immunity has our race? [*Meditatively.*] The pride and the prejudice, the dreams and the sacrifices, the traditions and the superstitions, the fasts and the feasts, things noble and things sordid—they must all into the Crucible.

MENDEL [*With prophetic fury*]. The Jew has been tried in a thousand fires and only tempered and annealed.[1]

DAVID. Fires of hate, not fires of love. That is what melts.

MENDEL [*Sneeringly*]. So I see.

DAVID. Your sneer is false. The love that melted me was not

---

1   To heat and then cool metal or glass to make it tougher and less brittle.

Vera's—it was the love *America* showed me—the day she gathered me to her breast.

MENDEL [*Speaking passionately and rapidly*]. Many countries have gathered us. Holland took us when we were driven from Spain—but we did not become Dutchmen. Turkey took us when Germany oppressed us, but we have not become Turks.

DAVID. These countries were not in the making. They were old civilisations stamped with the seal of creed. In such countries the Jew may be right to stand out. But here in this new secular Republic[1] we must look forward——

MENDEL [*Passionately interrupting*]. We must look backwards, too.

DAVID [*Hysterically*]. To what? To Kishineff? [*As if seeing his vision.*] To that butcher's face directing the slaughter? To those——?

MENDEL [*Alarmed*]. Hush! Calm yourself!

DAVID [*Struggling with himself*]. Yes, I will calm myself—but how else shall I calm myself save by forgetting all that nightmare of religions and races, save by holding out my hands with prayer and music toward the Republic of Man and the Kingdom of God! The Past I cannot mend—its evil outlines are stamped in immortal rigidity. Take away the hope that I can mend the Future, and you make me mad.

MENDEL. You are mad already—your dreams are mad—the Jew is hated here as everywhere—you are false to your race.

DAVID. I keep faith with America. I have faith America will keep faith with us. [*He raises his hands in religious rapture toward the flag over the door.*] Flag of our great Republic, guardian of our homes, whose stars and——

MENDEL. Spare me that rigmarole. Go out and marry your Gentile and be happy.

DAVID. You turn me out?

MENDEL. Would you stay and break my mother's heart? You know she would mourn for you with the rending of garments

---

1 A republic without an established religion.

and the seven days' sitting on the floor.[1] Go! You have cast off the God of our fathers!

DAVID [*Thundrously*]. And the God of our children—does *He* demand no service? [*Quieter, coming toward his uncle and touching him affectionately on the shoulder.*] You are right—I do need a wider world. [*Expands his lungs.*] I must go away.

MENDEL. Go, then—I'll hide the truth—she must never suspect—lest she mourn you as dead.

FRAU QUIXANO [*Outside, in the kitchen*]. Ha! Ha! Ha! Ha! Ha! [*Both men turn toward the kitchen and listen.*]

KATHLEEN. Ha! Ha! Ha! Ha! Ha!

FRAU QUIXANO AND KATHLEEN. Ha! Ha! Ha! Ha! Ha!

MENDEL [*Bitterly*]. A merry *Purim*! [*The kitchen door opens and remains ajar.* FRAU QUIXANO *rushes in, carrying* DAVID'S *violin and bow.* KATHLEEN *looks in, grinning.*]

FRAU QUIXANO [*Hilariously*]. Nu spiel noch! spiel![2] [*She holds the violin and bow appealingly toward* DAVID.]

MENDEL [*Putting out a protesting hand*]. No, no, David—I couldn't bear it.

DAVID. But I must! You said she mustn't suspect. [*He looks lovingly at her as he loudly utters these words, which are unintelligible to her.*] And it may be the last time I shall ever play for her. [*Changing to a mock merry smile as he takes the violin and bow from her.*] Gewiss,[3] Granny! [*He starts the same old Slavic dance.*]

FRAU QUIXANO [*Childishly pleased*]. He! He! He! [*She claps on a false grotesque nose from her pocket.*]

DAVID [*Torn between laughter and tears*]. Ha! Ha! Ha! Ha! Ha!

MENDEL [*Shocked*]. Mutter!

FRAU QUIXANO. Un' du auch![4] [*She claps another false nose on* MENDEL, *laughing in childish glee at the effect. Then she starts*

---

1 Very devout Jews, especially in earlier times, would treat an intermarried child as if he or she were dead. Tearing one's clothing and sitting on the floor or on a low stool are customs observed by Jewish mourners.
2 Yiddish: So play more! Play!
3 Yiddish: Certainly.
4 Yiddish: And you, too!

dancing to the music, and KATHLEEN *slips in and joyously dances beside her.*]

DAVID [*Joining tearfully in the laughter*]. Ha! Ha! Ha! Ha! Ha! [*The curtain falls quickly. It rises again upon the picture of* FRAU QUIXANO *fallen back into a chair, exhausted with laughter, fanning herself with her apron, while* KATHLEEN *has dropped breathless across the arm of the armchair;* DAVID *is still playing on, and* MENDEL, *his false nose torn off, stands by, glowering. The curtain falls again and rises upon a final tableau of* DAVID *in his cloak and hat, stealing out of the door with his violin, casting a sad farewell glance at the old woman and at the home which has sheltered him.*]

Act III

April, about a month later. The scene changes to MISS REVENDAL'S *sitting-room at the Settlement House on a sunny day. Simple, pretty furniture: a sofa, chairs, small table, etc. An open piano with music. Flowers and books about. Fine art reproductions on walls. The fireplace is on the left. A door on the left leads to the hall, and a door on the right to the interior. A servant enters from the left, ushering in* BARON *and* BARONESS REVENDAL *and* QUINCY DAVENPORT. *The* BARON *is a tall, stern, grizzled man of military bearing, with a narrow, fanatical forehead and martinet*[1] *manners, but otherwise of honest and distinguished appearance, with a short, well-trimmed white beard and well-cut European clothes. Although his dignity is diminished by the constant nervous suspiciousness of the Russian official, it is never lost; his nervousness, despite its comic side, being visibly the tragic shadow of his position. His English has only a touch of the foreign in accent and vocabulary and is much superior to his wife's, which comes to her through her French.*[2] *The* BARONESS *is pretty and dressed in red in the height of Paris fashion, but blazes with barbaric jewels at neck and throat and wrist. She gestures freely with her hand, which, when ungloved, glitters with heavy rings. She is much younger than the* BARON *and self-consciously fascinating. Her*

---

1 Strict military disciplinarian.
2 French was the language of the Russian aristocracy and nobility in the nineteenth century, so presumably the Baroness learned English through a French-speaking instructor. As mentioned earlier in the play, the Baron had studied English in hopes of furthering his career goals, and thus Vera had an English governess. Zangwill indicates the Baroness's French accent phonetically as he records her English speech.

parasol, which matches her costume, suggests the sunshine without.
QUINCY DAVENPORT *is in a smart spring suit with a motor dust-coat and cap, which last he lays down on the mantelpiece.*

SERVANT. Miss Revendal is on the roof-garden. I'll go and tell her. [*Exit, toward the hall.*]

BARON. A marvellous people, you Americans. Gardens in the sky!

QUINCY. Gardens, forsooth! We plant a tub and call it Paradise. No, Baron. New York is the great stone desert.

BARONESS. But ze big beautiful Park vere ve drove tru?

QUINCY. No taste, Baroness, modern sculpture and menageries! Think of the Medici gardens[1] at Rome.

BARONESS. Ah, Rome! [*With an ecstatic sigh, she drops into an armchair. Then she takes out a dainty cigarette-case, pulls off her right-hand glove, exhibiting her rings, and chooses a cigarette. The* BARON, *seeing this, produces his match-box.*]

QUINCY. And now, dear Baron Revendal, having brought you safely to the den of the lioness—if I may venture to call your daughter so—I must leave *you* to do the taming, eh?

BARON. You are always of the most amiable. [*He strikes a match.*]

BARONESS. *Tout à fait charmant.*[2] [*The* BARON *lights her cigarette.*]

QUINCY [*Bows gallantly*]. Don't mention it. I'll just have my auto take me to the Club, and then I'll send it back for you.

BARONESS. Ah, zank you—zat street-car looks horreeble. [*She puffs out smoke.*]

BARON. Quite impossible. What is to prevent an anarchist sitting next to you and shooting out your brains?[3]

---

1 Gardens surrounding the villa of the powerful Medici family, established in 1540 on the site of existing luxurious gardens and connected to the famed Borghese gardens.
2 French: Completely charming.
3 During this time period anarchism was a movement that threatened governments in Europe and the United States; acts of terrorism by anarchists were greatly feared, especially in Tsarist Russia.

QUINCY. We haven't much of that here—I don't mean brains. Ha! Ha! Ha!

BARON. But I saw desperadoes spying as we came off your yacht.

QUINCY. Oh, that was newspaper chaps.

BARON [*Shakes his head*]. No—they are circulating my appearance to all the gang in the states. They took snapshots.

QUINCY. Then you're quite safe from recognition. [*He sniggers.*] Didn't they ask you questions?

BARON. Yes, but I am a diplomat. I do not reply.

QUINCY. That's not very diplomatic here. Ha! Ha!

BARON. *Diable!*[1] [*He claps his hand to his hip pocket, half-producing a pistol. The* BARONESS *looks equally anxious.*]

QUINCY. What's up?

BARON [*Points to window, whispers hoarsely*]. Regard! A hooligan peeped in!

QUINCY [*Goes to window*]. Only some poor devil come to the Settlement.

BARON [*Hoarsely*]. But under his arm—a bomb!

QUINCY [*Shaking his head smilingly*]. A soup bowl.

BARONESS. Ha! Ha! Ha!

QUINCY. What makes you so nervous, Baron? [*The* BARON *slips back his pistol, a little ashamed.*]

BARONESS. Ze Intellectuals and ze *Bund*,[2] zey all hate my husband because he is faizful to Christ [*Crossing herself*] and ze Tsar.

QUINCY. But the Intellectuals are in Russia.

---

1 French: Devil!

2 German and Yiddish: union, federation, association. The Baron is likely referring to the General Jewish Workers' Bund in Lithuania, Poland, and Russia, a secular Jewish socialist party founded in the Russian Empire in 1897. The Bund sided with the Bolsheviks in the failed 1905 Revolution and was seen as a threat by the nobility. Russian intellectuals were also anti-Tsarist.

BARON. They have their branches here—the refugees are the leaders—it is a diabolical network.

QUINCY. Well, anyhow, *we're* not in Russia, eh? No, no, Baron, you're quite safe. Still, you can keep my automobile as long as you like—I've plenty.

BARON. A thousand thanks. [*Wiping his forehead.*] But surely no gentleman would sit in the public car, squeezed between working-men and shop-girls, not to say Jews and Blacks.

QUINCY. It *is* done here. But we shall change all that. Already we have a few taxi-cabs. Give us time, my dear Baron, give us time. You mustn't judge us by your European standard.

BARON. By the European standard, Mr. Davenport, you put our hospitality to the shame. From the moment you sent your yacht for us to Odessa——

QUINCY. Pray, don't ever speak of that again—you know how anxious I was to get you to New York.

BARON. Provided we have arrived in time!

QUINCY. That's all right, I keep telling you. They aren't married yet——

BARON [*Grinding his teeth and shaking his fist*]. Those Jew-vermin—all my life I have suffered from them!

QUINCY. We all suffer from them.

BARONESS. Zey are ze pests of ze civilisation.

BARON. But this supreme insult Vera shall not put on the blood of the Revendals—not if I have to shoot her down with my own hand—and myself after!

QUINCY. No, no, Baron, that's not done here. Besides, if you shoot her down, where do *I* come in, eh?

BARON [*Puzzled*]. Where *you* come in?

QUINCY. Oh, Baron! Surely you have guessed that it is not merely Jew-hate, but—er—Christian love. Eh? [*Laughing uneasily.*]

BARON. You!

BARONESS [*Clapping her hands*]. Oh, *charmant, charmant*! But it ees a romance!

BARON. But you are married!

BARONESS [*Downcast*]. *Ah, oui. Quel dommage,*[1] vat a peety!

QUINCY. You forget, Baron, we are in America. The law giveth and the law taketh away. [*He sniggers.*]

BARONESS. It ees a vonderful country! But your vife—*hein?*[2]—vould she consent?

QUINCY. She's mad to get back on the stage—I'll run a theatre for her. It's your daughter's consent that's the real trouble—she won't see me because I lost my temper and told her to stop with her Jew. So I look to you to straighten things out.

BARONESS. *Mais parfaitement.*[3]

BARON [*Frowning at her*]. You go too quick, Katusha. What influence have I on Vera? And *you* she has never even seen! To kick out the Jew-beast is one thing....

QUINCY. Well, anyhow, don't *shoot* her—shoot the beast rather. [*Sniggeringly.*]

BARON. Shooting is too good for the enemies of Christ. [*Crossing himself.*] At Kishineff we stick the swine.

QUINCY [*Interested*]. Ah! I read about that. Did you see the massacre?

BARON. Which one? Give me a cigarette, Katusha. [*She obeys.*] We've had several Jew-massacres in Kishineff.

QUINCY. Have you? The papers only boomed one—four or five years ago—about Easter time, I think——

BARON. Ah, yes—when the Jews insulted the procession of the Host![4] [*Taking a light from the cigarette in his wife's mouth.*]

QUINCY. Did they? I thought——[5]

---

1 The Baroness gives the translation in her accented English: "What a pity."

2 French: Eh?

3 French: But perfectly.

4 Bread used in the Christian communion ritual.

5 Quincy is correct in questioning the Baron. The cause that the Baron mentions was a false pretext likely circulated to justify the anti-Jewish violence.

BARON [*Sarcastically*]. I daresay. That's the lies they spread in the West. They have the Press in their hands, damn 'em. But you see I was on the spot. [*He drops into a chair.*] I had charge of the whole district.[1]

QUINCY [*Startled*]. You!

BARON. Yes, and I hurried a regiment up to teach the blaspheming brutes manners—— [*He puffs out a leisurely cloud.*]

QUINCY [*Whistling*]. Whew! ... I—I say, old chap, I mean Baron, you'd better not say that here.

BARON. Why not? I am proud of it.

BARONESS. My husband vas decorated for it—he has ze order of St. Vladimir.

BARON [*Proudly*]. Second class! Shall we allow these bigots to mock at all we hold sacred? The Jews are the deadliest enemies of our holy autocracy and of the only orthodox Church. Their *Bund* is behind all the Revolution.

BARONESS. A plague-spot muz be cut out!

QUINCY. Well, I'd keep it dark if I were you. Kishineff is a back number, and we don't take much stock in the new massacres. Still, we're a bit squeamish——

BARON. Squeamish! Don't you lynch and roast your niggers?[2]

QUINCY. Not officially. Whereas your Black Hundreds——[3]

BARON. Black Hundreds! My dear Mr. Davenport, they are the white hosts of Christ [*Crossing himself*] and of the Tsar, who is

---

1   The Baron is a fictional character, and the pogrom, which extended to Easter Monday, was in fact intensified due to a lack of leadership (see Judge 49–65, 139–40). It was, however, carried out viciously by local anti-Semites who were not stopped by the soldiers and police called to the scene. The complete information was likely not available when Zangwill wrote *The Melting-Pot*. The violence to people and property, however, was at least as brutal as Zangwill records it in the play.

2   Lynchings and burnings of African Americans by unofficial mobs were common in the American south from the 1860s to the 1960s. The term *nigger* was used more frequently and generally in 1908 than today, but its use by the Baron underscores his bigotry.

3   Ultranationalistic, anti-revolutionary, and antisemitic group active in Russia during and after the Revolution of 1905.

God's vicegerent on earth. Have you not read the works of our sainted Pobiedonostzeff, Procurator of the Most Holy Synod?[1]

QUINCY. Well, of course, I always felt there was another side to it, but still——

BARONESS. Perhaps he has right, Alexis. Our Ambassador vonce told me ze Americans are more sentimental zan civilised.

BARON. Ah, let them wait till they have ten million vermin overrunning *their* country—we shall see how long they will be sentimental. Think of it! A burrowing swarm creeping and crawling everywhere, ugh! They ruin our peasantry with their loans and their drink shops, ruin our army with their revolutionary propaganda, ruin our professional classes by snatching all the prizes and professorships, ruin our commercial classes by monopolising our sugar industries, our oil-fields, our timber-trade.... Why, if we gave them equal rights, our Holy Russia would be entirely run by them.

BARONESS. *Mon dieu! C'est vrai.*[2] Ve real Russians vould become slaves.

QUINCY. Then what are you going to do with them?

BARON. One-third will be baptized, one-third massacred, the other third emigrated here.[3] [*He strikes a match to relight his cigarette.*]

QUINCY [*Shudderingly*]. Thank you, my dear Baron,—you've already sent me one Jew too many. We're going to stop all alien immigration.[4]

BARON. To stop *all* alien—? But that is barbarous!

QUINCY, Well, don't let us waste our time on the Jew-problem ... our own little Jew-problem is enough, eh? Get rid of this little fiddler. Then *I* may have a look in. Adieu, Baron.

---

1 Konstantin Petrovich Pobyedonostsyev (1827–1907), Russian statesman and jurist who held the position of Procurator from 1880 to 1905. He was a reactionary and influential advisor to the Tsarist regime, and extremely antisemitic.
2 French: My God! It's true.
3 This statement has been attributed to Pobyedonostsyev.
4 Britain had already passed the restrictive Aliens Act of 1905 when Zangwill wrote *The Melting-Pot*. Americans would severely restrict immigration later, in 1924.

BARON. Adieu. [*Holding his hand.*] But you are not really serious about Vera? [*The* BARONESS *makes a gesture of annoyance.*]

QUINCY. Not serious, Baron? Why, to marry her is the only thing I have ever wanted that I couldn't get. It is torture! Baroness, I rely on your sympathy. [*He kisses her hand with a pretentious foreign air.*]

BARONESS [*In sentimental approval*]. Ah! *L'amour*! *L'amour!* [1] [*Exit* QUINCY DAVENPORT, *taking his cap in passing.*] You might have given him a little encouragement, Alexis.

BARON. Silence, Katusha. I only tolerated the man in Europe because he was a link with Vera.

BARONESS. You accepted his yacht and his——

BARON. If I had known his loose views on divorce——

BARONESS. I am sick of your scruples. You are ze only poor official in Bessarabia. [2]

BARON. Be silent! Have I not forbidden——?

BARONESS [*Petulantly*]. Forbidden! Forbidden! All your life you have served ze Tsar, and you cannot afford a single automobile. A millionaire son-in-law is just vat you owe me.

BARON. What I owe you?

BARONESS. Yes, ven I married you, I vas tinking you had a good position. I did not know you were too honest to use it. You vere not open viz me, Alexis.

BARON. You knew I was a Revendal. The Revendals keep their hands clean.... [*With a sudden start he tiptoes noiselessly to the door leading to the hall and throws it open. Nobody is visible. He closes it shamefacedly.*]

BARONESS [*Has shared his nervousness till the door was opened, but now bursts into mocking laughter*]. If you thought less about your precious safety, and more about me and Vera——

BARON. Hush! You do not know Vera. You saw I was even afraid to give my name. She might have sent me away as she sent away the Tsar's plate of mutton.

---

1 French: Love! love!
2 An area that today includes Moldova and parts of Ukraine. Kishinev is located there.

BARONESS. The Tsar's plate of——?

BARON. Did I never tell you? When she was only a school-girl—at the Imperial High School—the Tsar on his annual visit tasted the food, and Vera, as the show pupil, was given the honour of finishing his Majesty's plate.

BARONESS [*In incredulous horror*]. And she sent it away?

BARON. Gave it to a servant. [*Awed silence.*] And then you think I can impose a husband on her. No, Katusha, I have to win her love for myself, not for millionaires.

BARONESS [*Angry again*]. Alvays so affrightfully selfish!

BARON. I have no control over her, I tell you! [*Bitterly.*] I never could control my womenkind.

BARONESS. Because you zink zey are your soldiers. Silence! Halt! Forbidden! Right Veel! March!

BARON [*Sullenly*]. I wish I did think they were my soldiers—I might try the lash.

BARONESS [*Springing up angrily, shakes parasol at him*]. You British barbarian!

VERA [*Outside the door leading to the interior*]. Yes, thank you, Miss Andrews. I know I have visitors.

BARON [*Ecstatically*]. Vera's voice! [*The* BARONESS *lowers her parasol. He looks yearningly toward the door. It opens. Enter* VERA *with inquiring gaze.*]

VERA [*With a great shock of surprise*]. Father!!

BARON. *Verotschka!* My dearest darling! ... [*He makes a movement toward her, but is checked by her irresponsiveness.*] Why, you've grown more beautiful than ever.

VERA. You in New York!

BARON. The Baroness wished to see America. Katusha, this is my daughter.

BARONESS [*In sugared sweetness*]. And mine, too, if she vill let me love her.

VERA [*Bowing coldly, but still addressing her father*]. But how? When?

BARON. We have just come and——

BARONESS [*Dashing in*]. Zat charming young man lent us his yacht—he is adoràhble.

VERA. What charming young man?

BARONESS. Ah, she has many, ze little coquette—ha! ha! ha! [*She touches* VERA *playfully with her parasol.*]

BARON. We wished to give you a pleasant surprise.

VERA. It is certainly a surprise.

BARON [*Chilled*]. You are not very ... daughterly.

VERA. Do you remember when you last saw me? You did not claim me as a daughter then.

BARON [*Covers his eyes with his hand*]. Do not recall it; it hurts too much.

VERA. I was in the dock.[1]

BARON. It was horrible. I hated you for the devil of rebellion that had entered into your soul. But I thanked God when you escaped.

VERA [*Softened*]. I think I was more sorry for you than for myself. I hope, at least, no suspicion fell on you.

BARONESS [*Eagerly*]. But it did—an avalanche of suspicion. He is still buried under it. Vy else did they make Skovaloff Ambassador instead of him? Even now he risks everyting to see you again. Ah, *mon enfant*,[2] you owe your fazer a grand reparation!

VERA. What reparation can I possibly make?

BARON [*Passionately*]. You can love me again, Vera.

BARONESS [*Stamping foot*]. Alexis, you are interrupting——

VERA. I fear, father, we have grown too estranged—our ideas are so opposite——

BARON. But not now, Vera, surely not now? You are no longer [*He lowers his voice and looks around.*] a Revolutionist?

VERA. Not with bombs, perhaps. I thank Heaven I was caught before I had done any *practical* work. But if you think I accept

---

1   The place where a defendant sits in a criminal trial. Vera was on trial for revolutionary activities and sentenced to imprisonment in Siberia.

2   French: My child.

the order of things, you are mistaken. In Russia I fought against the autocracy——[1]

BARON. Hush! Hush! [*He looks round nervously.*]

VERA. Here I fight against the poverty. No, father, a woman who has once heard the call will always be a wild creature.

BARON. But [*Lowering his voice*] those revolutionary Russian clubs here—you are not a member?

VERA. I do not believe in Revolutions carried on at a safe distance. I have found my life-work in America.

BARON. I am enchanted, Vera, enchanted.

BARONESS [*Gushingly*]. Permit me to kiss you, *belle enfant*.[2]

VERA. I do not know you enough yet; I will kiss my father.

BARON [*With a great cry of joy*]. Vera! [*He embraces her passionately.*] At last! At last! I have found my little Vera again!

VERA. No, father, *your* Vera belongs to Russia with her mother and the happy days of childhood. But for their sakes—— [*She breaks down in emotion.*]

BARON. Ah, your poor mother!

BARONESS [*Tartly*]. Alexis, I perceive I am too many! [*She begins to go toward the door.*]

BARON. No, no, Katusha. Vera will learn to love you, too.

VERA [*To* BARONESS]. What does my loving you matter? I can never return to Russia.

BARONESS [*Pausing*]. But ve can come here—often—ven you are married.

VERA [*Surprised*]. When I am married? [*Softly, blushing.*] You know?

BARONESS [*Smiling*]. Ve know zat charming young man adores ze floor your foot treads on!

VERA [*Blushing*]. You have seen David?

BARON [*Hoarsely*]. David! [*He clenches his fist.*]

---

1 Government by absolute rule, in this case the tsar's regime.
2 French: Beautiful child.

BARONESS [*Half aside, as much gestured as spoken*]. Sh! Leave it to me. [*Sweetly.*] Oh, no, ve have not seen David.

VERA [*Looking from one to the other*]. Not seen—? Then what— whom are you talking about?

BARONESS. About zat handsome, quite adoràhble Mr. Davenport.

VERA. Davenport!

BARONESS. Who combines ze manners of Europe viz ze millions of America!

VERA [*Breaks into girlish laughter*]. Ha! Ha! Ha! So Mr. Davenport has been talking to you! But you all seem to forget one small point—bigamy is not permitted even to millionaires.

BARONESS. Ah, not boz at vonce, but——

VERA. And do you think I would take another woman's leavings? No, not even if she were dead.

BARONESS. You are insulting!

VERA. I beg your pardon—I wasn't even thinking of you. Father, to put an end at once to this absurd conversation, let me inform you I am already engaged.

BARON [*Trembling, hoarse*]. By name, David.

VERA. Yes—David Quixano.

BARON. A Jew!

VERA. How did you know? Yes, he is a Jew, a noble Jew.

BARON. A Jew noble! [*He laughs bitterly.*]

VERA. Yes—even as you esteem nobility—by pedigree. In Spain his ancestors were hidalgos, favourites at the Court of Ferdinand and Isabella; but in the great expulsion of 1492 they preferred exile in Poland to baptism.[1]

BARON. And you, a Revendal, would mate with an unbaptized dog?

---

1   The Inquisition, a tribunal begun by the Pope to rid the Roman Catholic Church of heresy, began in the twelfth century and took hold in Spain in 1481. It was not specifically aimed against Jews, but since many Jews had converted as a result, their loyalty was questioned and resulted in widespread use of the *auto da fe*, a test of faith   (*continued*)

VERA. Dog! You call my husband a dog!

BARON. Husband! God in heaven—are you married already?

VERA. No! But not being unemployed millionaires like Mr. Davenport, we hold even our troth eternal.[1] [*Calmer.*] Our poverty, not your prejudice, stands in the way of our marriage. But David is a musician of genius, and some day——

BARONESS. A fiddler in a beer-hall! She prefers a fiddler to a millionaire of ze first families of America!

VERA [*Contemptuously*]. First families! I told you David's family came to Poland in 1492—some months before America was discovered.

BARON. Christ save us! You have become a Jewess!

VERA. No more than David has become a Christian. We were already at one—all honest people are. Surely, father, all religions must serve the same God—since there is only one God to serve.

BARONESS. But ze girl is an ateist!

BARON. Silence, Katusha! Leave me to deal with my daughter. [*Changing tone to pathos, taking her face between his hands.*] Oh, Vera, *Verotschka*, my dearest darling, I had sooner you had remained buried in Siberia than that—— [*He breaks down.*]

VERA [*Touched, sitting beside him*]. For you, father, I *was* as though buried in Siberia. Why did you come here to stab yourself afresh?

BARON. I wish to God I had come here earlier. I wish I had not been so nervous of Russian spies. Ah, *Verotschka*, if you only knew how I have pored over the newspaper pictures of you, and the reports of your life in this Settlement!

---

by burning at the stake. Finally, in March 1492, Torquemada, leader of the Inquisition, convinced the Spanish monarchs Ferdinand and Isabella to issue a decree that expelled all Jews from the country; the expulsion was complete four months later. Most of these Sephardic (Spanish) Jews fled to Turkey and North Africa, but some went to Spanish colonies in the Americas and others to various parts of Europe, most notably Holland but also eastern Europe. This explains the unusual situation of a family with a Sephardic name and origins becoming victims of the Kishinev pogrom.

1 On opening night, this line read, "In the sight of that God we are: not being trueborn Americans, we hold even our troth eternal." See Introduction, p. 31.

VERA. You asked me not to send letters.

BARON. I know, I know—and yet sometimes I felt as if I could risk Siberia myself to read your dear, dainty handwriting again.

VERA [*Still more softened*]. Father, if you love me so much, surely you will love David a little too—for my sake.

BARON [*Dazed*]. I—love—a Jew? Impossible. [*He shudders.*]

VERA [*Moving away, icily*]. Then so is any love from me to you. You have chosen to come back into my life, and after our years of pain and separation I would gladly remember only my old childish affection. But not if you hate David. You must make your choice.

BARON [*Pitifully*]. Choice? I have no choice. Can I carry mountains? No more can I love a Jew. [*He rises resolutely.*]

BARONESS [*Who has turned away, fretting and fuming, turns back to her husband, clapping her hands*]. Bravo!

VERA [*Going to him again, coaxingly*]. I don't ask you to carry mountains, but to drop the mountains you carry—the mountains of prejudice. Wait till you see him.

BARON. I will not see him.

VERA. Then you will hear him—he is going to make music for all the world. You can't escape him, *papasha*, you with your love of music, any more than you escaped Rubinstein.

BARONESS. Rubinstein vas not a Jew.

VERA. Rubinstein was a Jewish boy-genius, just like my David.

BARONESS. But his parents vere baptized soon after his birth. I had it from his patroness, ze Grande Duchesse Helena Pavlovna.[1]

VERA. And did the water outside change the blood within? Rubinstein was our Court pianist and was decorated by the Tsar. And you, the Tsar's servant, dare to say you could not meet a Rubinstein.

BARON [*Wavering*]. I did not say I could not meet a *Rubinstein*.

VERA. You practically said so. David will be even greater than

---

1   The Grand Duchess Elena Pavlovna (1807–73), patron of Anton Rubinstein.

Rubinstein. Come, father, I'll telephone for him; he is only round the corner.

BARONESS [*Excitedly*]. Ve vill not see him!

VERA [*Ignoring her*]. He shall bring his violin and play to you. There! You see, little father, you are already less frowning—now take that last wrinkle out of your forehead. [*She caresses his forehead.*] Never mind! David will smooth it out with his music as his Biblical ancestor smoothed that surly old Saul.[1]

BARONESS. Ve vill not hear him!

BARON. Silence, Katusha! Oh, my little Vera, I little thought when I let you study music at Petersburg[2]——

VERA [*Smiling wheedlingly*]. That I should marry a musician. But you see, little father, it all ends in music after all. Now I will go and perform on the telephone, I'm not angel enough to bear one in here.[3] [*She goes toward the door of the hall, smiling happily.*]

BARON [*With a last agonized cry of resistance*]. Halt!

VERA [*Turning, makes mock military salute*]. Yes, *papasha.*

BARON [*Overcome by her roguish smile*]. You—I—he—do you love this J—this David so much?

VERA [*Suddenly tragic*]. It would kill me to give him up. [*Resuming smile.*] But don't let us talk of funerals on this happy day of sunshine and reunion. [*She kisses her hand to him and exit toward the hall.*]

BARONESS [*Angrily*]. You are in her hands as vax!

BARON. She is the only child I have ever had, Katusha. Her baby arms curled round my neck; in her baby sorrows her wet face nestled against little father's. [*He drops on a chair, and leans his head on the table.*]

BARONESS [*Approaching tauntingly*]. So you vill have a Jew son-in-law!

---

1   1 Samuel 16:14–23. Before Saul or David became kings, Saul called for David to play the harp to soothe him.
2   St. Petersburg, capital of Imperial Russia.
3   In 1908, a telephone would have been large and heavy, and possibly fixed to a wall.

BARON. You don't know what it meant to me to feel her arms round me again.

BARONESS. And a hook-nosed brat to call you grandpapa, and nestle his greasy face against yours.

BARON [*Banging his fist on the table*]. Don't drive me mad! [*His head drops again.*]

BARONESS. Then drive me home—I vill not meet him.... Alexis! [*She taps him on the shoulder with her parasol. He does not move.*] Alexis Ivanovitch! Do you not listen! ... [*She stamps her foot.*] Zen I go to ze hotel alone. [*She walks angrily toward the hall. Just before she reaches the door, it opens, and the servant ushers in* HERR PAPPELMEISTER *with his umbrella. The* BARONESS'S *tone changes instantly to a sugared society accent.*] How do you do, Herr Pappelmeister? [*She extends her hand, which he takes limply.*] You don't remember me? *Non?* [*Exit servant.*] Ve vere with Mr. Quincy Davenport at Wiesbaden—ze Baroness Revendal.

PAPPELMEISTER. *So!* [*He drops her hand.*]

BARONESS. Yes, it vas ze Baron's entousiasm for you zat got you your present position.

PAPPELMEISTER [*Arching his eyebrows*]. *So!*

BARONESS. Yes—zere he is! [*She turns toward the* BARON.] Alexis, rouse yourself! [*She taps him with her parasol.*] Zis American air makes ze Baron so sleepy.

BARON [*Rises dazedly and bows*]. Charmed to meet you, Herr——

BARONESS. Pappelmeister! You remember ze great Pappelmeister.

BARON [*Waking up, becomes keen*]. Ah, yes, yes, charmed—why do you never bring your orchestra to Russia, Herr Pappelmeister?

PAPPELMEISTER [*Surprised*]. Russia? It never occurred to me to go to Russia—she seems so uncivilised.

BARONESS [*Angry*]. Uncivilised! Vy, ve have ze finest restaurants in ze vorld! And ze best telephones!

PAPPELMEISTER. *So?*

BARONESS. Yes, and the most beautiful ballets—Russia is affrightfully misunderstood. [*She sweeps away in burning indignation.* PAPPELMEISTER *murmurs in deprecation. Re-enter* VERA *from the hall. She is gay and happy.*]

VERA. He is coming round at once—— [*She utters a cry of pleased surprise.*] Herr Pappelmeister! This is indeed a pleasure! [*She gives* PAPPELMEISTER *her hand, which he kisses.*]

BARONESS [*Sotto voce to the* BARON]. Let us go before he comes. [*The* BARON *ignores her, his eyes hungrily on* VERA.]

PAPPELMEISTER [*To* VERA]. But I come again—you have visitors.

VERA [*Smiling*]. Only my father and——

PAPPELMEISTER [*Surprised*]. Your fader? *Ach so!* [*He taps his forehead.*] Revendal!

BARONESS [*Sotto voce to the* BARON]. I vill not meet a Jew, I tell you.

PAPPELMEISTER. But you vill vant to talk to your fader, and all *I* vant is Mr. Quixano's address. De Irish maiden at de house says de bird is flown.

VERA [*Gravely*]. I don't know if I ought to tell you where the new nest is——

PAPPELMEISTER [*Disappointed*]. *Ach!*

VERA [*Smiling*]. But I will produce the bird.

PAPPELMEISTER [*Looks round*]. You vill broduce Mr. Quixano?

VERA [*Merrily*]. By clapping my hands. [*Mysteriously.*] I am a magician.

BARON [*Whose eyes have been glued on* VERA]. You are, indeed! I don't know how you have bewitched me. [*The* BARONESS *glares at him.*]

VERA. Dear little father! [*She crosses to him and strokes his hair.*] Herr Pappelmeister, tell father about Mr. Quixano's music.

PAPPELMEISTER [*Shaking his head*]. Music cannot be talked about.

VERA [*Smiling*]. That's a nasty one for the critics. But tell father what a genius Da— Mr. Quixano is.

BARONESS [*Desperately intervening*]. Good-bye, Vera. [*She thrusts out her hand, which* VERA *takes.*] I have a headache. You muz excuse me. Herr Pappelmeister, *au plaisir de vous revoir.*[1] [PAPPELMEISTER *hastens to the door, which he holds open. The* BARONESS *turns and glares at the* BARON.]

BARON [*Agitated*]. Let me see you to the auto——

BARONESS. You could see me to ze hotel almost as quick.

BARON [*To* VERA]. I won't say good-bye, *Verotschka*—I shall be back. [*He goes toward the hall, then turns.*] You will keep your Rubinstein waiting? [VERA *smiles lovingly.*]

BARONESS. You are keeping *me* waiting. [*He turns quickly. Exeunt* BARON *and* BARONESS.]

PAPPELMEISTER. And now broduce Mr. Quixano!

VERA. Not so fast. What are you going to do with him?

PAPPELMEISTER. Put him in my orchestra!

VERA [*Ecstatic*]. Oh, you dear! [*Then her tone changes to disappointment.*] But he won't go into Mr. Davenport's orchestra.

PAPPELMEISTER. It is no more Mr. Davenport's orchestra. He fired me, don't you remember? Now I boss—how say you in American?

VERA [*Smiling*]. Your own show.

PAPPELMEISTER. *Ja*, my own band. Ven I left dat comic opera millionaire, dey all shtick to me almost to von man.

VERA. How nice of them!

PAPPELMEISTER. All egsept de Christian—he vas de von man. He shtick to de millionaire. So I lose my brincipal first violin.

VERA. And Mr. Quixano is to—oh, how delightful! [*She claps her hands girlishly.*]

PAPPELMEISTER [*Looks round mischievously*]. *Ach*, de magic failed.

VERA [*Puzzled*]. Eh!

---

1   French: I hope to see you again; I hope to see you soon.

PAPPELMEISTER. You do not broduce him. You clap de hands—but you do not broduce him. Ha! Ha! Ha! [*He breaks into a great roar of genial laughter.*]

VERA [*Chiming in merrily*]. Ha! Ha! Ha! But I said I have to know everything first. Will he get a good salary?

PAPPELMEISTER. Enough to keep a vife and eight children!

VERA [*Blushing*]. But he hasn't a——

PAPPELMEISTER. No, but de Christian had—he get de same—I mean salary, ha! ha! ha! not children. Den he can be independent—vedder de fool-public like his American symphony or not—*nicht wahr?*[1]

VERA. You *are* good to us—— [*Hastily correcting herself.*] to Mr. Quixano.

PAPPELMEISTER [*Smiling*]. And aldough you cannot broduce him, I broduce his symphony. *Was?*

VERA. Oh, Herr Pappelmeister! You are an angel.

PAPPELMEISTER. *Nein, nein, mein liebes Kind!*[2] I fear I haf not de correct shape for an angel. [*He laughs heartily. A knock at the door from the hall.*]

VERA [*Merrily*]. Now I clap my hands. [*She claps.*] Come! [*The door opens.*] Behold him! [*She makes a conjurer's gesture.* DAVID, *bare-headed, carrying his fiddle, opens the door, and stands staring in amazement at* PAPPELMEISTER.]

DAVID. I thought you asked me to meet your father.

PAPPELMEISTER. She is a magician. She has changed us. [*He waves his umbrella.*] Hey presto, *was?* Ha! Ha! Ha! [*He goes to* DAVID, *and shakes hands.*] *Und wie geht's?*[3] I hear you've left home.

DAVID. Yes, but I've such a bully cabin——

PAPPELMEISTER [*Alarmed*]. You are sailing avay?

VERA [*Laughing*]. No, no—that's only his way of describing his two-dollar-a-month garret.

---

1 German: Isn't it so?
2 German: No, no, my dear child!
3 German: And how are you?

DAVID. Yes—my state-room on the top deck!

VERA [*Smiling*]. Six foot square.

DAVID. But three other passengers aren't squeezed in, and it never pitches and tosses. It's heavenly.

PAPPELMEISTER [*Smiling*]. And from heaven you flew down to blay in dat beer-hall. *Was?* [DAVID *looks surprised.*] *I* heard you.

DAVID. You! What on earth did you go *there* for?

PAPPELMEISTER. Vat on earth does one go to a beer-hall for? Ha! Ha! Ha! For vawter! Ha! Ha! Ha! Ven I hear you blay, I dink mit myself—if my blans succeed and I get Carnegie Hall[1] for Saturday Symphony Concerts, dat boy shall be one of my first violins. *Was?* [*He slaps* DAVID *on the left shoulder.*]

DAVID [*Overwhelmed, ecstatic, yet wincing a little at the slap on his wound*]. Be one of your first—— [*Remembering.*] Oh, but it is impossible.

VERA [*Alarmed*]. Mr. Quixano! You must not refuse.

DAVID. But does Herr Pappelmeister know about the wound in my shoulder?

PAPPELMEISTER [*Agitated*]. You haf been vounded?

DAVID. Only a legacy from Russia—but it twinges in some weathers.

PAPPELMEISTER. And de pain ubsets your blaying?

DAVID. Not so much the pain—it's all the dreadful memories—

VERA [*Alarmed*]. Don't talk of them.

DAVID. I *must* explain to Herr Pappelmeister—it wouldn't be fair. Even now [*Shuddering.*] there comes up before me the bleeding body of my mother, the cold, fiendish face of the Russian officer, supervising the slaughter——

VERA. Hush! Hush!

DAVID [*Hysterically*]. Oh, that butcher's face—there it is—hovering in the air, that narrow, fanatical forehead, that——

---

1   Prestigious concert hall in New York City, built in 1891.

PAPPELMEISTER [*Brings down his umbrella with a bang*]. *Schluss!*[1] No man ever dared break down under me. My baton will beat away all dese faces and fancies. Out with your violin! [*He taps his umbrella imperiously on the table.*] *Keinen Mut verlieren!*[2] [DAVID *takes out his violin from its case and puts it to his shoulder,* PAPPELMEISTER *keeping up a hypnotic torrent of encouraging German cries.*] *Also! Fertig! Anfangen!*[3] [*He raises and waves his umbrella like a baton.*] Von, dwo, dree, four——

DAVID [*With a great sigh of relief*]. Thanks, thanks—they are gone already.

PAPPELMEISTER, Ha! Ha! Ha! You see. And ven ve blay your American symphony——

DAVID [*Dazed*]. You will play my American symphony?

VERA [*Disappointed*]. Don't you jump for joy?

DAVID [*Still dazed but ecstatic*]. Herr Pappelmeister! [*Changing back to despondency.*] But what certainty is there your Carnegie Hall audience would understand me? It would be the same smart set. [*He drops dejectedly into a chair and lays down his violin.*]

PAPPELMEISTER. *Ach, nein.* Of course, some—ve can't keep peoble out merely because dey pay for deir seats. *Was?* [*He laughs.*]

DAVID. It was always my dream to play it first to the new immigrants—those who have known the pain of the old world and the hope of the new.

PAPPELMEISTER. Try it on the dog. *Was?*

DAVID. Yes—on the dog that here will become a man!

PAPPELMEISTER [*Shakes his head*]. I fear neider dogs nor men are a musical breed.

DAVID. The immigrants will not understand my music with their brains or their ears, but with their hearts and their souls.

VERA. Well, then, why shouldn't it be done here—on our Roof-Garden?

---

1   German: Stop! Put an end to this!
2   German: Lose no courage!
3   German: So! Done! Start!

DAVID [*Jumping up*]. *A Bas-Kôl! A Bas-Kôl!*[1]

VERA. What *are* you talking?

DAVID. Hebrew! It means a voice from heaven.

VERA. Ah, but will Herr Pappelmeister consent?

PAPPELMEISTER [*Bowing*]. Who can disobey a voice from heaven? ... But ven?

VERA. On some holiday evening.... Why not the Fourth of July?

DAVID [*Still more ecstatic*]. Another *Bas-Kôl*! ... My American Symphony! Played to the People! Under God's sky! On Independence Day! With all the—— [*Waving his hand expressively, sighs voluptuously.*] That will be too perfect.

PAPPELMEISTER [*Smiling*]. Dat has to be seen. You must permit me to invite——

DAVID [*In horror*]. Not the musical critics!

PAPPELMEISTER [*Raising both hands with umbrella in equal horror*]. *Gott bewahre!*[2] But I'd like to invite all de persons in New York who really undershtand music.

VERA. Splendid! But should we have room?

PAPPELMEISTER. Room? I vant four blaces.

VERA [*Smiling*]. You are severe! Mr. Davenport was right.

PAPPELMEISTER [*Smiling*]. Perhaps de oders vill be out of town. *Also!* [*Holding out his hand to* DAVID.] You come to Carnegie to-morrow at eleven. Yes? *Fräulein.* [*Kisses her hand.*] *Auf Wiedersehen!*[3] [*Going.*] On de Roof-Garden—*nicht wahr?*

VERA [*Smiling*]. Wind and weather permitting.

PAPPELMEISTER. I haf alvays mein umbrella. *Was?* Ha! Ha! Ha!

VERA [*Murmuring*]. Isn't he a darling? Isn't he——?

PAPPELMEISTER [*Pausing suddenly*]. But ve never settled de salary.

---

1 Hebrew: A heavenly voice or (literally) a bass voice; in Ashkenazic Hebrew or Yiddish, it can also be read as the daughter of a voice.

2 German: God forbid!

3 German: Goodbye.

DAVID. Salary! [*He looks dazedly from one to the other.*] For the honour of playing in your orchestra!

PAPPELMEISTER. Shylock!! ... Never mind—ve settle de pound of flesh to-morrow.[1] *Lebe wohl*[2] [*Exit, the door closes.*]

VERA [*Suddenly miserable*]. How selfish of you, David!

DAVID. Selfish, Vera?

VERA. Yes—not to think of your salary. It looks as if you didn't really love me.

DAVID. Not love you? I don't understand.

VERA [*Half in tears*]. Just when I was so happy to think that now we shall be able to marry.

DAVID. Shall we? Marry? On my salary as first violin?

VERA. Not if you don't want to.

DAVID. Sweetheart! Can it be true? How do you know?

VERA [*Smiling*]. *I'm* not a Jew. I asked.

DAVID. My guardian angel! [*Embracing her. He sits down, she lovingly at his feet.*]

VERA [*Looking up at him*]. Then you *do* care?

DAVID. What a question!

VERA. And you don't think wholly of your music and forget me?

DAVID. Why, you are behind all I write and play!

VERA [*With jealous passion*]. Behind? But I want to be before! I want you to love me first, before everything.

DAVID. I do put you before everything.

VERA. You are sure? And nothing shall part us?

DAVID. Not all the seven seas could part you and me.

VERA. And you won't grow tired of me—not even when you are world-famous——?

---

1 Shylock, a Jewish money-lender, is a central character in William Shakespeare's (1564–1616) *The Merchant of Venice* (c. 1596–99). He lends money to the merchant Antonio, who agrees to forfeit a pound of his flesh if he cannot repay.

2 German: Farewell.

DAVID [*A shade petulant*]. Sweetheart, considering I should owe it all to you——

VERA [*Drawing his head down to her breast*]. Oh, David! David! Don't be angry with poor little Vera if she doubts, if she wants to feel quite sure. You see father has talked so terribly, and after all I was brought up in the Greek Church, and we oughtn't to cause all this suffering unless——

DAVID. Those who love us *must* suffer, and *we* must suffer in their suffering. It is live things, not dead metals, that are being melted in the Crucible.

VERA. Still, we ought to soften the suffering as much as——

DAVID. Yes, but only Time can heal it.

VERA [*With transition to happiness*]. But father seems half-reconciled already! Dear little father, if only he were not so narrow about Holy Russia!

DAVID. If only *my* folks were not so narrow about Holy Judea! But the ideals of the fathers shall not be foisted on the children. Each generation must live and die for its own dream.

VERA. Yes, David, yes. You are the prophet of the living present. I am so happy. [*She looks up wistfully.*] You are happy, too?

DAVID. I am dazed—I cannot realise that all our troubles have melted away—it is so sudden.

VERA. You, David? Who always see everything in such rosy colours? Now that the whole horizon is one great splendid rose, you almost seem as if gazing out toward a blackness——

DAVID. We Jews are cheerful in gloom, mistrustful in joy. It is our tragic history——

VERA. But you have come to end the tragic history; to throw off the coils of the centuries.

DAVID [*Smiling again*]. Yes, yes, Vera. You bring back my sunnier self. I must be a pioneer on the lost road of happiness. To-day shall be all joy, all lyric ecstasy. [*He takes up his violin.*] Yes, I will make my old fiddle-strings *burst* with joy! [*He dashes into a jubilant tarantella. After a few bars there is a knock at the door leading from the hall; their happy faces betray no sign of hearing it; then the door slightly opens, and* BARON REVENDAL'S *head looks hesitatingly in. As* DAVID *perceives it, his features work convulsively, his string breaks with a tragic snap, and he totters backward into* VERA'S *arms. Hoarsely.*] The face! The face!

VERA. David—my dearest!

DAVID [*His eyes closed, his violin clasped mechanically*]. Don't be anxious—I shall be better soon—I oughtn't to have talked about it—the hallucination has never been so complete.

VERA. Don't speak—rest against Vera's heart—till it has passed away. [*The* BARON *comes dazedly forward, half with a shocked sense of* VERA'S *impropriety, half to relieve her of her burden. She motions him back.*] This is the work of your Holy Russia.

BARON [*Harshly*]. What is the matter with him? [DAVID'S *violin and bow drop from his grasp and fall on the table.*]

DAVID. *The voice!* [*He opens his eyes, stares frenziedly at the* BARON, *then struggles out of* VERA'S *arms.*]

VERA [*Trying to stop him*]. Dearest——

DAVID. Let me go. [*He moves like a sleep-walker toward the paralysed* BARON, *puts out his hand, and testingly touches the face.*]

BARON [*Shuddering back*]. Hands off!

DAVID [*With a great cry*]. A-a-a-h! It is flesh and blood. No, it is stone—the man of stone! Monster! [*He raises his hand frenziedly.*]

BARON [*Whipping out his pistol*]. Back, dog! [VERA *darts between them with a shriek.*]

DAVID [*Frozen again, surveying the pistol stonily*]. Ha! You want *my* life, too. Is the cry not yet loud enough?

BARON. The cry?

DAVID [*Mystically*]. Can you not hear it? The voice of the blood of my brothers crying out against you from the ground? Oh, how can you bear not to turn that pistol against yourself and execute upon yourself the justice which Russia denies you?

BARON. Tush! [*Pocketing the pistol a little shamefacedly.*]

VERA. Justice on himself? For what?

DAVID. For crimes beyond human penalty, for obscenities beyond human utterance, for——

VERA. You are raving.

DAVID. Would to heaven I were!

VERA. But this is my father.

DAVID. Your father! ... God! [*He staggers.*]

BARON [*Drawing her to him*]. Come, Vera, I told you——

VERA [*Frantically, shrinking back*]. Don't touch me!

BARON [*Starting back in amaze*]. Vera!

VERA [*Hoarsely*]. Say it's not true.

BARON. What is not true?

VERA. What David said. It was the mob that massacred—*you* had no hand in it.

BARON [*Sullenly*]. I was there with my soldiers.

DAVID [*Leaning, pale, against a chair, hisses*]. And you looked on with that cold face of hate—while my mother—my sister——

BARON [*Sullenly*]. I could not see everything.

DAVID. Now and again you ordered your soldiers to fire——

VERA [*In joyous relief*]. Ah, he *did* check the mob—he *did* tell his soldiers to fire.

DAVID. At any Jew who tried to defend himself.

VERA. Great God! [*She falls on the sofa and buries her head on the cushion, moaning.*] Is there no pity in heaven?

DAVID. There was no pity on earth.

BARON. It was the People avenging itself, Vera. The People rose like a flood. It had centuries of spoliation to wipe out. The voice of the People is the voice of God.

VERA [*Moaning*]. But you could have stopped them.

BARON. I had no orders to defend the foes of Christ and [*Crossing himself.*] the Tsar.[1] The People——

---

1 Although at the time it was believed that the tsar had ordered this and other pogroms, in fact the tsar had nothing to gain and much to lose from civil disorder. Recent research confirms that the pogrom was started by drunken adults and youths who began by (*continued*)

VERA. But you could have stopped them.

BARON. Who can stop a flood? I did my duty. A soldier's duty is not so pretty as a musician's.

VERA. But you could have stopped them.

BARON [*Losing all patience*]. Silence! You talk like an ignorant girl, blinded by passion. The *pogrom* is a holy crusade. Are we Russians the first people to crush down the Jew? No—from the dawn of history the nations have had to stamp upon him—the Egyptians, the Assyrians, the Persians, the Babylonians, the Greeks, the Romans——

DAVID. Yes, it is true. Even Christianity did not invent hatred. But not till Holy Church arose were we burnt at the stake, and not till Holy Russia arose were our babes torn limb from limb. Oh, it is too much! Delivered from Egypt four thousand years ago, to be slaves to the Russian Pharaoh to-day. [*He falls as if kneeling on a chair, and leans his head on the rail.*] O God, shall we always be broken on the wheel of history? How long, O Lord, how long?

BARON [*Savagely*]. Till you are all stamped out, ground into your dirt. [*Tenderly.*] Look up, little Vera! You saw how *papasha* loves you—how he was ready to hold out his hand—and how this cur tried to bite it. Be calm—tell him a daughter of Russia cannot mate with dirt.

VERA. Father, I will be calm. I will speak without passion or blindness. I will tell David the truth. I was never absolutely sure of my love for him—perhaps that was why I doubted his love for me—often after our enchanted moments there would come a nameless uneasiness, some vague instinct, relic of the long centuries of Jew-loathing, some strange shrinking from his Christless creed——

BARON [*With an exultant* cry]. Ah! She is a Revendal.

---

destroying Jewish commercial property after Easter services and festivities. The local governor, Rudolf von Raaben (on whose name Revendal may be loosely based) called for military support but then failed to issue orders, so the military for the most part stood by and did nothing to stop the violence. There were some reports that soldiers joined in, which may be the basis for David's story in this play. The violence he describes, however, matches all accounts, regardless of who was in charge of its commission. See Judge 49–69; Introduction, pp. 23–27.

VERA. But now—— [*She rises and walks firmly toward* DAVID.] now, David, I come to you, and I say in the words of Ruth, thy people shall be my people and thy God my God![1] [*She stretches out her hands to* DAVID.]

BARON. You shameless——! [*He stops as he perceives* DAVID *remains impassive.*]

VERA [*With agonised cry*]. David!

DAVID [*In low, icy tones*]. You cannot come to me. There is a river of blood between us.

VERA. Were it seven seas, our love must cross them.

DAVID. Easy words to you. You never saw that red flood bearing the mangled breasts of women and the spattered brains of babes and sucklings. Oh! [*He covers his eyes with his hands. The* BARON *turns away in gloomy impotence. At last* DAVID *begins to speak quietly, almost dreamily.*] It was your Easter, and the air was full of holy bells and the streets of holy processions—priests in black and girls in white and waving palms and crucifixes, and everybody exchanging Easter eggs and kissing one another three times on the mouth in token of peace and goodwill, and even the Jew-boy felt the spirit of love brooding over the earth, though he did not then know that this Christ, whom holy chants proclaimed re-risen, was born in the form of a brother Jew. And what added to the peace and holy joy was that our own Passover was shining before us. My mother had already made the raisin wine, and my greedy little brother Solomon had sipped it on the sly that very morning. We were all at home—all except my father—he was away in the little Synagogue at which he was cantor. Ah, such a voice he had—a voice of tears and thunder—when he prayed it was like a wounded soul beating at the gates of Heaven—but he sang even more beautifully in the ritual of home, and how we were looking forward to his hymns at the Passover table—— [*He breaks down. The* BARON *has gradually turned round under the spell of* DAVID'S *story and now listens hypnotised.*] I was playing my cracked little fiddle. Little Miriam was making her doll dance to it. Ah, that decrepit old china doll—the only one the poor child had ever had—I can see it now—one eye, no nose, half an arm. We were all laughing to see it caper to my music.... My father flies in through the door, desperately clasping to his breast the Holy Scroll. We cry out to

1 Ruth 1:16.

him to explain, and then we see that in that beloved mouth of song there is no longer a tongue—only blood. He tries to bar the door—a mob breaks in—we dash out through the back into the street. There are the soldiers—and the Face—— [VERA'S *eyes involuntarily seek the face of her father, who shrinks away as their eyes meet.*]

VERA [*In a low sob*]. O God!

DAVID. When I came to myself, with a curious aching in my left shoulder, I saw lying beside me a strange shapeless Something.... [DAVID *points weirdly to the floor, and* VERA, *hunched forwards, gazes stonily at it, as if seeing the horror.*] By the crimson doll in what seemed a hand I knew it must be little Miriam. The doll was a dream of beauty and perfection beside the mutilated mass which was all that remained of my sister, of my mother, of greedy little Solomon—Oh! You Christians can only see that rosy splendour on the horizon of happiness. And the Jew didn't see rosily enough for you, ha! ha! ha! the Jew who gropes in one great crimson mist. [*He breaks down in spasmodic, ironic, long-drawn, terrible laughter.*]

VERA [*Trying vainly to tranquillise him*]. Hush, David! Your laughter hurts more than tears. Let Vera comfort you. [*She kneels by his chair, tries to put her arms round him.*]

DAVID [*Shuddering*]. Take them away! Don't you feel the cold dead pushing between us?

VERA [*Unfaltering, moving his face toward her lips*]. Kiss me!

DAVID. I should feel the blood on my lips.

VERA. My love shall wipe it out.

DAVID. Love! Christian love! [*He unwinds her clinging arms; she sinks prostrate on the floor as he rises.*] For this I gave up my people—darkened the home that sheltered me—there was always a still, small voice[1] at my heart calling me back, but I heeded nothing—only the voice of the butcher's daughter. [*Brokenly.*] Let me go home, let me go home. [*He looks lingeringly at* VERA'S *prostrate form, but overcoming the instinct to touch and comfort her, begins tottering with uncertain pauses toward the door leading to the hall.*]

---

1 I Kings 19:12.

BARON [*Extending his arms in relief and longing*]. And here is your home, Vera! [*He raises her gradually from the floor; she is dazed, but suddenly she becomes conscious of whose arms she is in, and utters a cry of repulsion.*]

VERA. Those arms reeking from that crimson river! [*She falls back.*]

BARON [*Sullenly*]. Don't echo that babble. You came to these arms often enough when they were fresh from the battlefield.

VERA. But not from the shambles! You heard what he called you. Not soldier—butcher! Oh, I dared to dream of happiness after my nightmare of Siberia, but you—you—— [*She breaks down for the first time in hysterical sobs.*]

BARON [*Brokenly*]. Vera! Little Vera! Don't cry! You stab me!

VERA. You thought you were ordering your soldiers to fire at the Jews, but it was my heart they pierced. [*She sobs on.*]

BARON. ... And my own.... But we will comfort each other. I will go to the Tsar myself—with my forehead to the earth—to beg for your pardon![1] ... Come, put your wet face to little father's....

VERA [*Violently pushing his face away*]. I hate you! I curse the day I was born your daughter! [*She staggers toward the door leading to the interior. At the same moment* DAVID, *who has reached the door leading to the hall, now feeling subconsciously that* VERA *is going and that his last reason for lingering on is removed, turns the door-handle. The click attracts the* BARON'S *attention, he veers round.*]

BARON [*To* DAVID]. Halt! [DAVID *turns mechanically.* VERA *drifts out through her door, leaving the two men face to face. The* BARON *beckons to* DAVID, *who as if hypnotised moves nearer. The* BARON *whips out his pistol, slowly crosses to* DAVID, *who stands as if awaiting his fate. The* BARON *hands the pistol to* DAVID.] You were right! [*He steps back swiftly with a touch of stern heroism into the attitude of the culprit at a military execution, awaiting the bullet.*] Shoot me!

DAVID [*Takes the pistol mechanically, looks long and pensively at it as with a sense of its irrelevance. Gradually his arm droops and lets*

---

1   He will ask the tsar to pardon Vera for her revolutionary activities.

the pistol fall on the table, and there his hand touches a string of his violin, which yields a little note. Thus reminded of it, he picks up the violin, and as his fingers draw out the broken string he murmurs]. I must get a new string. [*He resumes his dragging march toward the door, repeating maunderingly.*] I must get a new string. [*The curtain falls.*]

Act IV

Saturday, July 4, evening. The Roof-Garden of the Settlement House, showing a beautiful, far-stretching panorama of New York, with its irregular sky-buildings on the left, and the harbour with its Statue of Liberty on the right.[1] Everything is wet and gleaming after rain. Parapet at the back. Elevator on the right. Entrance from the stairs on the left. In the sky hang heavy clouds through which thin, golden lines of sunset are just beginning to labour. DAVID is discovered on a bench, hugging his violin-case to his breast, gazing moodily at the sky. A muffled sound of applause comes up from below and continues with varying intensity through the early part of the scene. Through it comes the noise of the elevator ascending. MENDEL steps out and hurries forward.

MENDEL. Come down, David! Don't you hear them shouting for you? [*He passes his hand over the wet bench.*] Good heavens! You will get rheumatic fever!

DAVID. Why have you followed me?

MENDEL. Get up—everything is still damp.

DAVID [*Rising, gloomily*]. Yes, there's a damper over everything.

MENDEL. Nonsense—the rain hasn't damped your triumph in the least. In fact, the more delicate effects wouldn't have gone so well in the open air. Listen!

DAVID. Let them shout. Who told you I was up here?

MENDEL. Miss Revendal, of course.

DAVID [*Agitated*]. Miss Revendal? How should *she* know?

MENDEL [*Sullenly*]. She seems to understand your crazy ways.

---

1 According to Edna Nahshon, in performance the image of the Statue of Liberty was projected as the backdrop by a "stereopticon, a powerful multiple-lens magic lantern" (239).

DAVID [*Passing his hand over his eyes*]. Ah, *you* never understood me, uncle.... How did she look? Was she pale?

MENDEL. Never mind about Miss Revendal. Pappelmeister wants you—the people insist on seeing you. Nobody can quiet them.

DAVID. They saw me all through the symphony in my place in the orchestra.

MENDEL. They didn't know you were the composer as well as the first violin. Now Miss Revendal has told them. [*Louder applause*.] There! Eleven minutes it has gone on—like for an office-seeker. You *must* come and show yourself.

DAVID. I won't—I'm not an office-seeker. Leave me to my misery.

MENDEL. Your misery? With all this glory and greatness opening before you? Wait till you're *my* age—— [*Shouts of* "QUIXANO!"] You hear! What is to be done with them?

DAVID. Send somebody on the platform to remind them this is the interval for refreshments!

MENDEL. Don't be cynical. You know your dearest wish was to melt these simple souls with your music. And now——

DAVID. Now I have only made my own stony.

MENDEL. You are right. You are stone all over—ever since you came back home to us. Turned into a pillar of salt, mother says—like Lot's wife.[1]

DAVID. That was the punishment for looking backward. Ah, uncle, there's more sense in that old Bible than the Rabbis suspect. Perhaps that is the secret of our people's paralysis—we are always looking backward. [*He drops hopelessly into an iron garden-chair behind him.*]

MENDEL [*Stopping him before he touches the seat*]. Take care—it's sopping wet. You don't look backward enough. [*He takes out his handkerchief and begins drying the chair.*]

DAVID [*Faintly smiling*]. I thought you wanted the salt to melt.

---

1 Genesis 19:26.

MENDEL. It *is* melting a little if you can smile. Do you know, David, I haven't seen you smile since that *Purim* afternoon?

DAVID. You haven't worn a false nose since, uncle. [*He laughs bitterly.*] Ha! Ha! Ha! Fancy masquerading in America because twenty-five centuries ago the Jews escaped a *pogrom* in Persia. Two thousand five hundred years ago! Aren't we uncanny? [*He drops into the wiped chair.*]

MENDEL [*Angrily*]. Better you should leave us altogether than mock at us. I thought it was your Jewish heart that drove you back home to us; but if you are still hankering after Miss Revendal——

DAVID [*Pained*]. Uncle!

MENDEL. I'd rather see you marry her than go about like this. You couldn't make the house any gloomier.

DAVID. Go back to the concert, please. They have quieted down.

MENDEL [*Hesitating*]. And you?

DAVID. Oh, I'm not playing in the popular after-pieces. Pappelmeister guessed I'd be broken up with the stress of my own symphony—he has violins enough.

MENDEL. Then you don't want to carry this about. [*Taking the violin from* DAVID'S *arms.*]

DAVID [*Clinging to it*]. Don't rob me of my music—it's all I have.

MENDEL. You'll spoil it in the wet. I'll take it home.

DAVID. No—— [*He suddenly catches sight of two figures entering from the left—*FRAU QUIXANO *and* KATHLEEN *clad in their best, and wearing tiny American flags in honour of Independence Day.* KATHLEEN *escorts the old lady, with the air of a guardian angel, on her slow, tottering course toward* DAVID. *FRAU QUIXANO is puffing and panting after the many stairs.* DAVID *jumps up in surprise, releases the violin-case to* MENDEL.] They at my symphony!

MENDEL. Mother *would* come—even though, being *Shabbos*, she had to walk.[1]

---

1   This line makes clear that the settlement house is in Richmond, since one could only get to the other boroughs from Richmond by ferry. Historically, however, there were no settlement houses in Richmond at that time.

DAVID. But wasn't she shocked at my playing on the Sabbath?

MENDEL. No—that's the curious part of it. She said that even as a boy you played your fiddle on *Shabbos*, and that if the Lord has stood it all these years, He must consider you an exception.

DAVID. You see! She's more sensible than you thought. I daresay whatever I were to do she'd consider me an exception.

MENDEL [*In sullen acquiescence*]. I suppose geniuses *are*.

KATHLEEN [*Reaching them; panting with admiration and breathlessness*]. Oh, Mr. David! it was like midnight mass! But the misthress was ashleep.

DAVID. Asleep! [*Laughs half-merrily, half-sadly.*] Ha! Ha! Ha!

FRAU QUIXANO [*Panting and laughing in response*]. He! He! He! *Dovidel lacht widder.*[1] He! He! He! [*She touches his arm affectionately, but feeling his wet coat, utters a cry of horror.*] *Du bist nass!*[2]

DAVID. *Es ist gor nicht,*[3] Granny—my clothes are thick. [*She fusses over him, wiping him down with her gloved hand.*]

MENDEL. But what brought you up here, Kathleen?

KATHLEEN. Sure, not the elevator. The misthress said 'twould be breaking the *Shabbos* to ride up in it.

DAVID [*Uneasily*]. But did—did Miss Revendal send you up?

KATHLEEN. And who else should be axin' the misthress if she wasn't proud of Mr. David? Faith, she's a sweet lady.

MENDEL [*Impatiently*]. Don't chatter, Kathleen.

KATHLEEN. But, Mr. Quixano——!

DAVID [*Sweetly*]. Please take your mistress down again—don't let her walk.

KATHLEEN. But *Shabbos* isn't out yet!

MENDEL. Chattering again!

---

1 Yiddish: David laughs again.
2 Yiddish: You are wet!
3 Yiddish: It's nothing.

DAVID [*Gently*]. There's no harm, Kathleen, in going *down* in the elevator.[1]

KATHLEEN. Troth, I'll egshplain to her that droppin' down isn't ridin'.

DAVID [*Smiling*]. Yes, tell her dropping down is natural—not *work*, like flying up. [KATHLEEN *begins to move toward the stairs, explaining to* FRAU QUIXANO.] And, Kathleen! You'll get her some refreshments.

KATHLEEN [*Turns, glaring*]. Refreshments, is it? Give her refrishments where they mix the mate with the butther plates! Oh, Mr. David! [*She moves off toward the stairs in reproachful sorrow.*]

MENDEL [*Smiling*]. I'll get her some coffee.

DAVID [*Smiling*]. Yes, that'll keep her awake. Besides, Pappelmeister was so sure the people wouldn't understand me, he's relaxing them on Gounod and Rossini.[2]

MENDEL. Pappelmeister's idea of relaxation! *I* should have given them comic opera. [*With sudden call to* KATHLEEN, *who with her mistress is at the wrong exit*.] Kathleen! The elevator's *this* side!

KATHLEEN [*Turning*]. What way can that be, when I came up *this* side?

MENDEL. You chatter too much. [FRAU QUIXANO, *not understanding, exit*.] Come this way. Can't you see the elevator?

KATHLEEN [*Perceives* FRAU QUIXANO *has gone, calls after her in Irish-sounding Yiddish*]. Wu geht Ihr,[3] bedad? ... [*Impatiently*.] Houly Moses, komm' zurick![4] [*Exit anxiously, re-enter with* FRAU QUIXANO.] Begorra, we Jews never know

---

1 Despite his and Kathleen's reasoning, David is just being kind to his grandmother to spare her the exertion of walking downstairs. If riding up in an elevator is forbidden on the Sabbath, so is riding down. Today, many rabbis approve of Sabbath elevators programmed to stop at every floor, so that the rider is not doing the work of setting the elevator in motion or opening the door.

2 Charles Gounod (1818–93), French composer best known for his opera *Faust* (see p. 155, n. 1); Gioachino Rossini (1792–1868), best known for his operas *The Barber of Seville* and *William Tell*.

3 Yiddish: Where are you going? *Bedad*, like *begorra* (below), is an Irish exclamation.

4 Yiddish: Come back!

our way. [MENDEL, *carrying the violin, escorts his mother and* KATHLEEN *to the elevator. When they are near it, it stops with a thud, and* PAPPELMEISTER *springs out, his umbrella up, meeting them face to face. He looks happy and beaming over* DAVID'S *triumph.*]

PAPPELMEISTER [*In loud, joyous voice*]. *Nun, Frau Quixano, was sagen Sie?*[1] Vat you tink of your David?

FRAU QUIXANO. *Dovid? Er ist meshuggah.* [*She taps her forehead.*]

PAPPELMEISTER [*Puzzled, to* MENDEL]. *Meshuggah!* Vat means *meshuggah?* Crazy?

MENDEL [*Half-smiling*]. You've struck it. She says David doesn't know enough to go in out of the rain. [*General laughter.*]

DAVID [*Rising*]. But it's stopped raining, Herr Pappelmeister. You don't want your umbrella. [*General laughter.*]

PAPPELMEISTER. *So.* [*Shuts it down.*]

MENDEL. *Herein, Mutter.*[2] [*He pushes* FRAU QUIXANO'S *somewhat shrinking form into the elevator.* KATHLEEN *follows, then* MENDEL.] Herr Pappelmeister, we are all your grateful servants. [PAPPELMEISTER *bows; the gates close, the elevator descends.*]

DAVID. And you won't think *me* ungrateful for running away— you know my thanks are too deep to be spoken.

PAPPELMEISTER. And zo are my congratulations!

DAVID. Then, don't speak them, please.

PAPPELMEISTER. But you *must* come and speak to all de people in America who undershtand music.

DAVID [*Half-smiling*]. To your four connoisseurs? [*Seriously.*] Oh, please! I really could not meet strangers, especially musical vampires.

PAPPELMEISTER [*Half-startled, half-angry*]. Vampires? Oh, come!

DAVID. Voluptuaries, then—rich, idle æsthetes to whom art and

---

1 German: Now, Frau Quixano, what do you say?

2 Yiddish: Come in, Mother [spelled as in German].

life have no connection, parasites who suck our music——

PAPPELMEISTER [*Laughs good-naturedly*]. Ha! Ha! Ha! Vait till you hear vat dey say.

DAVID. I will wait as long as you like.

PAPPELMEISTER. Den I like to tell you now. [*He roars with mischievous laughter.*] Ha! Ha! Ha! De first vampire says it is a great vork, but poorly performed.

DAVID [*Indignant*]. Oh!

PAPPELMEISTER. De second vampire says it is a poor vork, but greatly performed.

DAVID [*Disappointed*]. Oh!

PAPPELMEISTER. De dird vampire says it is a great vork greatly performed.

DAVID [*Complacently*]. Ah!

PAPPELMEISTER. And de fourz vampire says it is a poor vork poorly performed.

DAVID [*Angry and disappointed*]. Oh! [*Then smiling.*] You see you *have* to go by the people after all.

PAPPELMEISTER [*Shakes head, smiling*]. *Nein.* Ven critics disagree—I agree mit mineself.[1] Ha! Ha! Ha! [*He slaps* DAVID *on the back.*] A great vork dat vill be even better performed next time! Ha! Ha! Ha! Ten dousand congratulations. [*He seizes* DAVID'S *hand and grips it heartily.*]

DAVID. Don't! You hurt me.

PAPPELMEISTER [*Dropping* DAVID'S *hand,—misunderstanding*]. Pardon! I forgot your vound.

DAVID. No—no—what does my wound matter? That never stung half so much as these clappings and congratulations.

PAPPELMEISTER [*Puzzled but solicitous*]. I knew your nerves vould be all shnapping like fiddle-shtrings. Oh, you cheniuses! [*Smiling.*] You like neider de clappings nor de criticisms,—*was?*

---

1   Zangwill plays on Oscar Wilde's aphorism "When critics disagree the artist is in accord with himself" (Preface to *The Picture of Dorian Gray* [1891]).

DAVID. They are equally—irrelevant. One has to wrestle with one's own art, one's own soul, *alone!*

PAPPELMEISTER [*Patting him soothingly*]. I am glad I did not let you blay in Part Two.

DAVID. Dear Herr Pappelmeister! Don't think I don't appreciate all your kindnesses—you are almost a father to me.

PAPPELMEISTER. And you disobey me like a son. Ha! Ha! Ha! Vell, I vill make your excuses to de—vampires. Ha! Ha! *Also*, David. [*He lays his hand again affectionately on* DAVID'S *right shoulder.*] *Lebe wohl!* I must go down to my popular classics. [*Gloomily.*] Truly a going down! *Was?*

DAVID [*Smiling*]. Oh, it isn't such a descent as all that. Uncle said you ought to have given them comic opera.

PAPPELMEISTER [*Shuddering convulsively*]. Comic opera.... Ouf! [*He goes toward the elevator and rings the bell. Then he turns to* DAVID.] Vat vas dat vord, David?

DAVID. What word?

PAPPELMEISTER [*Groping for it*]. *Mega—megasshu ...*

DAVID [*Puzzled*]. *Megasshu?* [*The elevator comes up; the gates open.*]

PAPPELMEISTER. *Megusshah!* You know. [*He taps his forehead with his umbrella.*]

DAVID. Ah, *meshuggah!*

PAPPELMEISTER [*Joyously*]. *Ja, meshuggah!* [*He gives a great roar of laughter.*] Ha! Ha! Ha! [*He waves umbrella at* DAVID.] Well, don't be ... *meshuggah*. [*He steps into the elevator.*] Ha! Ha! Ha! [*The gates close, and it descends with his laughter.*]

DAVID [*After a pause*]. Perhaps I am ... *meshuggah*. [*He walks up and down moodily, approaches the parapet at back.*] Dropping down is indeed natural. [*He looks over.*] How it tugs and drags at one! [*He moves back resolutely and shakes his head.*] That would be even a greater descent than Pappelmeister's to comic opera. One must fly upward—somehow. [*He drops on the chair that* MENDEL *dried. A faint music steals up and makes an accompaniment to all the rest of the scene.*] Ah! the popular classics! [*His head sinks on a little table. The elevator comes up again, but he does not raise his head.* VERA, *pale and sad, steps out and walks gently*

over to him; stands looking at him with maternal pity; then decides not to disturb him and is stealing away when suddenly he looks up and perceives her and springs to his feet with a dazed glad cry.]
Vera!

VERA [*Turns, speaks with grave dignity*]. Miss Andrews has charged me to convey to you the heart-felt thanks and congratulations of the Settlement.

DAVID [*Frozen*]. Miss Andrews is very kind.... I trust you are well.

VERA. Thank you, Mr. Quixano. Very well and very busy. So you'll excuse me. [*She turns to go.*]

DAVID. Certainly.... How are your folks?

VERA [*Turns her head*]. They are gone back to Russia. And yours?

DAVID. You just saw them all.

VERA [*Confused*]. Yes—yes—of course—I forgot! Good-bye, Mr. Quixano.

DAVID. Good-bye, Miss Revendal. [*He drops back on the chair. VERA walks to the elevator, then just before ringing turns again.*]

VERA. I shouldn't advise you to sit here in the damp.

DAVID. My uncle dried the chair. [*Bitterly.*] Curious how every one is concerned about my body and no one about my soul.

VERA. Because your soul is so much stronger than your body. Why, think! It has just lifted a thousand people far higher than this roof-garden.

DAVID. Please don't you congratulate me, too! That would be too ironical.

VERA [*Agitated, coming nearer*]. Irony, Mr. Quixano? Please, please, do not imagine there is any irony in my congratulations.

DAVID. The irony is in all the congratulations. How can I endure them when I know what a terrible failure I have made!

VERA. Failure! Because the critics are all divided? That is the surest proof of success. You have produced something real and new.

DAVID. I am not thinking of Pappelmeister's connoisseurs—*I* am the only connoisseur, the only one who knows. And every bar of my music cried "Failure! Failure!" It shrieked from the violins, blared from the trombones, thundered from the drums. It was written on all the faces——

VERA [*Vehemently, coming still nearer*]. Oh, no! no! I watched the faces—those faces of toil and sorrow, those faces from many lands. They were fired by your vision of their coming brotherhood, lulled by your dream of their land of rest. And I could see that you were right in speaking to the people. In some strange, beautiful, way the inner meaning of your music stole into all those simple souls——

DAVID [*Springing up*]. And *my* soul? What of *my* soul? False to its own music, its own mission, its own dream. That is what I mean by failure, Vera. I preached of God's Crucible, this great new continent that could melt up all race-differences and vendettas, that could purge and re-create, and God tried me with his supremest test. He gave me a heritage from the Old World, hate and vengeance and blood, and said, "Cast it all into my Crucible." And I said, "Even thy Crucible cannot melt this hate, cannot drink up this blood." And so I sat crooning over the dead past, gloating over the old blood-stains—I, the apostle of America, the prophet of the God of our children. Oh—how my music mocked me! And you—so fearless, so high above fate—how you must despise me!

VERA. I? Ah no!

DAVID. You must. You do. Your words still sting. Were it seven seas between us, you said, our love must cross them. And I—I who had prated of seven seas——

VERA. Not seas of blood—I spoke selfishly, thoughtlessly. I had not realised that crimson flood. Now I see it day and night. O God! [*She shudders and covers her eyes.*]

DAVID. There lies my failure—to have brought it to your eyes, instead of blotting it from my own.

VERA. No man could have blotted it out.

DAVID. Yes—by faith in the Crucible. From the blood of battle-fields spring daisies and buttercups. In the divine chemistry the very garbage turns to roses. But in the supreme moment my faith was found wanting. You came to me—and I thrust you away.

VERA. I ought not to have come to you.... I ought not to have come to you to-day. We must not meet again.

DAVID. Ah, you cannot forgive me!

VERA. Forgive? It is I that should go down on my knees for my father's sin. [*She is half-sinking to her knees. He stops her by a gesture and a cry.*]

DAVID. No! The sins of the fathers shall not be visited on the children.[1]

VERA. My brain follows you, but not my heart. It is heavy with the sense of unpaid debts—debts that can only cry for forgiveness.

DAVID. You owe me nothing——

VERA. But my father, my people, my country.... [*She breaks down. Recovers herself.*] My only consolation is, you need nothing.

DAVID [*Dazed*]. I—need—nothing?

VERA. Nothing but your music ... your dreams.

DAVID. And your love? Do I not need that?

VERA [*Shaking her head sadly*]. No.

DAVID. You say that because I have forfeited it.

VERA. It is my only consolation, I tell you, that you do not need me. In our happiest moments a suspicion of this truth used to lacerate me. But now it is my one comfort in the doom that divides us. See how you stand up here above the world, alone and self-sufficient. No woman could ever have more than the second place in your life.

DAVID. But you have the *first* place, Vera!

VERA [*Shakes her head again*]. No—I no longer even desire it. I have gotten over that womanly weakness.

DAVID. You torture me. What do you mean?

VERA. What can be simpler? I used to be jealous of your music, your prophetic visions. I wanted to come first—before them all!

---

1 Numerous verses in Hebrew scripture refer to the sins of the fathers being visited on their children—or not. See, for example, Exodus 34:7 and Deuteronomy 24:16.

Now, dear David, I only pray that they may fill your life to the brim.

DAVID. But they cannot.

VERA. They will—have faith in yourself, in your mission—good-bye.

DAVID [*Dazed*]. You love me and you leave me?

VERA. What else can I do? Shall the shadow of Kishineff hang over all your years to come? Shall I kiss you and leave blood upon your lips, cling to you and be pushed away by all those cold, dead hands?

DAVID [*Taking both her hands*]. Yes, cling to me, despite them all, cling to me till all these ghosts are exorcised, cling to me till our love triumphs over death. Kiss me, kiss me now.

VERA [*Resisting, drawing back*]. I dare not! It will make you remember.

DAVID. It will make me forget. Kiss me. [*There is a pause of hesitation, filled up by the Cathedral music from "Faust"[1] surging up softly from below.*]

VERA [*Slowly*]. I will kiss you as we Russians kiss at Easter—the three kisses of peace. [*She kisses him three times on the mouth as in ritual solemnity.*]

DAVID [*Very calmly*]. Easter was the date of the massacre—see! I am at peace.

VERA. God grant it endure! [*They stand quietly hand in hand.*] Look! How beautiful the sunset is after the storm! [DAVID *turns. The sunset, which has begun to grow beautiful just after* VERA'S *entrance, has now reached its most magnificent moment; below there are narrow lines of saffron and pale gold, but above the whole sky is one glory of burning flame.*]

DAVID [*Prophetically exalted by the spectacle*]. It is the fires of God round His Crucible. [*He drops her hand and points downward.*] There she lies, the great Melting Pot—listen! Can't you hear the roaring and the bubbling? There gapes her mouth [*He points east.*]—the harbour where a thousand mammoth feeders

---

1 Opera by Charles Gounod, first performed in 1859. The Cathedral scene represents a moment of crisis for the imperiled lovers, Faust and Marguerite.

come from the ends of the world to pour in their human freight. Ah, what a stirring and a seething! Celt and Latin, Slav and Teuton, Greek and Syrian,—black and yellow——

VERA [*Softly, nestling to him*]. Jew and Gentile——

DAVID. Yes, East and West, and North and South, the palm and the pine, the pole and the equator, the crescent and the cross—how the great Alchemist melts and fuses them with his purging flame! Here shall they all unite to build the Republic of Man and the Kingdom of God. Ah, Vera, what is the glory of Rome and Jerusalem where all nations and races come to worship and look back, compared with the glory of America, where all races and nations come to labour and look forward! [*He raises his hands in benediction over the shining city.*] Peace, peace, to all ye unborn millions, fated to fill this giant continent—the God of our *children* give you Peace. [*An instant's solemn pause. The sunset is swiftly fading, and the vast panorama is suffused with a more restful twilight, to which the many-gleaming lights of the town add the tender poetry of the night. Far back, like a lonely, guiding star, twinkles over the darkening water the torch of the Statue of Liberty. From below comes up the softened sound of voices and instruments joining in "My Country, 'tis of Thee." The curtain falls slowly.*]

APPENDIX A[1]

THE MELTING POT IN ACTION

ALIENS ADMITTED TO THE UNITED STATES IN THE YEAR ENDED JUNE 30TH, 1913[2]

African (black)	9,734
Armenian	9,554
Bohemian and Moravian	11,852
Bulgarian, Servian, Montenegrin	10,083
Chinese	3,487
Croatian and Slavonian	44,754
Cuban	6,121
Dalmatian, Bosnian, Herzegovinian	4,775
Dutch and Flemish	18,746
East Indian	233
English	100,062
Finnish	14,920
French	26,509
German	101,764
Greek	40,933
Hebrew	105,826
Irish	48,103
Italian (north)	54,171
Italian (south)	264,348
Japanese	11,672
Korean	74
Lithuanian	25,529
Magyar	33,561
Mexican	15,495
Pacific Islander	27

1 Zangwill added the following Appendices to his first published edition of *The Melting-Pot*, and they have been reprinted with the play ever since. His goal was to reinforce the importance of all immigrants in building America while at the same time documenting the horrors that Jewish immigrants, in particular, needed to escape. The Appendices were presumably drawn from contemporary sources, some of which Zangwill identifies in square brackets after the titles. Where I am able to add source information, it appears in footnotes. References to Appendices in the footnotes, however, refer to Appendices A through G in this Broadview Edition.

2 See *Statistical Abstract of the United States, 1915* (Washington, DC: Government Printing Office, 1916), p. 89.

Polish	185,207
Portuguese	14,631
Roumanian	14,780
Russian	58,380
Ruthenian (Russniak)	39,405
Scandinavian	51,650
Scotch	31,434
Slovak	29,094
Spanish	15,017
Spanish-American	3,409
Syrian	10,019
Turkish	2,132
Welsh	3,922
West Indian (except Cuban)	2,302
Other peoples	3,512
Total	1,427,227

APPENDIX B

THE POGROM

(I) A RUSSIAN ON ITS REASONS

[From *The Nation*, November 15, 1913][1]

It is now over thirty years since the crew of the sinking ship of Russian absolutism first tried this unworthy weapon to save their failing cause. This was when Plehve[2] organised an anti-Semitic agitation and Jewish pogroms in 1883 in South Russia, where the Jews formed almost the only merchant class in the villages, and where the ignorant peasants, together with some crafty Russian tradesmen, had a natural grudge against them. The result was that the prevailing discontent of the masses was diverted against the Jews. A large public meeting of protest was organised at that

---

1 See *The Nation and Athenaeum*, vol. 14, p. 318. Square brackets in Zangwill's source identifications are his.
2 Vyacheslav von Plehve (1846–1904), appointed Minister of the Interior
and Chief of Police for the Russian Imperial government in 1902.
Although this article accuses Plehve of organizing pogroms, more recent
opinion finds him guilty, rather, of doing little or nothing to stop them.

time in the London Mansion House, the Lord Mayor taking the chair. English public opinion rightly appreciated the value of this criminal method of using Jews as scapegoats for political purposes. Now we see merely a further, and let us hope a final, development of the same tactics. They have been used on many occasions since 1883. One of the largest Jewish pogroms of the latest series in Kishineff in 1903 has been clearly traced to the same experienced hand of Plehve, when the passive attitude of the local administration and the military was explained by the presence in the town of a mysterious colonel of the Imperial Gendarmerie who arrived with secret orders and a large supply of pogrom literature from St. Petersburg, and who organised the scum of the town population for the purpose of looting and killing Jews.

The repulsive stories of further pogroms all over the country immediately after the issue of the constitutional manifesto of October 17, 1905,[1] are fresh in the memory of the civilised world. At that time anti-Semitic doctrine was openly preached, not only against Jews, but against the whole constitutional and revolutionary upheaval. Pogroms against both were organised under the same pretext of saving the Tsar, the orthodoxy, and the Fatherland. Local police and military officials had secret orders to abstain from interference with the looting and murdering of Jews or "their hirelings." Processions of peaceful citizens and children were trampled down by the Cossack horses, and the Cossacks[2] received formal thanks from high quarters for their excellent exploits....

N. W. TCHAYKOVSKY.[3]

---

1   The October Manifesto was issued by the tsar to end the Revolution of 1905. It promised to transform the government into a constitutional monarchy with a Duma (Parliament) and increased civil liberties, including freedom of speech. Once the Revolution subsided, many of the promises of the manifesto were undone. However, as the article seems to imply, greater freedom of expression may have led to more open antisemitism, especially since Jews were associated with the failed Revolution.

2   Cossacks were originally freedom-seeking adventurers who lived in the steppes of Russia and Ukraine. By the early twentieth century, they supported ultra-nationalist movements in both countries and were known to be antisemitic as well as militaristic.

3   Nicholas Wassilievich Tchaykovsky (1850–1926) lectured and wrote about the 1905 Russian revolution in the United States, raising funds for the anti-Tsarist movement.

(II) A NURSE ON ITS RESULTS

[From *Public Health*, Nurses' Quarterly, Cleveland, Ohio, October 1913][1]

I was a Red Cross nurse on the battlefield.

The words of the chief doctor of the Jewish Hospital of Odessa[2] still ring in my ears. When the telephone message came, he said, "Moldvanko is running in blood; send nurses and doctors." This meant that the Pogrom (massacre) was going on.

Dr. P—— came into the wards with these words: "Sisters, there is no time for weeping. Those who have no one dependent upon them, come. Put on your white surgical gowns, and the red cross. Make ready to go on the battlefield at once. God knows how many of our sisters and brothers are already killed." Tears were just running down his cheeks as he spoke. In a minute twelve nurses and eight doctors had volunteered. There was one Red Cross nurse who was in bed waiting to be operated on. She got up and made ready too. Nobody could keep her from going with us. "Where my sisters and brothers fall, there shall I fall," she said, and with these words, jumped into the ambulance and went on to the City Hospital with us. There they had better equipment, and they sent out three times as many nurses as the Jewish Hospital. At the City Hospital they hung silver crosses about our necks. We wore the silver crosses so that we would not be recognised as Jewish by the Holiganes (Hooligans).

Then we went to Molorosiskia Street in the Moldvanko (slums). We could not see, for the feathers were flying like snow.[3] The blood was already up to our ankles on the pavement and in the yards. The uproar was deafening but we could hear the Holiganes' fierce cries of "Hooray, kill the Jews," on all sides. It was enough to hear such words. They could turn your hair grey, but

---

1 Full citation: "'The Massacre (Pogram [sic]) in Odessa, Russia in 1905,' by A St. Louis Visiting Nurse," *The Public Health Nurse Quarterly* (1913): 85–90. Zangwill only slightly abbreviates the account, and he regularizes the spellings of some Russian words.

2 Odessa is a large port city in southern Ukraine, about 173 km (107.5 miles) from Kishinev. Its population in the nineteenth and early twentieth centuries was internationally diverse and included many Jews.

3 Among the most prized possessions of Jews in eastern Europe and Russia were featherbeds (mattress-toppers) and feather pillows, made by hand in each family. During acts of violence against the Jews, marauders would slash these treasured items such that feathers filled the air.

we went on. We had no time to think. All our thoughts were to pick up wounded ones, and to try to rescue some uninjured ones. We succeeded in rescuing some uninjured who were in hiding. We put bandages on them to make it appear that they were wounded. We put them in the ambulance and carried them to the hospital, too. So at the Jewish Hospital we had five thousand injured and seven thousand uninjured to feed and protect for two weeks. Some were left without homes, without clothes, and children were even without parents. [...][1]

My dear reader, I want to tell you one thing before I describe the scenes of the massacre any further; do not think that you are reading a story which could not happen! No, I want you to know that everything you read is just exactly as it was. My hair is a little grey, but I am surprised it is not quite white after what I witnessed.

The procession of the Pogrom was led by about ten Catholic (Greek) Sisters[2] with about forty or fifty of their school children. They carried ikons or pictures of Jesus and sang "God Save the Tsar." They were followed by a crowd containing hundreds of men and women murderers yelling "Bey Zhida," which means "Kill the Jews." With these words they ran into the yards where there were fifty or a hundred tenants. They rushed in like tigers. Soon they began to throw children out of the windows of the second, third, and fourth stories. They would take a poor, innocent six-months-old baby, who could not possibly have done any harm in this world and throw it down on to the pavement. You can imagine it could not live after it struck the ground, but this did not satisfy the stony-hearted murderers. They then rushed up to the child, seized it and broke its little arm and leg bones into three or four pieces, then wrung its neck too. They laughed and yelled, so carried away with pleasure at their successful work.

I do wish a few Americans could have been there to see, and they would know what America is, and what it means to live in the United States. It was not enough for them to open up a woman's abdomen and take out the child which she carried, but they took time to stuff the abdomen with straw and fill it up. Can you imagine human beings able to do such things? I do not think anybody could, because I could not imagine it myself when a few years before I read the news of the massacre in Kishineff, but now I have seen it with my own eyes. It was not enough for them to

---

1 Here Zangwill omits a paragraph without indicating ellipsis.
2 Nuns of the Russian Orthodox (Greek Orthodox) Church.

cut out an old man's tongue and cut off his nose, but they drove nails into the eyes also. You wonder how they had enough time to carry away everything of value—money, gold, silver, jewels—and still be able to do so much fancy killing, but oh, my friends, all the time for three days and three nights was theirs.

The last day and night it poured down rain, and you would think that might stop them, but no, they worked just as hard as ever. We could wear shoes no longer. Our feet were swollen, so we wore rubbers over our stockings, and in this way worked until some power was able to stop these horrors. They not only killed, but they had time to abuse young girls of twelve and fourteen years of age, who died immediately after being operated upon.

I remember what happened to my own class-mates. They were two who came from a small town to Odessa to become midwives. These girls ran to the school to hide themselves as it was a government school, and they knew the Holiganes would not dare to come in there. But the dean of the school had ordered they should not be admitted, because they were Jewish, as if they had different blood running in their veins. So when they came, the watchman refused to open the doors, according to his instructions. The crowd of Holiganes found them outside the doors of the hospital. They abused them right there in the middle of the street. One was eighteen years old and the other was twenty. One died after the operation and the other went insane from shame.

Some people ask why the Jews did not leave everything and go away. But how could they go and where could they go? The murderers were scattered throughout the Jewish quarters. All they could do was hide where they were in the cellars and garrets. The Holiganes searched them out and killed them where they were hidden. Others may ask, why did they not resist the murderers with their knives and pistols? The grown men organised by the second day. They were helped by the Vigilantes, too, who brought them arms. The Vigilantes were composed of students at the University and high-school boys, and also the strongest man from each Jewish family. There were a good many Gentiles among the students who belonged to the Vigilantes because they wanted justice. So on the second day the Vigilantes stood before the doors and gave resistance to the murderers. Some will ask where were the soldiers and the police? They were sent to protect, but on arriving, joined in with the murderers. However, the police put disguises on over their uniforms. Later, when they were brought to the hospital with other wounded, we found their uniforms underneath their disguises.

When the Vigilantes took their stations, the scene was like a battlefield. Bullets were flying from both sides of the Red Cross carriages. We expected to be killed any minute, but notwithstanding, we rushed wherever there were shots heard in order to carry away the wounded. Whenever we arrived we shouted "Red Cross, Red Cross," in order to help make them realise we were not Vigilantes. Then they would stop and let us pick up the wounded. They did this on account of their own wounded.

The Vigilantes could not stop the butchery entirely because they were not strong enough in numbers. On the fourth day, the Jewish people of Odessa, through Dr. P——, succeeded in communicating to the Mayor of a different State. Soldiers from outside, strangers to the murderers, came in and took charge of the city. The city was put under martial law until order could be restored.

On the fifth day the doctors and nurses were called to the cemetery, where there were four hundred unidentified dead. Their friends and relatives who came to search for them were crazed and hysterical and needed our attention. Wives came to look for husbands, parents hunting children, a mother for her only son, and so on. It took eight days to identify the bodies and by that time four hundred of the wounded had died, and so we had eight hundred to bury. If you visit Odessa, you will be shown two long graves, about one hundred feet long, beside the Jewish Cemetery. There lie the victims of the massacre. Among them are Gentile Vigilantes whose parents asked that they be buried with the Jews....[1]

Another case I knew was that of a married man. He left his wife, who was pregnant, and three children, to go on a business trip. When he got back the massacre had occurred. His home was in ruins, his family gone. He went to the hospital, then to the cemetery. There he found his wife with her abdomen stuffed with straw, and his three children dead. It simply broke his heart, and he lost his mind. But he was harmless, and was to be seen wandering about the hospital as though in search of some one, and daily he grew more thin and suffering.

This story is told in the hope that Americans will appreciate the safety and freedom in which they live and that they will help others to gain that freedom.

---

1 Zangwill indicates omission of a paragraph here, an example of a mother who goes insane after the murder of her son.

APPENDIX C

THE STORY OF DANIEL MELSA[1]

Another example of Nature aping Art is afforded by the romantic story of Daniel Melsa, a young Russo-Jewish violinist who has carried audiences by storm in Berlin, Paris and London, and who had arranged to go to America last November. The following extract from an interview in the *Jewish Chronicle*[2] of January 24, 1913, shows the curious coincidence between his beginnings and David Quixano's:

"Melsa is not yet twenty years of age, but he looks somewhat older. He is of slight build and has a sad expression, which increased to almost a painful degree when recounting some of his past experiences. He seems singularly devoid of any affectation, while modesty is obviously the keynote of his nature.

"After some persuasion, Melsa put aside his reticence, and, complying with the request, outlined briefly his career, the early part of which, he said, was overshadowed by a great tragedy. He was born in Warsaw, and, at the age of three, his parents moved to Lodz,[3] where shortly after a private tutor was engaged for him.

"'Although I exhibited a passion for music quite early, I did not receive any lessons on the subject till my seventh birthday, but before that my father obtained a cheap violin for me upon which I was soon able to play simple melodies by ear.'

"By chance a well-known professor of the town heard him play, and so impressed was he with the talent exhibited by the boy

---

1 Daniel Melsa (1892–1952) performed throughout the world and was the author of *The Art of Violin Playing* (1927). According to Paul French, Melsa taught violin at the Broadhurst Academy in Shanghai in the late 1920s, returning to London by 1934, when he performed concerts for the BBC and in other venues. His first wife was the actress Joan Carr ("Daniel Melsa, Prodigy Violinist and his Shanghai Sojourn," *China Rhyming: A Gallimaufry of Random China History and Research Interests*, http://www.chinarhyming.com/2015/12/20/daniel-melsa-prodigy-violinist-and-his-shanghai-sojourn/).

2 The leading English-language Jewish newspaper in Britain, founded in 1841.

3 Warsaw is the capital of Poland, and Lodz is a large city about 75 miles southwest of the capital. Before the Holocaust (1939–45), Warsaw had the largest Jewish community in Poland and the second largest in the world (after New York City); Lodz had the second largest Jewish community in Poland.

that he advised the father to have him educated. Acting upon this advice, as far as limited means allowed, tutors were engaged, and so much progress did he make that at the age of nine he was admitted to the local Conservatorium of Professor Grudzinski, where he remained two years. It was at the age of eleven that a great calamity overtook the family, his father and sister falling victims to the pogroms.

"Melsa's story runs as follows:

"'It was in June of 1905, at the time of the pogroms, when one afternoon my father, accompanied by my little sister, ventured out into the street, from which they never returned. They were both killed,' he added sadly, 'by Cossacks. A week later I found my sister in a Christian churchyard riddled with bullets, but I have not been able to trace the remains of my father, who must have been buried in some out-of-the-way place. During this awful period my mother and myself lived in imminent danger of our lives, and it was only the recollection of my playing that saved us also falling a prey to the vodka-besodden Cossacks.'"

APPENDIX D

BEILIS AND AMERICA[1]

The close relation in Jewish thought between Russo-Jewish persecution and America as the land of escape from it is well illustrated by the recent remarks of the *Jewish Chronicle* on the future of the victim of the Blood-Ritual Prosecution in Kieff. "So long as Beilis continues to live in Russia, his life is unsafe. The Black Hundreds, he himself says, have solemnly decided on his death, and we have seen, in the not distant past, that they can carry out diabolical plots of this description with complete immunity.... He would gladly go to America, provided he was sure of a living. The

---

1 Menahem Mendel Beilis (1874–1934), generally known as Mendel Beilis, was falsely accused of murdering a Christian boy in March 1911. It was a case of blood libel, the centuries-old false accusation that Jews kidnapped and murdered Christian children to use their blood in rituals. Beilis was imprisoned until he was placed on trial in 1913, when he was acquitted. He emigrated to then-Palestine and finally to the United States. His prosecution was followed worldwide and became famous as an example of Russian antisemitism. This article must have appeared before Beilis had left Russia. See also Introduction, pp. 24–25.

condition should not be difficult to fulfil, and if this victim of a barbarous *régime*—we cannot say latest victim, for, as we write, comes the news of an expulsion order against 1200 Jewish students of Kieff—should find a home and place under the sheltering wing of freedom, it would be a fitting ending to a painful chapter in our Jewish history."

That it is the natural ending even the Jew-baiting Russian organ, the *Novoe Vremya*,[1] indirectly testifies, for it has published a sneering cartoon representing a number of Jews crowded on the Statue of Liberty to welcome the arrival of Beilis. One wonders that the Russian censor should have permitted the masses to become aware that Liberty exists on earth, if only in the form of a statue.

APPENDIX E

THE ALIEN IN THE MELTING POT[2]

Mr. Frederick J. Haskin has recently published in the *Chicago Daily News* the following graphic summary of what immigrants have done and do for the United States:

I am the immigrant.

Since the dawn of creation my restless feet have beaten new paths across the earth.

My uneasy bark has tossed on all seas.

My wanderlust was born of the craving for more liberty and a better wage for the sweat of my face.

I looked towards the United States with eyes kindled by the fire of ambition and heart quickened with new-born hope.

I approached its gates with great expectation.

I entered in with fine hopes.

I have shouldered my burden as the American man of all work.

I contribute eighty-five per cent. of all the labour in the slaughtering and meat-packing industries.

---

1 Russian: *New Times*. Published 1868–1917.

2 Frederic J. Haskin collected many of his essays on immigration in *The Immigrant: An Asset and a Liability* (1913). Despite the title, the book reflects the very positive view of immigration presented here, as well as the statistics; the one liability Haskin points out is the failure of some immigrants to assimilate into American society, as he also suggests here.

I do seven-tenths of the bituminous coal mining.

I do seventy-eight per cent. of all the work in the woollen mills.

I contribute nine-tenths of all the labour in the cotton mills.

I make nine-twentieths of all the clothing.

I manufacture more than half the shoes.

I build four-fifths of all the furniture.

I make half of the collars, cuffs, and shirts.

I turn out four-fifths of all the leather.

I make half the gloves.

I refine nearly nineteen-twentieths of the sugar.

I make half of the tobacco and cigars.

And yet, I am the great American problem.

When I pour out my blood on your altar of labour, and lay down my life as a sacrifice to your god of toil, men make no more comment than at the fall of a sparrow.[1]

But my brawn is woven into the warp and woof of the fabric of your national being.

My children shall be your children and your land shall be my land because my sweat and my blood will cement the foundations of the America of To-Morrow.

If I can be fused into the body politic, the Melting-Pot will have stood the supreme test.

Afterword[2]

I

The Melting Pot is the third of the writer's plays to be published in book form, though the first of the three in order of composition. But unlike *The War God* and *The Next Religion*, which are dramatisations of the spiritual duels of our time, *The Melting Pot* sprang directly from the author's concrete experience as President of the Emigration Regulation Department of the Jewish Territorial Organisation, which, founded shortly after the great massacres of Jews in Russia, will soon have fostered the settle-

---

1 See Matthew 10:29; Shakespeare, *Hamlet* (c. 1601) 5.2.233.

2 As becomes clear, Zangwill wrote this Afterword for the 1914 publication of the play to respond to negative dramatic criticisms as well as to complaints about the drama's themes of intermarriage and "racial fusion." For examples of reviews and other critiques, see Appendices A and B in this edition.

ment of ten thousand Russian Jews in the West of the United States.[1]

"Romantic claptrap," wrote Mr. A. B. Walkley in the *Times* of "this rhapsodising over music and crucibles and statues of Liberty."[2] As if these things were not the homeliest of realities, and rhapsodising the natural response to them of the Russo-Jewish psychology, incurably optimist. The statue of Liberty is a large visible object at the mouth of New York harbour; the crucible, if visible only to the eye of imagination like the inner reality of the sunrise to the eye of Blake, is none the less a roaring and flaming actuality. These things are as substantial, if not as important, as Adeline Genée and Anna Pavlova,[3] the objects of Mr. Walkley's own rhapsodising. Mr. Walkley, never having lacked Liberty, nor cowered for days in a cellar in terror of a howling mob, can see only theatrical exaggeration in the enthusiasm for a land of freedom, just as, never having known or never having had eyes to see the grotesque and tragic creatures existing all around us, he has doubted the reality of some of Balzac's[4] creations. It is to be feared that for such a play as *The Melting Pot* Mr. Walkley is far from being the χαρίεις[5] of Aristotle. The ideal spectator must have known and felt more of life than Mr. Walkley, who resembles too much the library-fed man of letters whose denunciation by Walter Bagehot[6] he himself quotes

---

1   Zangwill's play *The War God* was first produced in 1911, *The Next Religion* in 1912. Zangwill founded the Jewish Territorial Organization (known as the ITO) in 1905 to find a homeland anywhere in the world for Jews "who cannot or will not remain in the lands in which they at present live." The project he refers to here is Jacob Schiff's Galveston Plan to resettle Russian Jews through the port of Galveston, Texas, a program in which the ITO had a significant role.

2   See Walkley's (A12) and others' reviews in Appendix A of this edition.

3   Adeline Genée (1878–1970), Danish-born ballet dancer who performed in British theater; in 1936 she founded what became the Royal Academy of Dancing, and in 1950 was made a Dame of the British Empire. Anna Pavlova (1881–1931), world-famous Russian prima ballerina who performed with the Imperial Russian Ballet and Sergei Diaghilev's Ballets Russes. In 1911 she formed her own company.

4   Honoré de Balzac (1799–1850), French novelist and innovator of the novel form known for his realistic portrayals of contemporary life.

5   Greek: *Kharieis*, a refined or cultivated gentleman, or in this case an ideal. The term appears in Book IV of Aristotle's *Nichomachean Ethics* (350 BCE).

6   Walter Bagehot (1826–77), leading British economist, journalist, and editor who wrote on literary as well as political and economic subjects.

without suspecting *de te fabula narratur*.[1] Even the critic, who has to deal with a refracted world, cannot dispense with primary experience of his own. For "the adventures of a soul among masterpieces"[2] it is not only necessary there should be masterpieces, there must also be a soul. Mr. Walkley, one of the wittiest of contemporary writers and within his urban range one of the wisest, can scarcely be accused of lacking a soul, though Mr. Bernard Shaw's[3] long-enduring misconception of him as a brother in the spirit is one of the comedies of literature. But such spiritual vitality as Oxford failed to sterilise in him has been largely torpified by his profession of play-taster, with its divorcement from reality in the raw. His cry of "romantic claptrap" is merely the reaction of the club armchair to the "drums and tramplings" of the street. It is in fact (he will welcome an allusion to Dickens almost as much as one to Aristotle) the higher Podsnappery.[4] "Thus happily acquainted with his own merit and importance, Mr. Podsnap settled that whatever he put behind him he put out of existence.... The world got up at eight, shaved close at a quarter past, breakfasted at nine, went to the City at ten, came home at half-past five, and dined at seven."

Mr. Roosevelt,[5] with his multifarious American experience as soldier and cowboy, hunter and historian, police-captain and President, comes far nearer the ideal spectator, for this play at least, than Mr. Walkley. Yet his enthusiasm for it has been dismissed by our critic as "stupendous *naïveté*." Mr. Roosevelt apparently falls under that class of "people who knowing no rules, are at the mercy of their undisciplined taste," which Mr. Walkley excludes altogether from his classification of critics, in despite of Dr. Johnson's[6] opinion that "natural

---

1 Latin: The story applies to you. From the first of Horace's *Satires* (35–34 BCE), the quotation implies that an unflattering description could in fact apply to the reader, listener, or speaker.
2 Definition of a critic attributed to French writer Anatole France (1844–1924).
3 (George) Bernard Shaw (1856–1950), major British playwright. Shaw parodied Walkley in the character of Mr. Trotter, a pompous theatre critic, in *Fanny's First Play* (1911).
4 Mr. Podsnap is a character in *Our Mutual Friend* (1865) by Charles Dickens (1812–70). His narrow-minded complacency came to be known as Podsnappery.
5 President Theodore Roosevelt (1858–1919), who attended the opening night performance of the play and praised it heartily.
6 Samuel Johnson (1709–84), English critic, poet, biographer, and lexicographer.

judges" are only second to "those who know but are above the rules." It is comforting, therefore, to find Mr. Augustus Thomas,[1] the famous American playwright, who is familiar with the rules to the point of contempt, chivalrously associating himself, in defence of a British rival, with Mr. Roosevelt's "stupendous *naïveté*."

"Mr. Zangwill's 'rhapsodising' over music and crucibles and statues of Liberty is," says Mr. Thomas, "a very effective use of a most potent symbolism, and I have never seen men and women more sincerely stirred than the audience at *The Melting Pot*. The impulses awakened by the Zangwill play were those of wide human sympathy, charity, and compassion; and, for my own part, I would rather retire from the theatre and retire from all direct or indirect association with journalism than write down the employment of these factors by Mr. Zangwill as mere claptrap."

"As a work of art for art's sake," also wrote Mr. William Archer,[2] "the play simply does not exist." He added: "but Mr. Zangwill would not dream of appealing to such a standard." Mr. Archer had the misfortune to see the play in New York side by side with his more cynical *confrère*, and thus his very praise has an air of apologia to Mr. Walkley and the great doctrine of "art for art's sake." It would almost seem as if he even takes a "work of art" and a "work of art for art's sake" as synonymous. Nothing, in fact, could be more inartistic. "Art for art's sake" is one species of art, whose right to existence the author has amply recognised in other works. (*The King of Schnorrers* was even read aloud by Oscar Wilde to a duchess.)[3] But he roundly denies that art is any the less artistic for being inspired by life, and seeking in its turn to inspire life. Such a contention is tainted by the very

---

1 Thomas (1857–1934) wrote a play with a Christian-Jewish marriage theme, *As a Man Thinks*, in 1911.

2 "Art for art's sake" was the motto of the Aesthetic movement of the late nineteenth century, which asserted that the purpose of art was to be beautiful, not to convey moral meaning. Zangwill did not adhere to the tenets of that movement, although he had respect for some of its practitioners. William Archer (1856–1924), British theatre critic and theorist; Archer championed the avant-garde realist drama of Norwegian playwright Henrik Ibsen (1828–1906).

3 *The King of Schnorrers* (1893–94), Zangwill's comic novel (a collection of connected comic vignettes), later turned into a play. The work of Oscar Wilde (1854–1900)—playwright, essayist, fiction writer—epitomizes the theory and practice of art for art's sake.

Philistinism[1] it would repudiate, since it seeks a negative test of art in something outside art—to wit, purpose, whose presence is surely as irrelevant to art as its absence. The only test of art is artistic quality, and this quality *occurs* perhaps more frequently than it is achieved, as in the words of the Hebrew prophets, or the vision of a slum at night, the former consciously aiming at something quite different, the latter achieving its beauty in utter unconsciousness.

II

It will be seen from the official table of immigration that the Russian Jew is only one and not even the largest of the fifty elements that, to the tune of nearly a million and a half a year, are being fused in the greatest "Melting Pot" the world has ever known; but if he has been selected as the typical immigrant, it is because he alone of all the fifty has no homeland.[2] Some few other races, such as the Armenians, are almost equally devoid of political power, and, in consequence, equally obnoxious to massacre;[3] but except the gipsy,[4] whose essence is to be homeless, there is no other race—black, white, red, or yellow—that has not remained at least a majority of the population in some area of its own. There is none, therefore, more in need of a land of liberty, none to whose future it is more vital that America should preserve that spirit of William Penn which President Wilson[5] has so

---

1 Conventionality, materialism, antagonism to the arts and intellectual life. Matthew Arnold (1822–88) created this use of the term in his critique of the Victorian middle classes in *Culture and Anarchy* (1869). It derives from the biblical Philistines, warriors and enemies of the Israelites, as described in the books of Judges and Kings.

2 The modern State of Israel was not established until 1948. In 1914, when Zangwill wrote this Afterword, his Jewish Territorial Organization was seeking to establish a land for the Jews wherever one might be found. At the same time, he worked to keep doors of immigration open to Jews who were being persecuted. See Introduction, pp. 15–16.

3 Indeed, in 1915 Turkey carried out what may be considered genocidal massacres against Armenians.

4 More commonly spelled *gypsy* (now a derogatory term), a reference to the Roma people of Europe and elsewhere, a nomadic group believed originally to have migrated from India.

5 William Penn (1644–1718), British Quaker leader and supporter of religious freedom who founded the American colony of Pennsylvania. Woodrow Wilson was president of the United States from *(continued)*

nobly characterised. And there is assuredly none which has more valuable elements to contribute to the ethnic and psychical amalgam of the people of to-morrow.

The process of American amalgamation is not assimilation or simple surrender to the dominant type, as is popularly supposed, but an all-round give-and-take by which the final type may be enriched or impoverished. Thus the intelligent reader will have remarked how the somewhat anti-Semitic Irish servant of the first act talks Yiddish herself in the fourth. Even as to the ultimate language of the United States, it is unreasonable to suppose that American, though fortunately protected by English literature, will not bear traces of the fifty languages now being spoken side by side with it, and of which this play alone presents scraps in German, French, Russian, Yiddish, Irish, Hebrew, and Italian.

That in the crucible of love, or even co-citizenship, the most violent antitheses of the past may be fused into a higher unity is a truth of both ethics and observation, and it was in order to present historic enmities at their extremes that the persecuted Jew of Russia and the persecuting Russian race have been taken for protagonists—"the fell incensèd points of mighty opposites."[1]

The Jewish immigrant is, moreover, the toughest of all the white elements that have been poured into the American crucible, the race having, by its unique experience of several thousand years of exposure to alien majorities, developed a salamandrine[2] power of survival. And this asbestoid fibre is made even more fireproof by the anti-Semitism of American uncivilisation. Nevertheless, to suppose that America will remain permanently afflicted by all the old European diseases would be to despair of humanity, not to mention super-humanity.

III

Even the negrophobia is not likely to remain eternally at its present barbarous pitch. Mr. William Archer, who has won a new fame as student of that black problem, which is America's

---

1913 to 1921, and so was president at the time of this publication. In a 1913 address at Swarthmore College, Wilson referred to Penn "as a sort of spiritual knight who went out upon his adventures to carry the torch that had been put in his hands, so that other men might have the path illuminated for them which led to justice and to liberty."

1 *Hamlet* 5.2.61–62. Fell: fierce, savage, dreadful.

2 Like a salamander, able to change appearance to fit into its surroundings.

nemesis for her ancient slave-raiding, and who favours the creation of a Black State as one of the United States,[1] observes: "It
is noteworthy that neither David Quixano nor anyone else in the
play makes the slightest reference to that inconvenient element in
the crucible of God—the negro." This is an oversight of Mr.
Archer's, for Baron Revendal defends the Jew-baiting of Russia
by asking of an American: "Don't you lynch and roast your
niggers?" And David Quixano expressly throws both "black and
yellow" into the crucible. No doubt there is an instinctive antipathy which tends to keep the white man free from black blood,
though this antipathy having been overcome by a large minority
in all the many periods and all the many countries of their conti-
guity, it is equally certain that there are at work forces of attraction as well as of repulsion, and that even upon the negro the
"Melting Pot" of America will not fail to act in a measure as it has
acted on the Red Indian, who has found it almost as facile to
mate with his white neighbours as with his black. Indeed, it is as
much social prejudice as racial antipathy that to-day divides black
and white in the New World; and Sir Sydney Olivier has recorded
that in Jamaica the white is far more on his guard and his dignity
against the half-white than against the all-black, while in Guiana,
according to Sir Harry Johnston in his great work "The Negro in
the New World," it is the half-white that, in his turn, despises the
black and succeeds in marrying still further whitewards.[2] It might
have been thought that the dark-white races on the northern
shore of the Mediterranean—the Spaniards, Sicilians, &c.—who
have already been crossed with the sons of Ham[3] from its southern shore, would, among the American immigrants, be the
natural links towards the fusion of white and black, but a similar
instinct of pride and peril seems to hold them back. But whether

---

1   Archer proposes this "solution" in *Through Afro-America: An English
    Reading of the Race Problem* (London: Chapman & Hall, 1910), 237–44.
2   Olivier (1859–1943), British governor of Jamaica for several terms
    between 1900 and 1913; Johnston (1858–1927), British scientist and
    colonial administrator who played a significant role in the late nine-
    teenth-century colonization of Africa. The language and discourse Zang-
    will uses in this part of the Afterword—discussing "antipathies," degrees
    of blackness, and various stereotypes—cannot help but be viewed as
    racist in the twenty-first century. It provides an example, however, of the
    conflicted ideas and attitudes of early-twentieth-century British and
    American liberals.
3   See Genesis 9:18. Ham, Noah's fourth son, is the ancestor of Canaan,
    and the phrase in English refers to African peoples.

the antipathy in America be a race instinct or a social prejudice, the accusations against the black are largely panic-born myths, for the alleged repulsive smell of the negro is consistent with being shaved by him, and the immorality of the negress is consistent with her control of the nurseries of the South. The devil is not so black nor the black so devilish as he is painted. This is not to deny that the prognathous[1] face is an ugly and undesirable type of countenance or that it connotes a lower average of intellect and ethics, or that white and black are as yet too far apart for profitable fusion. Melanophobia, or fear of the black, may be pragmatically as valuable a racial defence for the white as the counter-instinct of philoleucosis, or love of the white, is a force of racial uplifting for the black. But neither colour has succeeded in monopolising all the virtues and graces in its specific evolution from the common ancestral ape, and a superficial acquaintance with the work of Dr. Arthur Keith[2] teaches that if the black man is nearer the ape in some ways (having even the remains of throat-pouches), the white man is nearer in other ways (as in his greater hairiness).

And besides being, as Sir Sydney Olivier says, "a matrix of emotional and spiritual energies that have yet to find their human expression," the African negro has obviously already not a few valuable ethnic elements—joy of life, love of colour, keen senses, beautiful voice, and ear for music—contributions that might somewhat compensate for the dragging-down of the white and, in small doses at least, might one day prove a tonic to an anæmic and art-less America. A musician like Coleridge-Taylor is no despicable product of the "Melting Pot," while the negroes of genius whom the writer has been privileged to know—men like Henry O. Tanner, the painter, and Paul Laurence Dunbar, the poet[3]— show the potentialities of the race even without white admixture; and as men of this stamp are capable of attracting cultured white wives, the fusing process, beginning at the top with types like these, should be far less unwelcome than that which starts with

---

1 Having a projecting jaw.
2 Keith (1866–1955), proponent of "scientific racism" and segregation. The supposedly scientific views in this passage are racist products of their time.
3 Samuel Coleridge-Taylor (1875–1912), British composer and conductor of European and African descent. He made three concert tours of the United States between 1904 and 1910. Among his works were settings for poems by African-American poet Paul Laurence Dunbar (1872–1906). Henry Ossawa Tanner (1859–1937) is considered the first African-American painter to gain international acclaim.

the dregs of both races. But the negroid hair and complexion being, in Mendelian[1] language, "dominant," these black traits are not easy to eliminate from the hybrid posterity; and in view of all the unpleasantness, both immediate and contingent, that attends the blending of colours, only heroic souls on either side should dare the adventure of intermarriage. Blacks of this temper, however, would serve their race better by making Liberia[2] a success or building up an American negro State, as Mr. William Archer recommends, or at least asserting their rights as American citizens in that sub-tropical South which without their labour could never have been opened up. Meantime, however scrupulously and justifiably America avoids physical intermarriage with the negro, the comic spirit cannot fail to note the spiritual miscegenation[3] which, while clothing, commercialising, and Christianising the ex-African, has given "rag-time" and the sex-dances that go to it, first to white America and thence to the whole white world.

The action of the crucible is thus not exclusively physical—a consideration particularly important as regards the Jew. The Jew may be Americanised and the American Judaised without any gamic interaction.[4]

IV

Among the Jews *The Melting Pot*, though it has in some instances served to interpret to each other the old generation and the new, has more frequently been misunderstood by both. While a distinguished Christian clergyman wrote that it was "calculated to do for the Jewish race what 'Uncle Tom's Cabin'[5] did for the coloured man," the Jewish pulpits of America have resounded with denunciation of its supposed solution of the Jewish problem by dissolution. As if even a play with a purpose could do more than suggest and interpret! It is true that its leading figure, David Quixano, advocates absorption in America, but even he is speak-

---

1 Referring to Gregor Mendel (1822–84), founder of modern genetics.
2 The oldest republic in Africa, founded in 1847 by freed slaves from the United States and the Caribbean.
3 The physical mixing of groups through marriage or sexual relations.
4 Interaction of gametes—germ cells such as sperm and egg. Here Zangwill seeks to reassure those who see the play as promoting intermarriage between Jews and Gentiles.
5 Anti-slavery novel by Harriet Beecher Stowe (1811–96), published in 1852.

ing solely of the American Jews and asks his uncle why, if he objects to the dissolving process, he did not work for a separate Jewish land. He is not offering a panacea for the Jewish problem, universally applicable.[1] But he urges that the conditions offered to the Jew in America are without parallel throughout the world.

And, in sooth, the Jew is here citizen of a republic without a State religion—a republic resting, moreover, on the same simple principles of justice and equal rights as the Mosaic Commonwealth from which the Puritan Fathers drew their inspiration. In America, therefore, the Jew, by a roundabout journey from Zion, has come into his own again.[2] It is by no mere accident that when an inscription was needed for the colossal statue of Liberty in New York Harbour, that "Mother of Exiles" whose torch lights the entrance to the New Jerusalem, the best expression of the spirit of Americanism was found in the sonnet of the Jewess, Emma Lazarus:

> *Give me your tired, your poor,*
> *Your huddled masses yearning to breathe free,*
> *The wretched refuse of your teeming shore.*
> *Send these, the homeless, tempest-tost to me,*
> *I lift my lamp beside the golden door.*[3]

And if, alas! passing through the golden door, the Jew finds his New Jerusalem as much a caricature by the crumbling of its early ideals as the old became by the fading of the visions of Isaiah and Amos,[4] he may find his mission in fighting for the preservation of the original Hebraic pattern. In this fight he will not be alone, and intermarriage with his fellow-crusaders in the new Land of

---

1   For a more complete statement of Zangwill's views on "the melting pot" of assimilation versus Jewish life in a Jewish state, see Appendix B, specifically the debate with Daniel Guggenheim in the *New York Sunday Herald Magazine* (B1).

2   The Puritans in the Massachusetts Bay Colony saw the Bible—including the Five Books of Moses, the Pentateuch—as the basis for government. Thus *Zion*, which commonly refers to Jerusalem or the biblical promised land, might also be seen as the "Mosaic Commonwealth" that inspired founders of the United States.

3   These are the final lines of "The New Colossus," reprinted in full in Appendix D1. The poem was written by Jewish American poet Emma Lazarus (1849–87) in 1883, as part of the effort to raise funds for the pedestal of the Statue of Liberty.

4   Hebrew prophets.

Promise will naturally follow wherever, as with David Quixano and Vera Revendal, no theological differences divide. There will be neither Jew nor Greek.[1] Intermarriage, wherever there is social intimacy, will follow, even when the parties stand in opposite religious camps; but this is less advisable as leading to a house divided against itself and to dissension in the upbringing of the children. It is only when a common outlook has been reached, transcending the old doctrinal differences, that intermarriage is denuded of those latent discords which the instinct of mankind divines, and which keep even Catholic and Protestant wisely apart.

These discords, together with the prevalent anti-Semitism and his own ingrained persistence, tend to preserve the Jew even in the "Melting Pot," so that his dissolution must be necessarily slower than that of the similar aggregations of Germans, Italians, or Poles. But the process for all is the same, however tempered by specific factors. Beginning as broken-off bits of Germany, Italy, or Poland, with newspapers and theatres in German, Italian, or Polish, these colonies gradually become Americanised, their vernaculars, even when jealously cherished, become a mere medium for American conceptions of life; while in the third generation the child is ashamed both of its parents and their lingo, the newspapers dwindle in circulation, the theatres languish. The reality of this process has been denied by no less distinguished an American than Dr. Charles Eliot, ex-President of Harvard University, whose prophecy of Jewish solidarity in America and of the contribution of Judaism to the world's future is more optimistic than my own. Dr. Eliot[2] points to the still unmelted heaps of racial matter, without suspecting—although he is a chemist—that their semblance of solidity is only kept up by the constant immigration of similar atoms to the base to replace those liquefied at the apex. Once America slams her doors, the crucible will roar like a closed furnace.[3]

Heaven forbid, however, that the doors shall be slammed for centuries yet. The notion that the few millions of people in America have a moral right to exclude others is monstrous.

1 Galatians 3:28. This passage has a specifically Christian meaning in its original context.
2 Charles William Eliot (1834–96) served forty years as Harvard's president (1869–1909), during which time he turned it into a major research university.
3 That is, in Zangwill's view, once new immigration ends, assimilation will take over completely.

Exclusiveness may have some justification in countries, especially when old and well-populated; but for continents like the United States—or for the matter of that Canada and Australia—to mistake themselves for mere countries is an intolerable injustice to the rest of the human race.

The exclusion of criminals even is as impossible in practice as the exclusion of the sick and ailing is unchristian. Infinitely more important were it to keep the gates of *birth* free from undesirables. As for the exclusion of the able-bodied, whether illiterate or literate, that is sheer economic madness in so empty a continent, especially with the Panama Canal to divert them to the least developed States. Fortunately, any serious restriction will avenge itself not only by the stagnation of many of the States, but by the paralysis of the great liners which depend on steerage passengers, without whom freights and fares will rise and saloon passengers be docked of their sailing facilities. Meantime the inquisition at Ellis Island has to its account cruelties no less atrocious than the ancient Spanish—cruelties that only flash into momentary prominence when some luxurious music-hall lady of dubious morals has a taste of the barbarities meted out daily to blameless and hard-working refugees from oppression or hunger, who, having staked their all on the great adventure, find themselves hustled back, penniless and heartbroken, to the Old World.[1]

V

Whether any country will ever again be based like those of the Old World upon a unity of race or religion is a matter of doubt. New England, of course, like Pennsylvania and Maryland, owes its inception to religion, but the original impulse has long been submerged by purely economic pressures. And the same motley[2] immigration from the Old World is building up the bulk of the coming countries. At most, the dominant language gives a semblance of unity and serves to attract a considerable stream of immigrants who speak it, as of Portuguese to Brazil, Spaniards to the Argentine. But the chief magnet remains economic, for Brazil draws six times as many Italians as Portuguese, and the Argentine two and a half times as many Italians as Spanish. It may be urged, of course, that the Italian gravitation to these countries is still a

---

1   See Zangwill's short story "The Land of Promise" in Appendix D3.
2   Disparate or diverse, with a sense of incongruity or odd humorousness attached.

matter of race, and that, in the absence of an El Dorado[1] of his own, the Italian is attracted towards States that are at least Latin. But though Brazil and the Argentine be predominantly Latin, the minority of Germans, Austrians, and Swiss is by no means insignificant. The great modern steamship, in fact—supplemented by its wandering and seductive agent—is playing the part in the world formerly played by invasions and crusades, while the "economic" immigrant is more and more replacing the refugee, just as the purely commercial company working under native law is replacing the Chartered Company[2] which was a law to itself. How small a part in the modern movement is played by patriotism proper may be seen from the avidity with which the farmers of the United States cross the borders to Canada to obtain the large free holdings which enable them to sell off their American properties. How little the proudest tradition counts against the environment is shown in the shame felt by Argentine-born children for the English spoken by their British parents.

The difference in the method of importing the ingredients makes thus no difference to the action of the crucible. Though the peoples now in process of formation in the New World are being recruited by mainly economic forces, it may be predicted they will ultimately harden into homogeneity of race, if not even of belief. For internationalism in religion seems to be again receding in favour of national religions (if, indeed, these were ever more than superficially superseded), at any rate in favour of nationalism raised into religion.

If racial homogeneity has not yet been evolved completely even in England—and, of course, the tendency can never be more than asymptotic[3]—it is because cheap and easy transport and communication, with freedom of economic movement, have been late developments and are still far from perfect. Hence, there has never been a thorough shake-up and admixture of elements, so that certain counties and corners have retained types and breeds peculiar to them. But with the ever-growing interconnection of all parts of the country, and with the multiplication of labour bureaux, these breeds and types will be—alas, for local colour!—increasingly absorbed in the general mass. For fusion and unification are part of the historic life-process. "Normans

---

1 A place of great riches believed by sixteenth-century explorers to exist in South America; a mythical land of great riches.
2 European company formed for exploration and colonization.
3 Mathematics: becoming increasingly exact as it approaches infinity.

and Saxons and Danes"[1] are we here in England, yes and Huguenots and Flemings and Gascons and Angevins and Jews and many other things.

In fact, according to Sir Harry Johnston, there is hardly an ethnic element that has not entered into the Englishman, including even the missing link, as the Piltdown skull would seem to testify. The earlier discovery at Galley Hill showed Britannia rising from the apes with an extinct Tasmanian type, not unlike the surviving aboriginal Australian.[2] Then the west of Britain was invaded by a negroid type from France followed by an Eskimo type of which traces are still to be seen in the West of Ireland and parts of Scotland. Next came the true Mediterranean white man, the Iberian, with dark hair and eyes and a white skin; and then the round-headed people of the Bronze Age, probably Asiatic. And then the Gael, the long-headed, fair-haired Aryan, who ruled by iron and whose Keltic vocabulary was tinged with Iberian, and who was followed by the Brython or Belgian. And, at some unknown date, we have to allow for the invasion of North Britain by another Germanic type, the Caledonian, which would seem to have been a Norse stock, foreshadowing the later Norman Conquest. And, as if this mish-mash was not confusion enough, came to make it worse confounded the Roman conquerors, trailing like a mantle of many colours the subject-races of their far-flung Empire.

Is it wonderful if the crucible, capable of fusing such a motley of types into "the true-born Briton,"[3] should be melting up its Jews like old silver? The comparison belongs to Mr. Walkley, who was more moved by the beauty of the old and the pathos of its passing than by the resplendence of the new, and who seemed to forget that it is for the dramatist to register both impartially— their conflict constituting another of those spiritual duels which are peculiarly his affair. Jews are, unlike negroes, a "recessive" type, whose physical traits tend to disappear in the blended offspring. There does not exist in England to-day a single represen-

---

1   See "A Welcome to Alexandra" (1863) by Alfred, Lord Tennyson (1809–92).

2   The Piltdown Skull, discovered in 1912, and the skeletal remains of Galley Hill man found in 1888 were each believed to be the "missing link" between apes and humans predicted by Darwinian evolution. Decades later (and decades after Zangwill wrote about them), each of these finds was definitively judged a hoax. Tasmania, an island off the south coast of Australia, has been an Australian state since 1901.

3   See the 1701 poem "The True-Born Englishman," by British writer Daniel Defoe (1660–1731).

tative of the Jewish families whom Cromwell admitted,[1] though their lineage may be traced in not a few noble families. Thus every country has been and is a "Melting Pot." But America, exhibiting the normal fusing process magnified many thousand diameters and diversified beyond all historic experience, and fed not by successive waves of immigration but by a hodge-podge of simultaneous hordes, is, in Bacon's phrase, an "ostensive instance"[2] of a universal phenomenon. America is *the* "Melting Pot."

Her people has already begun to take on such a complexion of its own, it is already so emphatically tending to a new race, crossed with every European type, that the British illusion of a cousinly Anglo-Saxon people with whom war is unthinkable is sheer wilful blindness. Even to-day, while the mixture is still largely mechanical not chemical, the Anglo-Saxon element is only preponderant; it is very far from being the sum total.

VI

While our sluggish and sensual English stage has resisted and even burked[3] the writer's attempt to express in terms of the theatre our European problems of war and religion, and to interpret through art the "years of the modern, years of the unperformed,"[4] it remains to be acknowledged with gratitude that this play, designed to bring home to America both its comparative rawness and emptiness and its true significance and potentiality for history and civilisation, has been universally acclaimed by Americans as a revelation of Americanism, despite that it contains only one native-born American character, and that a bad one. Played throughout the length and breadth of the States since its original production in 1908, given, moreover, in Universities and Women's Colleges, passing through edition after edition in

---

1 The Jews were expelled from England in 1290 by an edict of King Edward I. In 1656, after discussions with Manasseh Ben Israel, a leader of the Dutch Jewish community, Oliver Cromwell (1599–1658) agreed not to uphold the edict and, although there was no official readmission, Jews began to return, joining those who had never left.

2 Francis Bacon (1561–1626) discussed the importance of such clearly demonstrative examples in writings that developed the scientific method such as his *Novum Organum* (1620).

3 Suppressed indirectly.

4 Walt Whitman (1819–92), "Years of the Modern" (1900), line 1.

book form, cited by preachers and journalists, politicians and Presidential candidates, even calling into existence a "Melting Pot" Club in Boston, it has had the happy fortune to contribute its title to current thought, and, in the testimony of Jane Addams,[1] to "perform a great service to America by reminding us of the high hopes of the founders of the Republic."

I. Z.
January 1914.

---

1 Addams (1860–1935), leader of women's suffrage and peace organizations, founded Hull-House, one of the first settlement houses, in Chicago in 1889; see Appendices E1–2 and Introduction, pp. 27–30.

Appendix A: Contemporary Reviews

[After a trial run of one August performance in Littlehampton, near Zangwill's home in Sussex, *The Melting-Pot* opened in Washington, DC, on 5 October 1908. From there it travelled to Chicago and numerous other North American cities before opening in New York in September 1909. It did not open in London until late January 1914, when two performances by the non-profit Play Actors at the Court Theatre gave way to the February premiere at the Queen's. Taken from a massive collection of reviews, this selection of extracts, presented in roughly chronological order, reflects American and British, including Jewish, opinions of these first productions.]

1. From "The Theater: Columbia Theater," *Evening Star* [Washington, DC] (6 October 1908): 20[1]

A remarkable play was exhibited at the Columbia Theater last night. "The Melting Pot" has the interest that must attach to something written from the heart. Outside the stage technique, of which Mr. Zangwill should, with his frequent experiences in theatric production, be a master, and beyond the literary charm which has so long distinguished his work, there is in this play the expression of intense feeling which has the shock and appeal of a human cry. The author has embodied in this work a sob of protest against the sufferings that a devout and sensitive people have endured for ages gone by and an outburst of joy as the light shines on the future. It is a sociological drama; one in which hard, solid thought takes the place of sentimentality; a work of great artistic value and of philosophic suggestion. It discusses the world and its assemblage of nations in the same spirit that Ibsen discusses the home.[2]

---

1 Israel Zangwill had reviews sent to him by a clipping service and kept them in scrapbooks that are now held by the Central Zionist Archives of Jerusalem (CZA). Reviews of *The Melting-Pot* make up by far the largest collection and appear in three files, A120/164 (divided into two parts) and A120/165. I indicate the file numbers for all the reviews that I found in this archive for which other publication data is incomplete; there are a few that I located separately.

2 Henrik Ibsen's (1828–1906) plays of the 1880s and 1890s (such as *A Doll's House* [1879] and *Ghosts* [1881]) deal provocatively with issues of marriage and family.

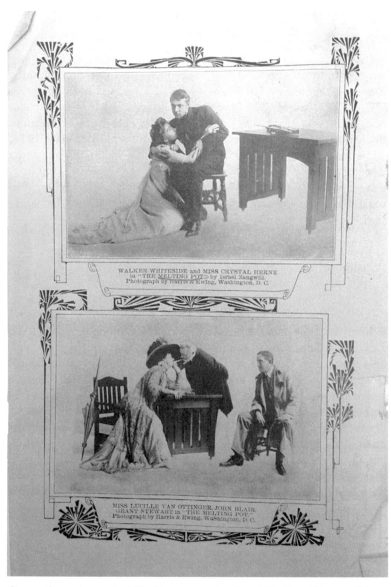

WALKER WHITESIDE and MISS CRYSTAL HERNE
in "THE MELTING POT" by Israel Zangwill.
Photograph by Harris & Ewing, Washington, D. C.

MISS LUCILLE VAN OTTINGER, JOHN BLAIR,
GRANT STEWART in "THE MELTING POT."
Photograph by Harris & Ewing, WaShington, D. C.

Scenes from the original Washington production, Billy Rose Theatre Division, New York Public Library.

2. From "The Alien's Opportunity," *Washington Post* (7 October 1908): n.p.; clipping in CZA A120/165

In his latest play Israel Zangwill, the Jewish author, has attempted to express in dramatic form the new era which opens for the alien when he lands on American shores, and he symbolizes the state of society in this country by calling it the melting pot. This is an apt phrase. Without doubt, the United States has become the melting pot of the races. Nations, creeds, and colors, diverse and conglomerate streams of blood, reach our shores; they step in and are lost forever, fused into one indistinguishable mass called the American people.

This is, perhaps, as it should be. Certainly there does not appear any present way of preventing it. But what if some portion of that alien stream which flows to us is evil? Will it not irremediably taint, in time, the whole body of American national life? There is but one way of keeping this great pool clean; no streams must be allowed to feed it which are foul.

If Mr. Zangwill's play means anything, it means that the hope of his own people lies in their being completely absorbed by the American nation through marriage. This means, of course, the utter obliteration of their race history, their religion, and those separate institutions which they have cherished for forty centuries. It is hard to see the body of Mr. Zangwill's people accepting this as their material salvation, and equally difficult to credit the author with advancing it; yet surely nothing less can be adduced from his play. There seems but one alternative. It is that the author did not mean to confine his doctrine to the absorption of his own people merely, but meant to express, in the particular instance, a universal idea. In other words, that the hope of all the dissatisfied and oppressed peoples lies in America.

If this is his idea, it will be as difficult for Americans to accept it as it is to reconcile the orthodox Jewish conviction with his more restricted theory. [...] However well Mr. Zangwill's play may be received for its artistic and dramatic qualities, it is to be feared that the doctrines he endeavors to preach will never become popular in this country.

Speaking to a general theory, also, it is a mistake to encourage the immigrant in the thought that whatever advantages accrue to him in this country are those prepared and waiting for him here. The stupid, the unambitious, the lazy, and the vicious, in Russia or the Balkans, are likely to remain the same after they land in America. What America offers to the alien is opportunity.

3. From Burns Mantle, "News of the Theaters: The Melting Pot," *Chicago Daily Tribune* (20 October 1908): 10

And lo, there came from out the center of Europe in the first years of the twentieth century a prophet with a message for America. A Jew he was, a refugee from the bloodstained streets of Kisheneff,[1] and he came to preach Americanism to Americans. [...]

He is the hero of Mr. Zangwill's new play, "The Melting Pot," is this new prophet, and last night in the Grand opera house he brought an audience of these same fusing Americans to a pitch of intense excitement by the ardor of his plea and the magnificent sincerity with which it was presented. Nothing spiritually finer, nothing dramatically more tremendous has been accomplished in the local theaters than the voicing of the prophet's message by a company of players fairly tingling with the author's own soul fed enthusiasm, and no applause more sincere than that following its most impressive climax has been heard in a local playhouse this season.

From the standpoint of the fusing American, therefore, "The Melting Pot" is to be accepted as something of a master work, for three of its four acts at least.[2] But it is likewise a work to which you must give something in order that you may receive more. It demands, for instance, that you must banish from your heart all narrowness and selfishness, and the quality of patriotism they beget, and accept the world, not as a subdivided planet of a hundred nations but as the home of a mighty family, a house of many mansions,[3] wherein the peace and good and happiness of all are the object of each. It comes as a text book drama with a lesson for all peoples and all communities, but with a special application to America—the America that the prophet would see become "a republic of men and a kingdom of God."

If it shall displease any, it will be he who finds it hard to open his heart and his mind and welcome the suggestion that America is, indeed, the "melting pot" and that we do represent as a people only the fused and fusing forces of older civilizations. In our deepest hearts we know it is true. [...] But it is not into his deepest heart that the average play goer is anxious to delve for certain truths, and so we are at a loss to estimate just what measure of popularity the new play will achieve.

---

1 This is one of several spellings of the name of the city where the 1903 massacre took place. In more recent times it has been known as Kishinev, but since the Republic of Moldova's independence from the Soviet Union in 1991, the city's official name is Chişinău, and it is Moldova's capital.

2 Quite a few reviewers were disappointed by Act IV.

3 John 14:2: In my Father's house are many mansions.

Sympathetically its appeal is strong and true, but it is a sympathy demanded for an alien people.

4. From Constance Skinner, "'Melting Pot,' at Grand, Play to Remember," *Chicago Evening American* (21 October 1908): n.p.; clipping in CZA A120/165

"The Melting Pot"—the great crucible alight with "the fires of God" —is America. Into that crucible the nations of the world are pouring; there they are being fused into the American of To-Morrow. [...]

Season after season our dramatists have aimed to produce "the great American play" by writing of America's social conditions, her money kings, her poor, her politics and her fleeting fashions. They have shown us her execrescences [sic] of materialism—the barnacles on Plymouth Rock.[1] And we have said:

"Yes, this is well done; we see the barnacles. But what of the Rock?"

Israel Zangwill has ploughed through the sands of our fluctuating social conditions. With the keen blade of insight he has scraped off the barnacles and laid bare the Rock. It is Zangwill, who is not of ours, who has written the great American play; for he has shown us the white soul of America and interpreted to all lands her message.[2]

5. From Amy Leslie, "Grave Play at Grand," *Chicago Daily News* (21 October 1908): n.p.; clipping in CZA A120/165

Israel Zangwill, throbbing with enthusiastic racial amalgamation ideas, comes with an avalanche of brilliant arguments steeped in red, white and blue, with a kind of mongrel spread-eagle[3] screaming liberty, fraternity and great inequality in his play, "The Melting Pot," which inaugurates the third settlement work play the Grand opera house has presented this season.

Mr. Zangwill knows nothing of the check rein of eloquence which divides spirit from frenzy of realism from excessive naturalism and with so inviting and vividly melodramatic a theme as the advanced Jew in America he has swamped a magnificent theory in rhetorical excess, framed some vivid and tragic tableaux of Kishinev in anguish too tor-

---

1 Traditionally held to be the site on the coast of Massachusetts where the Pilgrims landed in 1620.

2 The allusion to Zangwill as "not of ours" reminds readers that he was British, not American. The "white soul" of America most likely refers to spiritual purity.

3 An image of an eagle with wings and legs extended outward, or the kind of American patriotism such an image might represent.

turing to be endured and by his own luxurious genius for Yiddish hysteria, picturesque but ineffectual, he has nearly written a long Niagara[1] of the woes and faults of Judea,[2] instead of a startling American drama. [...]

Sermons, stirring and vital, teem in the play and satire mostly directed against the American, while America itself is on the laudation pan[3] all evening. The first act has a charming touch of simple realism and except for obstreperous Irish comedy in juxtaposition to the Jewish simplicity and truth, sincerity and drab seriousness, it is really interesting. The second is gauche,[4] impish and inconsequent and the others tremble under the weight of their own ambitions to roar in brute strength against existing calamities, social and racial, and to intensify the chance of melting up genuine metal with the dross of humanity, while the divine fires are kindled about this Zangwill crucible of elimination. Jews do not want to be melted up, however, and Americans are not anxious to be melted up with them or the Irish or the Dutch or the Hottentots[5] and the rest any more than any other nation is, so "The Melting Pot" fails of its mission, though its magnificent message is given in gorgeous flights of emotional hope and prophecy.

6. From "Grand Opera House," *Chicago Israelite* (23 October 1908): 8

[Reviews in the Jewish press were often mixed, with praise of this powerful play by a well-known Jewish writer combined with expressions of concern and disapproval regarding its themes. This review and the next, however, of the Chicago performance, are unreservedly laudatory.]

A remarkable play by Israel Zangwill was exhibited at the Grand Opera House Monday night and was received with wonderful enthusiasm. "The Melting Pot" has the interest that must attach to something written from the heart. The proposition submitted by the players is that America—or, rather, New York—is the greatest melting pot, in

---

1 The massive falls at the border of Canada and the United States (Ontario and New York), which include the largest and most powerful waterfall in North America.
2 Like Hebrews, another term for the Jewish people.
3 Possibly "laudation panegyric," a formal public speech of praise.
4 Awkward or graceless.
5 The Khoikhoi people of South Africa, formerly called Hottentots by Dutch settlers. The term is now considered offensive.

which racial hatreds must be fused and transformed. An example of the bitterest persecution known to history, the persecution of the Jewish people by the Russians, forms the basis of the plot.

7. From Leon Zolotkoff, "Zangwill's Great Success," *Daily Jewish Courier* [Chicago] (13 November 1908): n.p.; clipping in CZA A120/165

[This article, from a Yiddish newspaper, appears in the archive in both a copy of the original Yiddish and a typescript English translation. The translator is not indicated, but the author is identified as the State Attorney General, Chicago.]

Out of all the dramatic works ever written by Mr. Zangwill, "The Melting Pot" is undoubtedly the greatest masterpiece. In all his previous plays [...] he is only an artist, [...] But in his "Melting Pot" he is more than an artist, for there he is also a philosopher, a poet, and a prophet, with a deep insight into the future.

America is a novel experiment throughout the world. There is no precedent within the memory of mankind of a case of dozens of peoples and tongues, from various climates and with a different past, flowing to the same country, coming into contact with one another, and slowly getting closer to one another, all learning one language, and gradually merging into one nation. Though this process has now been going on for a couple of centuries, it has never occurred to anybody to present that process in a literary and artistic form, with a prophecy as to its results, and an indication of the intellectual and moral possibilities involved for humanity in such a fusion, until the arrival of Mr. Zangwill with his "Melting Pot." [...]

Many critics object to the fourth act, where the Jewish boy of Kishineff is united to the Christian girl, who is the daughter of the Russian anti-Semitic Baron. They charge Mr. Zangwill with preaching amalgamation, which many nationalities, especially Jews, are unwilling and unable to accept. But those critics close their eyes, and refuse to see that such fusions are of very frequent occurrence in the melting pot, whether the critics like it or not.[1] Zangwill does not preach but merely points out what is going on in the melting pot, and we know that it is true. "The Melting Pot" is a play that has a future, and is bound to gain more and more in importance as time goes on.

---

1   See Appendix B.

8. From [Adolph Klauber?,] "New Zangwill Play Cheap and Tawdry," *New York Times* (7 September 1909): 9

[Adolph Klauber (1879–1933) was the drama critic for the *New York Times* for twelve years beginning in 1906. Although this review is not signed, its similarities to his signed review in the Sunday edition suggest that it is by his hand.]

From time to time there has been born[e] in upon this community the intimation that in "The Melting Pot" Mr. Israel Zangwill had writ[t]en a most important play. The billboards have carried the endorsements of men of prominence in civic and National affairs, and even Col. Roosevelt, while still President, was quoted as among its most enthusiastic admirers. This merely goes to prove that even a President may be mistaken. "The Melting Pot" is not important.

It is, in fact, a very bad play viewed from almost any point of view. It is assumed to deal with a subject, which, as far as it goes, is big and vital, but it handles that subject in a cheap and tawdry way. As drama, it is hardly second rate. It is awkward in structure, clumsy in workmanship, and deficient as literature, if to be literary in such a case means to clothe a subject with language appropriate to its people and situations and to present those people in situations which are suggestively plausible and real. [...]

Mr. Zangwill, however, is true neither to his Jews nor his Gentiles, though in the case of the former he does introduce occasional glimpses of customs and racial characteristics that are genuine enough and give the figures color. It may be doubted, however, whether even he, with exceptional opportunity for studying the race, has ever seen a typical orthodox mother in Israel making merry on the Purim with an Irish housemaid as companion in the dance and a false nose to emphasize a racial trait. [...]

"The Melting Pot" is sentimental trash masquerading as a human document. That is the sum and substance of it.

9. From Adolph Klauber, "A Spread-Eagle Play by Israel Zangwill," *New York Times* (12 September 1909): X10

The worst of Mr. Israel Zangwill's play, "The Melting Pot," apart from its insincerity as a work of art, its obvious spread-eagleism and appeal to claptrap[1] patriotism, is its failure to develop the theme which the author lays down as the sum and substance of its purpose. [...] the

---

1 Pretentious, empty language.

tardy discovery on David's part that his natural antipathy to the Russian butcher and his progeny has given way to the more generous realization of the necessity for the peace on earth, good-will to men theory,[1] fails to convey any strong sense of increased Americanism on the part of the hero.

As a matter of fact Mr. Zangwill's hero succeeds in impressing himself upon the imagination as a neurotic sentimentalist, with a fine idea buzzing around in his head, but not very much mental balance. Does this describe a genius? Very well, let it go at that, and there would be no occasion to quarrel were the play designed as a purely romantic structure. But it is put forth as a human document, as a significant thing.

10. From "Zangwill Play Opens New Comedy Theatre," *New York Herald* (7 September 1909): n.p.; CZA A120/165[2]

In choosing Mr. Israel Zangwill's new play, "The Melting Pot," in which to open their new theatre, the Comedy, the Messrs. Shubert[3] got as far away as possible from the title of their playhouse. A story built upon the massacres of Jews in Russia and the race hatred of centuries can hardly have in it much of comedy, even when an exiled Jew, whose entire family was slain in the massacres, wins the love of the daughter of the Russian Baron who urged on the slaughter—and that is Mr. Zangwill's play.

With a poorer company than was seen last night, "The Melting Pot" might easily have been made too gloomy and too tragic, but with such a cast as presented the play to its first New York audience one forgot that it had little action and a great deal of dialogue in the excellent work of the players.

---

1 See Luke 2:14.

2 A note in the header that precedes the text of the review indicates that it will be cabled to Paris for inclusion in the European edition.

3 The Shubert brothers, Jewish immigrants from the Russian Empire who came to the United States as children, developed the Broadway theatre district of New York in the first half of the twentieth century. Their legacy continues in several major New York theatres (although not the Comedy, which was demolished in 1942) and in the Shubert Foundation, which supports performing arts organizations.

COMEDY THEATRE

SAM. S. and LEE SHUBERT (Inc.), Lessees

BEGINNING MONDAY EVENING, DEC. 27, 1909

Evenings at 8.15—Matinees Wednesday and Saturday at 2.15

WALKER WHITESIDE

In the New Play by Israel Zangwill

Treating of the amalgamation of the races in the making of the American

"THE MELTING POT"

LIEBLER & CO., Managers

The Cast

MENDEL QUIXANO	Sheridan Block
BARON REVENDAL	John Blair
QUINCY DAVENPORT, JR.	Grant Stewart
HERR PAPPELMEISTER	Henry Vogel
VERA REVENDAL	Florence Fisher
BARONESS REVENDAL	Leonora von Ottinger
FRAU QUIXANO	Louise Muldener
KATHLEEN O'REILLY	Nellie Butler
and	
DAVID QUIXANO	MR. WHITESIDE

Scenes in the Play

ACT I—The living-room in the house of the Quixanos in the Borough of Richmond, New York (at 5 o'clock of an afternoon in February).

Intermission three minutes between Acts I and II

ACT II—The Same (on an afternoon in March).

ACT III—Miss Revendal's room at the Settlement House (on an afternoon in April).

ACT IV—The roof-garden of the Settlement House (on the evening of the Fourth of July).

Program page, Comedy Theatre, first New York production, Billy Rose Theatre Division, New York Public Library.

11. From J.J. [?], "The Tragedy of Kishineff: Israel Zangwill's 'Melting Pot,'" *American Hebrew and Jewish Messenger* (10 September 1909): 1–2

Mr. Israel Zangwill's much-heralded play, "The Melting Pot," reached New York on Monday evening, the 6th inst., when it served as the opening play for the cozy new Comedy Theatre, in 41st street. Judging by the reception given at the premiere to the third act—the critical climax of all modern plays—it has come to stay. Call it sentimental, hysterical, melodramatic, clap-trap, what you will, the fact remains that the third act grips you, thrills you, and that is a sufficiently rare achievement in the modern drama to insure success. Indeed, "The Melting Pot" has already lived out a year's life on the boards,[1] and this

---

1 That is, it has already been performed onstage for nearly a year, in theatres outside New York.

fact alone proves that it has powers of appealing to the general public and the Jewish public, which argues for a continued run in its new environment. Still, New York is not Chicago and what may have pleased the somewhat garish taste of the West may not appeal to the more blasé sensibilities of New Yorkers. [...]

"The Melting Pot" is a problem play in the guise of a melodrama. [...] But in "The Melting Pot" it is rather difficult to determine exactly what is the problem raised by the melodrama. The title would seem to indicate that it is the noble function of America to assimilate all the nations which come to its shores into one uniform excellence with which the future of humanity is bound up, instead of effete[1] Europe. But assimilation is not necessarily coincident with intermarriage, yet the main problem raised in "The Melting Pot" is intermarriage. So far as one can see, David Quixano has become as assimilated as any immigrant could be. [...] This assimilation tendency had been effected before his meeting with Vera Revendal and might have continued if he had married an equally assimilated Jewess. The problem of his relation with Vera is the old tragedy of personal love as against parental or family misdeeds, and might have been transferred to Russian soil without any loss of effectiveness, or rather with an increase of it. This is the fundamental weakness of the play, considered as a problem drama.

Considered as a contribution to the Jewish problem in general,[2] the play is even less satisfactory. There is some attempt to discuss this between Quixano and the uncle, but the latter, at every important stage in the argument, weakly reiterates "I have to go to my lesson and cannot discuss that." The hero at one moment declares that his alternative solution of the Jewish question is "America or Zion," but this is scarcely novel or sufficient. Still, after all, the problem play need not necessarily have its cut and dried solution. If it raises the problem in a dramatic form it has achieved its purpose. Mr. Zangwill's play raises many problems, and some of them in a dramatic form. With its appeal to the American patriotism above the tier of boxes,[3] and to Jewish sentimentality below, its first success is perhaps sufficiently explained.

---

1 Overly refined, ineffectual.
2 The "Jewish problem" or "Jewish question" was a subject of debate in Europe and America from the eighteenth or nineteenth centuries through the early twentieth century. It concerned the status and treatment of Jews as a minority. Use of the phrase eventually became associated with antisemitism, especially when Nazis referred to the Holocaust as "the Final Solution to the Jewish question."
3 Boxes in a theatre, separate seating for small groups of people, are usually the most expensive seats in the house. One can assume from the context that wealthier, non-Jewish audience members sat above the box level while poorer immigrant Jews sat below.

12. From [A.B. Walkley,] "Some New York Plays," *Times* [London] (24 November 1909): 4

[Arthur Bingham Walkley (1855–1926) was the drama critic for the *Times* of London for twenty-six years beginning in 1900. He wrote its review of the New York production, excerpted below, and Zangwill took his highly negative criticism as the starting point for his Afterword in the 1914 publication of the play.]

Is it to gratify the American, or his own passion for romance that Mr. Zangwill has written *The Melting Pot*, now being played at the Comedy Theatre? It has all the old romantic machinery: the young long-haired fiddler, who "plays like an angel" [...]; the fair but steel-tempered Nihilist[1] heroine; wicked Russian spies with revolvers, and languourous baronesses with superciliously aristocratic *lorgnettes*.[2] According to the programme the play treats of the amalgamation of the races in the making of the American, and, to be sure, young David Quixano, the Jew musician escaped from Kichineff, does rhapsodize upon this, among other themes. [...] To him the Statue of Liberty is a mother holding out welcoming arms to all the weary and heavy-laden of the Old World, and promising them peace.

Well, peace is not exactly the most prominent characteristic of New York to a casual eye, and there are perhaps less romantic aspects of the great immigration question than this one [...]. Nor is it strictly accurate to speak of the Old World in the lump as a mere matter of *pogroms* and Kicheneffs [sic]. But then David is a dreamer and a musician, and what have statistics to do with symphonies? [...] Was it Mr. Taft[3] or Mr. Roosevelt who said not long ago that *The Melting Pot* was "one of the best plays he had ever seen"? What a stupendous *naïveté* there is in such a statement as that! For, after all, what is this glorification of the amalgamated immigrants, this exaggerated contrast of the freshness of the New World and the staleness of the Old, this rhap-

---

1 Nihilism (the term taken from the Latin word *nihil*, meaning "nothing") was a revolutionary movement that took hold in Russia in the 1860s and continued through the late nineteenth century. Revolutionary activity continued in Russia, and Nihilist is often a shorthand term to describe those, such as Vera, who participated in it. The term is not used in *The Melting-Pot*, however.

2 Eyeglasses or opera glasses held in front of the face by a long handle at the side.

3 William Howard Taft (1857–1930) was president of the United States when *The Melting-Pot* opened in New York in 1909. Then-president Theodore Roosevelt had been in the audience at its Washington premiere in October 1908, a few weeks before the presidential election.

sodizing over music and crucibles and Statues of Liberty, but romantic claptrap?

Naturally enough, when the optimistic idealism and general high falutin'[1] of the play are eagerly fastened upon, its one really valuable element passes almost unobserved. I refer to its delicately sympathetic and quietly toned picture of old-fashioned orthodox Judaism, forlorn but faithful amid strange and hostile surroundings, the simple, solemn ritual of the Sabbath, the pathetic clinging to what to outsiders seem "lost causes and forgotten beliefs,"[2] to be seen in the aged Frau Quixano and her son Mendel. Here, of course, Mr. Zangwill is at home; he knows the beauty of Jewish character and tradition, handles it reverently, and makes of it an exquisite thing. So exquisite a thing that, on one observer[3] at any rate, his play has produced just the opposite of its intended effect. What are "melting pots" generally used for? Is it not to melt down choice old silver, masterpieces of craftsmanship, the heirlooms of the ages, into a mere mass of metal? Well, it seems to me not a good thing, but a grievous pity, that these fine old products of the ages, these richly-toned masterpieces of tradition, the authentic orthodox Jews represented by the elder Quixanos, should be cast into the melting pot to come out—what? Americans, if you will have it so, but at any rate crude, shiny, brand-new Americans. Here is Mendel Quixano, the son of a learned Rabbi, wearing his shabby black frock-coat with something of Oriental dignity [...]. You cast Mendel into the "melting pot" and out he comes chewing gum and drinking cocktails, holding on by one hand to a subway strap and reading one of Mr. Hearst's papers[4] in the other [...]. Is the Jewish immigrant, is America, is anybody to be congratulated upon such a transformation as this? Mr. Zangwill of all men, one feels sure, does not really think so.

13. From "Court Theatre. 'The Melting-Pot,'" *Star* [London] (27 January 1914): n.p.; clipping in CZA A120/164

Mr. Zangwill's prophetic soul was no doubt right in warning him that the critics would ask with regard to "The Melting Pot" that question

---

1 Pomposity, pretentiousness; the proper spelling is *highfalutin*, but Walkley's apostrophe at the end seems to accentuate the word's common American usage.

2 Victorian writer and critic Matthew Arnold (1822–88) referred to the Oxford University of his day as "the home of lost causes and forgotten beliefs."

3 The reviewer himself.

4 William Randolph Hearst (1863–1951) owned the largest chain of newspapers in America. The papers were noted for their sensationalism.

which Mr. Kipling puts in the mouth of the Father of Criticism: "It's pretty, but is it Art?"[1] If we are wedded to the current definitions of dramatic Art, I fear the answer must be in the negative. The matter of the play is melodramatic, the manner rhetorical—of that there can be no doubt. It is not a good play of the Ibsen type, or the Galsworthy type, or the Barker type, or the Synge type:[2] it is full of crudities both of action and speech, from which any one of these sensitive technicians would shrink. But after all is said and done, it is an extremely interesting play of the Zangwill type, which has, I take it, as good a right to exist as any other. It is a palpitating human document; it brings us into living touch with the tragic destiny of an ancient, much enduring, indomitable race; and it utters the passionate faith of a prophet of the larger, saner age that is dawning over the world. I first saw the play in New York, with the "melting pot" seething all around me, and my pulses did not fail to respond to Mr. Zangwill's exultant Hymn of Praise to America as the great haven of refuge for the oppressed and down-trodden of the world. Mr. Walkley,[3] I remember, was with me that evening, and I am sorry to say that our two hearts did not beat as one. [...] Undoubtedly he was right as a critic; but my experience at the Court[4] yesterday afternoon convinced me that I was not wrong as a human being.

14. From "'The Melting Pot.' Mr. Zangwill's Play at the Court Theatre," *Jewish Chronicle* (30 January 1914): 16–17; 23

[The *Jewish Chronicle* was the leading organ of opinion for English-speaking British Jews.]

A play by Mr. Zangwill necessarily calls for the closest attention, as indeed does the product of any genius such as he. [...] Thus, when we

---

1 Rudyard Kipling (1865–1936), English journalist, fiction writer, and poet. In his satirical poem "The Conundrum of the Workshops" (1890), the Devil looks at Adam scratching a figure in the dirt of Eden and asks the question quoted.

2 John Galsworthy (1867–1933) and Harley Granville-Barker (1877–1946) were contemporary British realist playwrights; John Millington Synge (1871–1909), also a contemporary, was a leader of the Irish literary revival and a founder of the Abbey Theatre in Dublin.

3 See Appendix A12.

4 The Court Theatre, London, where the Play Actors performed *The Melting-Pot* before its commercial opening at the Queen's.

come to consider a play like "The Melting Pot" we have, if we would appreciate its reality, to dig deep below the surface and, ignoring for the moment the representation as a mere piece of dramatic art, bend ourselves to the true meaning that underlies the author's effort. What lesson did Mr. Zangwill desire to teach when he produced his play? Was it the economic, social, and religious consequences which are likely to result to the Jew from his migration in huge numbers to the American continent? Or was it the outcome for America—a vast continent which but a few years ago was sparsely populated, and to-day has still need of an enormous immigration year by year—which is likely to result in the history of the future? [...]

But it is sufficient for our purposes to confine ourselves to one of the problems which Mr. Zangwill's play suggests. It can be stated shortly:—The Jew, what will he become? Two millions of him we know are already in America; the only other large Jewish aggregation in the world is in Russia.[1] [...] The active persecution of our people in that country has been in progress for a little over thirty years [...] The misery of the Russian Pale must inevitably find its effects upon even the sturdy Jewish race. The privation and the suffering must have cut deep scars into the stamina of Russian Jewry. [...] On the other hand, the conditions in America are such that the status accorded to the individual Jew is an encouragement to our race there to grow sturdy and strong. [...] And now comes Mr. Zangwill with a message which none of us Jews can ignore. He tells us that the great inlet for our persecuted people, the great salvation that has been reckoned upon to heal their sores and bind up their wounds, the great goal for the stricken of Israel in these latter days—that America is a veritable death-trap to our people, as Jews, because all who enter there are bound to become immured in a vast crucible in which the Jew in the immigrant has to be eliminated, his mission being not to remain a Jew in America but merely to provide his quota to whatever may come out of the "melting pot." [...]

If this indeed were the destiny of our people, its miserable outlook in the future would well-nigh excuse, if it did not justify, a quicker ending—a throwing up of the sponge, a suicide of the race. But happily for the Jewish people their faith, their belief, their culture, their ideals, are based not—as is David Quixano's in Mr. Zangwill's play—on a faith in the God of our children, but a faith in the God of our fathers. [...] There are a certain number of our people there, victims of the "melting-pot," and in process of time there will be more. And yet there will of a surety, even in the United States, be manifested an

---

1   The State of Israel was not created until 1948.

answer to the eternal prayer of the Jew—that the remnant of Israel shall be saved[, ...] and who shall say that, even as we look, there are no signs in American Jewry of the revolt of our people against the "melting pot," and a determination to stay outside of it?

Let us not forget, however, that the message which Mr. Zangwill felt impelled to deliver it was his business to deliver without qualification and without equivocation. [...] The prophets painted their pictures, which they intended should attract attention, in definite colours, without light and shade, and it would be absurd to expect that Mr. Zangwill in delivering his "prophecy" should do otherwise than present it in a lurid, even if you like in a turgid form. Otherwise he could never hope to impress.

15. From J.T. Grein, "The Week's Premieres, (1) Court: 'The Melting Pot,'" *Sunday Times* [London] (1 February 1914): 6

[Jacob Thomas Grein (1862–1935) was a Dutch Jew who emigrated to England in 1885. He is best known as the founder of the Independent Theatre, which brought Ibsen's *A Doll's House* and *Ghosts* to the London stage as private performances. According to Edna Nahshon, Zangwill recommended Grein for his first position as a theatre critic, with the London weekly *Life*.[1] Here he reviews the non-profit production at the Court Theatre.]

There was one thought paramount in my mind as I listened to the play. Was Mr. Zangwill's original intention really a panegyric on the United States? Or did he—as others have done—temporarily resent the lesser appreciation of his dramatic work by his countrymen, and assign to America what rightly belongs to his native heath?[2] For let us be plain about this. The real Melting Pot, the land of freedom where peoples may commingle to new creation is not the States which the Russian refugee, David Quixano, hails as a republic of men, anon[3] Kingdom of God. The States may well call itself the land of the free—but there are serious qualifications. What about the differentiation of black and white? What about the ban against the yellow race?[4] What

---

1 Nahshon 17.
2 Native land.
3 Soon, shortly.
4 The Chinese Exclusion Act of 1882, renewed in 1902, prohibited nearly all Chinese immigration to the United States. The "Gentlemen's Agreement" of 1907 severely restricted Japanese immigration.

about the "third degree"?[1] What about Ellis Island? And there are others. The real Melting Pot is these Islands,[2] where the alien is only rejected with reluctance for stringent reasons of health or antecedents; where the foreigner so keenly strives to become one of the land that too often he unlearns his language, disowns his name, breaks away from his own country for ever, where his children more and more ignore the paternal idiom and in their—"I am an Englishman" become *plus royaliste que le roi*.[3] We who sat in front and listened to the work of an Englishman, therefore, felt little enthusiasm for the vapourings of the voluble young Jew. They seemed exotic (and, of course, quixotic, for David was a very young man); to a certain extent they sounded like the voice of the renegade. There was a flavour of currying favour against better knowledge.

[The next week, Grein wrote the following regarding the Queen's Theatre production (from *Sunday Times* [London] [8 February 1914]: 9).]

Last week I devoted a column to this play, which is now rightly promoted to the evening bill.[4] It is, therefore, scarcely necessary to dwell on the merits and defects which I then tried to weigh in careful analysis—it is merely an occasion to rejoice that a play of such earnest purpose and depth of thought has been made accessible to a wider public by the enterprise of Mr. Gaston Mayer.[5]

---

1 Intense questioning of prospective immigrants, such as at Ellis Island (see Appendix D).
2 The islands of Great Britain and Ireland.
3 French: more royalist than the king.
4 Evening performances at a commercial theatre.
5 The producer (d. 1923).

Appendix B: Intermarriage and Assimilation Debates

[Although *The Melting-Pot* was very popular with immigrant Jewish audiences, many communal leaders deplored what seemed to be its promotion of intermarriage with non-Jews and complete assimilation into non-Jewish American culture. At the time of the play the two seemed to go together: Christianity was the majority faith and Jews often suffered from subtle or overt antisemitism, so intermarriage generally meant the adoption of Christian ways. Fears of Jewish leaders and the reasons behind them are reflected in the extracts that follow, some in direct response to a newspaper debate between Zangwill and Jewish business leader Daniel Guggenheim, immediately below. For related observations in reviews of the play, see Appendix A.]

1. From Rupert Hughes, "Should Jews Marry Christians?: Israel Zangwill, the English Author, and Daniel Guggenheim, the Colorado Millionaire, Accept the Herald's Invitation to Discuss an Important Race Question," *New York Herald*, Sunday Magazine (8 November 1908): 1–2

"There is no Jewish problem in this country. Any Jew can get anything he has a right to, and get into any circle where he belongs. The trouble with those who complain is that they want more than they have earned. There is absolutely no limit to the opportunities open to a Jew in the United States."

People usually contradict their own theories by their own lives, but here was a speaker who was his own best proof of his argument. For Mr. Daniel Guggenheim, as he spoke, sat in his apartments in the St. Regis,[1] after a day among the magnates of the metropolis. His brother is a Senator of the United States, and he is himself a member of a family firm so wealthy and so honorable that it could and did voluntarily forfeit more than a million dollars for a principle,[2] and so pow-

---

1   Elegant hotel in New York City.
2   In its obituary of Guggenheim, who died at the age of 74 in 1930, the *New York Times* wrote that the Guggenheim brothers had "decreed that no outside investor who joined in any of their enterprises should lose a cent. This creed [...] was exemplified in 1906, when the firm paid up $1,500,000 losses incurred by those who joined them in underwriting Canadian mines" ("Daniel Guggenheim dies suddenly at 74," *New York Times* [29 September 1930]: 5).

erful that it is looked upon as the chief instrument in opening up the empire of banks.

His enthusiasm, however, was not fully shared by his guest, the eminent English novelist and playwright, Mr. Israel Zangwill, who is so discontented with the estate of Jews in the world that he is giving his life to the re-establishment of the race on a soil of its own.[1] [...]

These two exemplars of Jewish ability, one in high art and one in high finance, sat together at tea [...], and it was my privilege and pleasure to set them by the ears over the question that is agitating all the world—What to do with the Jews.[2]

These two leaders of their race are agreed upon one thing—that the solution of the problem is in their own hands. The great conundrum is not "What shall the world do with the Jews?" but "What shall the Jews do with the Jews?"

Mr. Zangwill believes that the trouble arises from the fact that the Jews are a race without a home. Until that condition can be changed he feels that his people are bound to be absorbed more or less by the peoples among whom they pitch their tents. He would, therefore, have all the Jews that can and will return to Palestine, or, failing that, any practicable territory, and form anew the nation that gave the world so much of the world's best. But he recognizes that a large proportion of them do not even desire such a change for themselves, and he thinks that these should make the best of their conditions. A certain amount of intermarriage with the Gentile he finds inevitable and much more common than people realize. "Did not Moses himself intermarry with a Gentile woman?" he asked. "And does not tradition make David, the epical hero of the race, a descendant from Ruth?"[3]

Mr. Guggenheim, however, thinks that the Jew is doing very well as a Jew and that he should maintain himself in his traditions.

"I am a Jew and proud of it. My objection to intermarriage is that it tends to fritter the race away."

"There has always been since earliest times an enormous leakage from our race," said Mr. Zangwill. "It can't be stopped. The Jews are

---

1 Hughes refers to Zangwill's Zionist and Territorialist efforts (see Introduction, pp. 15–16).

2 In the early twentieth century, the Jews were a minority in every country they inhabited. The "Jewish question" or "Jewish problem," discussed since at least the eighteenth century, concerned the status Jews should have in the nations of western Europe and suggests that Jews commonly lived with political and social disabilities.

3 Moses married a Midianite woman, and Ruth is considered the first convert to Judaism, adopting her mother-in-law's religion when her first husband died. Exodus 2:16–22, 18:1; Ruth 1:16.

among the most prolific of people. Yet there are only some twelve millions of us in the world. There would be at least a hundred millions if so many Jews and Jewesses had not married Gentiles throughout the Christian era. The result is that there is vastly more Jewish strain in the make-up of various nations than many people dream." [...]

The more than heathen cruelties which Christians have practised against his race for nearly twenty centuries constitute in Mr. Guggenheim's mind one of the chief reasons for hating the idea of conversion.

"Of all people, the Jew has the least excuse for adopting the Christian religion," he said. "Our race has throughout history suffered so long and so much from the Christians that a Jew should be ashamed to go over to their churches [...]."

"If the Jews don't want to have mixed marriages," Mr. Zangwill objected, "they ought to go where they won't have mixed societies. That is why I believe in the Zionist movement. At present there is an awful muddle and mischief in the very word 'Jew.' It is used both for a race and for a religion. This causes confusion everywhere, among the Jews especially. If we had a territory of our own, where we were all compact together, there would be no more probability of intermarriage than between French and Germans. [...] For nearly two thousand years [the Jew] has had no home, no fatherland. His religion is his home. I believe that we Jews are vitally in need of a real territorial home, a concrete country. Until we get such a land those who are compelled to live among foreign conditions should adapt themselves to them as best they can. And they do. That is the theme of my new play. America is the great melting pot of peoples. The Jews who come here to stay throw themselves into the crucible and come out good Americans, whether they intermarry or not."

"You mean, then, that they forget their religion?" I asked.

"Not necessarily. There is a great deal of orthodoxy in America. I have every sympathy with the idea of Jewish *religious* separation. Those, however, who do not believe in orthodox Judaism any longer must have full liberty of conscience to intermarry with Gentiles of the same ethical standards as themselves.[1] But the rest, if they wish to preserve themselves, must work harder than they have ever done." [...]

Mr. Zangwill anxiously explained:—"My view and my views are not the same. What I observe and what I desire are different. My ideals are a pure Jewish religion and a solid Jewish nation. What I see is the broken fragments of a homeless race struggling to maintain its religion and race in the face of almost hopeless obstacles and prejudices. I see

---

1   This is in fact what Zangwill did in 1903, when he married Edith Ayrton, a non-Jewish woman who shared his universalist ethical beliefs.

Jews, with little pride of race and with no remnants of the old faith, changing their names, denying their parentage and losing themselves in the new conditions. I see more and more intermarriages. [...] As a Jew I may lament, as an artist I can only record the truth. [...] I have a mixed ambition—the prosperity of my religion, the prosperity of my race as a unit and the prosperity of its individuals. It is for the individual to decide whether or not it is best for him to throw himself into the melting pot."

Mr. Guggenheim agreed with this only in part:—

"I have nothing to say against any act of conscience," he said, "but I am too good a Jew to approve of the Jew who gives up his religion for profit."

2. From "Shall the Jew Intermarry? Views of Prominent New Yorkers on this Subject," *Jewish Tribune* (4 December 1908): n.p.; CZA A120/165

[A month after the debate in the Herald appeared, the *Jewish Tribune* published a page of eight brief responses to the intermarriage question, the first from Daniel Guggenheim, one from the editor of another Jewish paper, and the rest from rabbis. All opposed intermarriage. Those quoted in full, below, cover the range of explanations prevalent at the time.]

Rev. Dr. Joseph Silverman, rabbi of Temple *Emanu-El*:[1] "The marriage of Jews and non-Jews would be a severe blow to the advance of the Jewish race. It would mean the disorganization of the home and the prevention of real home life. I am unalterably opposed to such intermarriage."

Dr. Stephen S. Wise, rabbi of the Free Synagog [sic]:[2] "It has been asserted that intermarriage is the solution of the Jewish problem. On the contrary, it would mean the dissolution of the Jewish people. Intermarriage would mean the passing of the Jew. He would be dissolved in the melting pot of Christianity; and since, in my opinion, the Jew should continue to exist, I am opposed to intermarriage. The message of the Jew to humanity has not as yet been fully proclaimed, and his prophetic ideals have not been fully realized. The Jew must preserve

---

1 Prominent Reform synagogue in Manhattan.

2 Stephen Wise (1874–1949) founded the Free Synagogue as a Reform synagogue in which anyone might address the congregation without prior review of the speech, as had been the custom at Temple Emanu-El. The Free Synagogue, on the Upper West Side of Manhattan, has thus always had a progressive orientation. In 1914, Wise was one of the co-founders of the NAACP.

his religion and racial integrity to the end, in order that he may yet greatly benefit the world."

Dr. Samuel Schulman, of Temple *Beth-El*:[1] "I recently preached a sermon on 'Judaism in Its Relations to Intermarriage with Christians,' in which I opposed such intermarriages. If the Jews had followed the precepts and example of Israel Zangwill, there would today be no Judaism in America."

Rabbi Aaron Eiseman, of the Congregation *Beth Israel Bikur Cholim*, Seventy-second street and Lexington avenue:[2] "Whenever there is intermarriage there is sure to be religious death. In ninety-nine out of a hundred cases Judaism will die in families founded by men and women holding opposite religious views. Trace the genealogy of any family and you will find that the first intermarriage led to alienation and estrangement from Judaism."

3. From "Mentor," "In the Communal Armchair: The 'Melting Pot' and the Jew. Some Stray Thoughts," *Jewish Chronicle* [London] (30 January 1914): 9

["Mentor" was the pseudonym of Leopold J. Greenberg (1861–1931), editor of the *Jewish Chronicle* from 1907 to his death in 1931. His weekly column commented on issues important to Britain's English-speaking Jewish community, and he relates Zangwill's play to their own situation.]

An observation that reached the ears of the present writer when, at the Court Theatre on Monday, he was among the audience who witnessed Mr. Zangwill's play, appears worthy of record. A lady, beneficent and kindly-looking, who appeared to be enraptured by Mr. Zangwill's work, observed: "What a pity that such a fine and sturdy people—so interesting—should go into the 'Melting Pot'"! It must be confessed that the dear old lady translated accurately the sentiments of at least one other[3] who witnessed this play of more than one problem. [...]

There is one point that emerges from Mr. Zangwill's play which in these columns has been frequently referred to. The assimilation of our people is going on with a rapidity which is appalling to those who

---

1 Prominent synagogue on the Upper East Side of Manhattan, which merged with nearby Temple Emanu-El in 1927.
2 This synagogue apparently no longer exists. However, like the others whose rabbis are represented in this symposium, it was in a fashionable neighbourhood of Manhattan.
3 The writer of this column.

would see the Jewish race maintained. Exter-marriages[1] in this country are frequent, not alone, as was once the case, among the rich and those prone to dip deep into the flesh-pots of Egypt,[2] but among all classes. The immigrant coming to the East End[3] is exhibiting a proneness to exter-marriage. In the very Pale of Russia itself exter-marriages and baptisms are only a little less constant than manifestations of our people's rejection of Judaism for sheer nothingarianism.[4] If we turn to any of the large centres in Europe, or to Australia, or to Africa, we find the same story repeated as we find in America.[5] Amid Jews of Asia, assimilation is constantly claiming its trophies. Thus the question arises for those of us who think for a moment of the Jewish destiny: Is the end to be as Mr. Zangwill has predicted it before our eyes? Is the great Jewish people to go down into the "Melting Pot"?

Here, in fact, is the main objection to Mr. Zangwill's play. It presents a state of affairs in America as if it were the doom of the entire Jewish people, and a doom in which they should delight. It ignores facts about our people's history, facts which show that we have survived despite countless "Melting Pots." [...] Persistency in the face of suffering, determination in the face of every drawback—there we have the psychology of the Jew, there we have what has been his traditional quality.

The fact is that to-day, as ever, there is a simple formula. The Jew, worthy as Jew, will not be embroiled in any "Melting Pot," and—well—the "Melting Pot" is welcome to the rest! [...] It is, as the unknown lady declared, a pity that a fine and sturdy race should go over into the "Melting Pot." But the finest and the sturdiest of the race do not.

None the less, constant vigilance, constant care, constant regard to the forces that are ever ready to overbear us, must be our charge. [...] When we find thousands and thousands of our children brought up with not a glimmer or scintilla of religious education, then we know that we are giving our young over to the "Melting Pot" as assuredly as if we took them corporeally and dropped them into some molten mass in which they would quickly be dissolved. Where we find such an utter

---

1 Marriages out of one's group, or intermarriages.
2 Exodus 16:3: the abundant food of Egypt remembered by the Israelites in the desert. The phrase later attained a metaphorical meaning suggesting illicit sexuality, and here Greenberg uses it to refer to alien objects of desire.
3 The East End of London, a site of Jewish immigrant settlement comparable to the Lower East Side of New York.
4 For no religion.
5 Large numbers of Jews from the Russian Empire emigrated to British and other colonies in Australia and Africa.

disregard of the tenets of our faith that grown men and women are ignorant of precepts which but a few years ago were well-known to tiny little children, then we may be sure that the "Melting Pot" is doing its work. [... And] as it is doing its work so it is laying up for us as a people trouble and sorrow, difficulty and dilemma. For the "Melting Pot" into which Jews skip so gaily is not liked or appreciated of the peoples among whom we live. They feel it a pity that so fine and sturdy a people should go over into the "Melting Pot." Their pity is soon turned into contempt, and their contempt into hatred.

Appendix C: The Kishinev Pogrom

[What came to be known as the Kishinev Pogrom took place on Easter Sunday and Monday, 6–7 April 1903 (20–21 April according to the calendar used in western Europe and the United States). This appendix contains extracts from contemporary accounts of the pogrom in the American and British press, which subsequent studies have shown to be largely accurate, as well as photographs of the pogrom's aftermath. Further background appears in the Introduction, pp. 23–27.]

1. From "The Kishineff Outbreak. Russian Publication's Account[1] of the Assault on Jews in Streets and Synagogues," *New York Times* (11 May 1903): 3

"In Kishineff all was quiet until Easter Sunday, when at noon the crowd on the Chuplinsky place,[2] where amusement and other booths had been erected, became excited. Several Jews, who came to watch the Christians enjoying themselves, were attacked. They ran away. The cry 'Kill the Jews!' was raised, and the mob, which swelled instantly, followed in hot pursuit, particularly through Alexandrowsky Street to the new bazaar, where a fearful riot took place.

"It is impossible to account the amount of goods destroyed in a few hours. The 'hurrahs' of the rioters and the pitiful cries of the victims filled the air. Wherever a [J]ew was met he was savagely beaten into insensibility. One Jew was dragged from a street car and beaten until the mob thought he was dead. The air was filled with feathers from torn bedding. About 3 o'clock in the afternoon the rioters were signaling and whistling in the principal streets. The miscreants began there by breaking windows.

"At nightfall quiet was restored, at least in the centre of the city, and it was presumed that the disturbance was at an end. Police, troops, and mounted gendarmes[3] patroled the streets, but the real assault only began on Monday morning, when, armed with axes and crowbars, the mob set upon its work of destruction, damaging the best houses and shops, clothing themselves in pillaged clothing and carrying away huge bundles of loot.

---

1 Report of the "Central Committee for the Relief of the Kishineff Sufferers."
2 Chuflinskii Square, a large open area in the town.
3 French: soldiers acting as police, or armed police officers.

"The mob ignored the order of the patrols and the police to disperse, and continued to rob, destroy, and kill.[1] Every Jewish household was broken into and the unfortunate Jews in their terror endeavored to hide in cellars and under roofs. The mob entered the synagogues, desecrated them, destroyed the biggest house of worship, and defiled the scrolls of the law.

"The conduct of the intelligent Christians was disgraceful. They made no attempt to check the rioting. It is disgraceful. They simply walked around enjoying the frightful 'sport.'

"On Tuesday, the third day, when it became known that the troops had received orders to shoot, the rioting ceased. The Jews then came out of their houses. The streets were piled up with the debris and they presented a horrible appearance. The big Jewis[h] Hospital is filled with dead and wounded. Some bodies are mutilated beyond identification. From a distance there could be heard heart-rending groans and pitiable wailings of widows and orphans. The misery of the Jews is indescribable. There is an actual famine. The prices of all living commodities have gone up. Relief is being organized."

2. From [A Correspondent,] "The Anti-Semitic Riots in South Russia," *Times* [London] (2 May 1903): 7–8

It seems now to be established beyond doubt that the affrays of Sunday and Monday last in the streets of Kishineff, in Bessarabia, were the result of a supposed "ritual murder" by the Jews of Dubossari.[2] According to the account which has just reached me, anti-Jewish feeling has been running very high in Bessarabia and portions of other governments in South Russia for some time past; and Dubossari contains a considerable Jewish element. The Jewish Easter this year commenced on the 12th inst.[3] A few days before this date the son of a Russian[4] mysteriously disappeared, and a rumour gained currency that he had been done to death by Jews for the sake of his blood. After several days' diligent search the body was discovered. Popular

---

1 According to Judge, the governor of the province, Rudolf von Raaben, refused to act or to give orders to the soldiers: "Lacking clear instructions, and sympathizing in some instances with the anti-Jewish crowds, they made only sporadic and ineffective efforts to restore order" (65).

2 Now spelled Dubăsari, a city in Moldova 43 km from Kishinev/Chişinău. It is also spelled Dubossary in English-language accounts.

3 I.e., Passover began on 12 April (according to the Gregorian calendar, used outside the Russian Empire; on the Russian calendar it would have been 30 March).

4 A 14-year-old boy named Mikhail Rybachenko.

hatred against the local Jews had meantime been thoroughly aroused. The police in vain attempted to allay Russian suspicion of Jewish foul play by declaring that the body had been discovered without any sign of an open wound having been inflicted, and in order to convince the populace an official *post mortem* examination was decided upon without delay. The official verdict, however, failed to allay the popular suspicion and disorders immediately followed. [...] Meantime the editor of the Kishineff newspaper, the *Bessarabyetz*, a Russian of the name of Krou-shevan, had published in the *Bessarabyetz* several inflammatory articles against the Jews. [...] An especially venomous article against the Jews was published in the *Bessarabyetz* just before the commencement of the Russian holidays, and it was apparent that serious trouble was brewing for last Sunday, the first day of the Russian Easter.

The population of Kishineff is estimated at about 140,000, of whom about one-third are Jews.[1] Several influential Jews had pointed out to the Governor of Bessarabia, M. von Raabe, the necessity for taking precautionary measures for the preservation of the peace during the holidays,[2] but the Governor's answer was he considered it inexpedient to take any exceptional measures. At dawn on Sunday morning,[3] within about two or three hours after the general exodus from the long midnight services in the Russian churches, gangs of stonemasons, carpenters, labourers, and others began to break open the Jewish shops in one of the principal streets of Kishineff. By 8 a.m. riot had spread throughout most of the principal business quarters of the town. Windows and doors were smashed in, and the contents of the shops either appropriated or thrown into the streets and destroyed. [...] In one quarter of the town the Jews showed fight, and thenceforward Jews and Jewesses were assaulted with sticks, clubs, and knives wherever met with. By Sunday night several streets had been wrecked from end to end, about a dozen Jews killed outright, and close on a

---

1   Goldberg lists the total population of the city as 125,000, nearly half of them (approximately 62,500) Jewish. Judge indicates a smaller number, approximately 48,000 (21). This is closer to the 46,600 suggested by the article, but, in any case, it is clear that Jews formed a significant percentage of the city's inhabitants. Full citations to sources by J.J. Goldberg and Edward H. Judge are in notes to the Introduction.

2   Judge notes that "rumors had circulated for several weeks about impending Easter violence, and despite the fact that Jewish leaders had more than once appealed to the authorities for protection, relatively little had been done to anticipate trouble" (51–52). As with other non-English proper nouns, von Raaben's name is spelled in a variety of ways in contemporary reports.

3   This conflicts with the accounts of afternoon trouble in Chuflinskii Square, as given by Judge and in the *New York Times* article, Appendix C1 above.

hundred severely injured. During Sunday night there was a lull, but early on Monday morning the riots were renewed with increased fury. Several thousand *mujiks*[1] had tramped into the town and joined the rioters with hay-forks or whatever came first to hand. Murder and pillage were frequent, and several cases of rape too horrible for detailed description. In one quarter of the town some Jewish families sought safety in the topmost storeys of their houses, but the crowd succeeded in forcing its way into the rooms in which they were and threw them out of the windows on to the basement [sic][2] below. On Monday afternoon a telegram was received from St. Petersburg authorizing the use of the rifle and the bayonet if by no other means the riots could be suppressed. Various portions of the town were promptly occupied by bodies of Cossacks, dragoons, and other troops; a few volleys were fired into the air as a warning to the rioters, and in the space of an hour or two the riots were over. [...]

The total number of Jews and Jewesses killed is now put down at between 60 and 70,[3] and the number of seriously injured is estimated at about 500. There is a difficulty in ascertaining with accuracy the number of Russians killed and injured, but it is known that in several quarters of the town mainly occupied by Jewish butchers and artisans Russians were very severely handled.

---

1 Russian peasants.

2 By *basement* the reporter may have meant some kind of ground-floor courtyard.

3 In the end, it was 49.

3. Photographs of the Aftermath of the Kishinev Pogrom from the Archives of the YIVO Institute for Jewish Research, New York

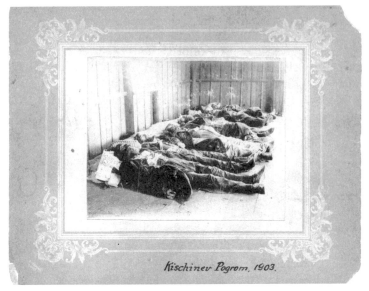

Kischinev Pogrom, 1903.

Kishinev 1903: After the pogrom: corpses of victims laid out on the floor.

גניזת ספרי התורה הנקרעים
בקעשענוב י״ג מנחם אב תרס״ג.

Kishinev 1903: After the pogrom: men pose behind desecrated Torah scrolls which have been placed on stretchers prior to burial (from the newspaper *Der Fraynd* [*The Friend*]).

4. From Chaim Nachman Bialik,[1] "The City of Slaughter," trans. Helena Frank,[2] *Selected Poems*, ed. Meyer W. Weisgal (New York: The New Palestine, 1926), 65–75

Of steel and iron, cold and hard and dumb,
Now forge thyself a heart, O man! and come
And walk the town of slaughter. Thou shalt see
With walking eyes, and touch with conscious hands,
On fences, posts, and doors,
On paving in the street, on wooden floors,
The black, dried blood, commingled here and there
With brains and splintered bone.

[...]

Then, creep to attics, clamber over roofs,
Peep in where all the black and yawning holes
Appear like ragged wounds that neither wait
Nor hope for healing more in all this world.
Outside, the sultry air is thick with feathers,
And thou shalt think to wade as in a river,
A flow of human sweat, the sweat of anguish.
Thou stumblest over heaps of goods and chattels—
They're just whole lives of men, whole lives of men,

---

1 Bialik (1873–1934; first name also spelled Haim and various other ways),
leading and much admired Hebrew poet and proponent of the development
of modern Hebrew literature. Born in Volozhin (a town now in Belarus),
Bialik lived in various places throughout the Pale of Settlement and wrote in
Hebrew long before emigrating to Palestine in 1924.

2 Helena Frank's (1872–1954) translation is the only one in the anthology not
done by Maurice Samuel (1895–1972). Frank translated from Bialik's own
Yiddish translation (of his Hebrew original) at some time prior to 1914, when
Samuel Roth (1893–1974) wrote in his collection *New Songs of Zion: A Zionist
Anthology* (New York: Judaean P, 1914), "Concerning my translation of 'The
City of Slaughter' I want to add that had I known from the start that Miss
Helena Frank had already labored successfully in that field I would never have
undertaken it. But I became aware of the existance [sic] of Miss Frank's
translation only after mine was already in press" (64). A memorial in *Jewish
Quarterly* indicates that Frank's mother was a non-Jewish British aristocrat
("Lady Agnes Grosvenor, sister of the Duke of Westminster") and her father
"of Jewish extraction," but she became a major translator and conserver of
Yiddish literature (Olga Somech Phillips, "The late Helena Frank," *Jewish
Quarterly* 1.4 [1954]: 32). The poem is often titled, as in the Hebrew, "In the
City of Slaughter."

Like broken potsherds,[1] past all mending ever—
Thou walkest, runnest, fallest in the wreckage,
In cushions, tinsel, linings, silk and satin,
All dragged and rent and torn to bits and trampled—
They're holidays and Sabbaths, joy of feast-days—
And scarfs and prayer-books, parchments, scraps of Torah,[2]
The white and holy wrappings of thy soul.
Look, look! they fold themselves about thy feet,
They kiss thy very footmarks in the dust ...
Thou fleest! whither? back to light and air?
Run, run! the sky will laugh thee, man, to scorn!
The sun will blind thee with his glowing spears,
Acacias hung with tassels white and green
Will poison thee with smells of blood and flowers,
And blossoms and feathers fall on thee in showers.
A thousand, thousand shivered bits of glass
Shall twinkle in thy dazzled eyes—behold!
For now is given thee a wondrous thing,
A twofold gift, a slaughter and a spring!

[...]

Thou seek'st the shelter of a court![3] in vain!
A heap of refuse. They beheaded twain:
A Jew—his dog, with hatchets, yesterday,
Toward the centre of the court. This morning
A hungry pig came by and dragged them hither,
And routed, grunting, in their mingled blood.
Let be! tomorrow there will fall a shower
And wash the blood into the drain, and stifle
Its cry to heaven for vengeance; [...]

The old grey spider spinning in the garret.
She knows a lot of stories—bid her tell them!
A story of a belly stuffed with feathers,
Of nostrils and of nails, of heads and hammers,
Of men who, after death, were hung head downward,

---

1   Pieces of broken ceramic pots. Well-known Jewish liturgical works compare
    human beings to clay in the hand of a divine potter.
2   The first five books of the Bible, inscribed by hand in a scroll, to be read
    during religious services. The phrase indicates literal scraps of parchment, but
    also the words and phrases on them.
3   Courtyard.

Like geese, along the rafter.
A story of a suckling child asleep,
A dead and cloven breast between its lips,
And of another child they tore in two,
Thus cutting short its last and loudest scream,
For "Ma-," was heard, but "Mama" never finished.

[...]

Appendix D: Ellis Island and Arrival in America

1. Emma Lazarus, "The New Colossus" (1883)

[Lazarus (1849–87), the daughter of a prominent New York Jewish family, was a well-known poet during her short life and corresponded with many famous literary figures. Of ancestry both Sephardic and Ashkenazic, Emma Lazarus became interested in the persecuted Russian Jews and she visited Ward's Island (precursor to Ellis Island) to meet with the immigrants themselves. She wrote the sonnet "The New Colossus" for an auction in support of the Bartholdi Pedestal Fund, which raised money to build a pedestal for Auguste Bartholdi's statue of *Liberty Enlightening the World* (the full name of the Statue of Liberty). The sonnet was read at the auction and, in 1903, engraved on a plaque that was placed in the pedestal. "The New Colossus" helped to identify the Statue of Liberty with immigration.]

Not like the brazen giant of Greek fame,[1]
With conquering limbs astride from land to land;
Here at our sea-washed, sunset gates shall stand
A mighty woman with a torch, whose flame
Is the imprisoned lightning, and her name
Mother of Exiles. From her beacon-hand
Glows world-wide welcome; her mild eyes command
The air-bridged harbor that twin cities frame.[2]

---

1   The Colossus of Rhodes, to which the title refers. It was built on the island of Rhodes in the third century BCE to commemorate a military victory, and was destroyed by an earthquake about 70 years after its construction, in 226 BCE. The idea that it straddled the harbor (line 2) is now considered a myth, but depictions indicate that it was a monumental statue of the Greek sun god Helios, with rays surrounding the head and an arm upraised, either with or without a torch. It was thus a clear model for Bartholdi's now famous statue.

2   Gregory Eiselein believes these "twin cities" are Jersey City and New York City, between which (more or less) the statue stands in New York harbour (*Emma Lazarus: Selected Poems and Other Writings* [Peterborough, ON: Broadview P, 2002], 233). Esther Schor suggests, more symbolically, that the phrase may refer to New York and Paris, since the statue came from France (*"The New Colossus," by Emma Lazarus, An Interactive Poem Annotated by Esther Schor*, http://nextbookpress.com/new-colossus/). In her biography of Lazarus, Schor indicates that Brooklyn (a separate city at the time) and New York were considered twin cities (*Emma Lazarus* [New York: Random House, 2006], 9).

"Keep, ancient lands, your storied pomp!" cries she
With silent lips. "Give me your tired, your poor,
Your huddled masses yearning to breathe free,
The wretched refuse of your teeming shore.
Send these, the homeless, tempest-tost to me,
I lift my lamp beside the golden door!"[1]

2. Illustrated Postcard, published in England by Raphael Tuck & Sons, n.d.

Ink "Pots"

Mr Zangwill.

From the collection of the late Philip Kleinberg, photocopy, gift to Meri-Jane Rochelson.

---

1 Zangwill quotes these last famous lines in his Afterword to *The Melting-Pot*, stating it is "no mere accident" that their author is a Jew (p. 176).

3. **Israel Zangwill, "The Land of Promise," *"They That Walk in Darkness": Ghetto Tragedies* (New York: Macmillan, 1899), 127–55**

[In this early story, Zangwill considers from a different perspective than *The Melting-Pot* the hardships of emigration from Russia and issues of assimilation in New York. His description of arrival procedures at Ellis Island is historically accurate.]

I

"Telegraph how many pieces you have."

In this wise did the Steamship Company convey to the astute agent its desire to know how many Russian Jews he was smuggling out of the Pale into the steerage of its Atlantic liner.[1]

The astute agent's task was simple enough. The tales he told of America were only the clarification of a nebulous vision of the land flowing with milk and honey that hovered golden-rayed before all these hungry eyes. To the denizens of the Pale, in their cellars, in their gutter-streets, in their semi-subterranean shops consisting mainly of shutters and annihilating one another's profits; to the congested populations newly reinforced by the driving back of thousands from beyond the Pale, and yet multiplying still by an improvident reliance on Providence; to the old people pauperized by the removal of the vodka business to Christian hands, and the young people dammed back from their natural outlets by Pan-Slavic ukases, and clogged with whimsical edicts and rescripts[2]—the astute agent's offer of getting you through Germany, without even a Russian passport, by a simple passage from Libau[3] to New York, was peculiarly alluring.

---

1   In the years of the Great Wave of Jewish immigration to the United States (1880–1920), most immigrants would purchase third-class tickets allowing them to travel in steerage, the lowest level of accommodation both in quality and in location on the ship. Russian Jews travelled from the Pale of Settlement, the area in the western Russian empire where Jews were permitted to live. Smuggling, as the narrator makes clear further on, was often needed at the border between Russia and Germany, from which many of the immigrants sailed. Mary Antin describes this situation in *From Plotsk to Boston* (1899; New York: Markus Wiener, 1986), 23–28, and more briefly in *The Promised Land* (1912; New York: Modern Library, 2001), 145–47.

2   Ukase is the Russian term for an edict or rescript, an official order or proclamation. Some Tsarist orders restricted the kinds of occupations Jews could hold, as well as in what parts of the Empire they could live.

3   One of the main ports of the Russian Empire, now in Latvia.

It was really almost an over-baiting of the hook on the part of the too astute agent to whisper that he had had secret information of a new thunderbolt about to be launched at the Pale; whereby the period of service for Jewish conscripts would be extended to fifteen years, and the area of service would be extended to Siberia.[1]

"Three hundred and seventy-seven pieces," ran his telegram in reply. In a letter he suggested other business he might procure for the line.

"Confine yourself to freight," the Company wrote cautiously, for even under sealed envelopes you cannot be too careful. "The more the better."

Freight! The word was not inexact. Did not even the Government reports describe these exploiters of the Muzhik[2] as in some places packed in their hovels like salt herrings in a barrel; as sleeping at night in serried masses in sties which by day were tallow or leather factories?

To be shipped as cargo came therefore natural enough. Nevertheless, each of these "pieces," being human after all, had a history, and one of these histories is here told.

II

Nowhere was the poverty of the Pale bitterer than in the weavers' colony, in which Srul betrothed himself to Biela.[3] The dowries, which had been wont to kindle so many young men's passions, had fallen to freezing-point; and Biela, if she had no near prospect of marriage, could console herself with the knowledge that she was romantically loved. Even the attraction of *kest*[4]—temporary maintenance of the young couple by the father-in-law—was wanting in Biela's case, for the simple reason that she had no father, both her parents having died of the effort to get a living. For marriage-portion and *kest*, Biela could only bring her dark beauty, and even that was perhaps less than it seemed. For you scarcely ever saw Biela apart from her homely quasi-mother, her elder sister Leah, who, like the original Leah, had "tender eyes,"[5] which combined with a pock-marked face to ensure for her

---

1 Many Jews emigrated to avoid conscription into the Tsarist army, where Jews experienced particularly harsh treatment.
2 Russian peasant; the statement is ironic, presumably reflecting government views.
3 The name Biela, in Russian, has the connotation of white or pure, innocent. Srul is a Yiddish nickname for the Hebrew name Yisrael (Israel).
4 The Yiddish term means "chestnut," as well as "room and board."
5 See Genesis 29:17.

premature recognition as an old maid. The inflamed eyelids were the only legacy Leah's father had left her.

From Srul's side, though his parents were living, came even fainter hope of the wedding-canopy. Srul's father was blind—perhaps a further evidence that the local hygienic conditions were nocuous to the eye in particular—and Srul himself, who had occupied most of his time in learning to weave Rabbinic webs,[1] had only just turned his attention to cloth, though Heaven was doubtless pleased with the gear of *Gemara* he had gathered in his short sixteen years. The old weaver had—in more than one sense—seen better days before his affliction and the great factories came on: days when the independent hand-weaver might sit busily before the loom from the raw dawn to the black midnight, taking his meals at the bench; days when, moreover, the "piece" of satin-faced cloth was many ells shorter. "But they make up for the extra length," he would say with pathetic humour, "by cutting the pay shorter."[2]

The same sense of humour enabled him to bear up against the forced rests that increasing slackness brought the hand-weavers, while the factories whirred on. "Now is the proverb fulfilled," he cried to his unsmiling wife, "for there are two Sabbaths a week." Alas! as the winter grew older and colder, it became a week of Sabbaths. The wheels stood still; in all the colony not a spool was reeled. It was unprecedented. Gradually the factories had stolen the customers. Some sat waiting dazedly for the raw yarns they knew could no longer come at this season; others left the suburb in which the colony had drowsed from time immemorial, and sought odd jobs in the town, in the frowning shadows of the factories. But none would enter the factories themselves, though these were ready to suck them in on one sole condition.

Ah! here was the irony of the tragedy. The one condition was the one condition the poor weavers could not accept. It was open to them to reduce the week of Sabbaths to its ancient and diurnal dimensions, provided the Sabbath itself came on Sunday. Nay, even the working-day offered them was less, and the wage was more than their own. The deeper irony within this irony was that the proprietor of every one of

---

1 Young Jewish men in the Pale of Settlement often spent their youth studying Talmud, a weblike compendium of Jewish law and commentary in two components, *Mishnah* and *Gemara*, mentioned later in the sentence.

2 An ell is a unit of measure. The factories employ former weavers for piece-work, for which they are paid by the number of pieces completed rather than hours worked.

these factories was a brother in Israel! Jeshurun grown fat and kicking.[1]

Even the old blind man's composure deserted him when it began to be borne in on his darkness that the younger weavers meditated surrender. The latent explosives generated through the years by their perusal of un-Jewish books in insidious "Yiddish" versions, now bade fair to be touched to eruption by this paraded prosperity of wickedness; wickedness that had even discarded the caftan and shaved the corners of its beard.[2]

"But thou, apple of my eye," the old man said to Srul, "thou wilt die rather than break the Sabbath?"

"Father," quoted the youth, with a shuddering emotion at the bare idea, "I have been young and now I am old, but never have I seen the righteous forsaken, nor his seed begging for bread."[3]

"My son! A true spark of the Patriarchs!" And the old man clasped the boy to his arms and kissed him on the pious cheeks down which the ear-locks dangled.

"But if Biela should tempt thee, so that thou couldst have the wherewithal to marry her," put in his mother, who could not keep her thoughts off grandchildren.

"Not for apples of gold, mother, will I enter the service of these serpents."

"Nevertheless, Biela is fair to see, and thou art getting on in years," murmured the mother.

"Leah would not give Biela to a Sabbath-breaker," said the old man reassuringly.

"Yes, but suppose she gives her to a bread-winner," persisted the mother. "Do not forget that Biela is already fifteen, only a year younger than thyself."

But Leah kept firm to the troth she had plighted on behalf of Biela, even though the young man's family sank lower and lower, till it was at last reduced from the little suburban wooden cottage, with the spacious courtyard, to one corner of a large town-cellar, whose population became amphibious when the Vistula[4] overflowed.

---

1   See Deuteronomy 32:15. The idea is that when the Jewish people grew comfortable they forgot about God. Jews are forbidden to work on the Sabbath, from Friday at dusk to Saturday at dusk, but most employers required a six-day work week, with Sundays, not Saturdays, off. The difficulty of this situation for immigrant Jews appears in several of Zangwill's stories.

2   The caftan was traditional Jewish dress. Cutting the corners of the beard is forbidden in Leviticus 19:27; this creates the ear-locks mentioned a few paragraphs later.

3   Srul quotes Psalms 37:25.

4   The longest river in Poland.

And Srul kept firm to the troth Israel had plighted with the Sabbath-bride, even when his father's heart no longer beat, so could not be broken. The old man remained to the last the most cheerful denizen of the cellar: perhaps because he was spared the vision of his emaciated fellow-troglodytes.[1] He called the cellar "Arba Kanfôs," after the four-cornered garment of fringes which he wore;[2] and sometimes he said these were the "Four Corners" from which, according to the Prophets, God would gather Israel.

III

In such a state of things an agent scarcely needed to be astute. "Pieces" were to be had for the picking up. The only trouble was that they were not gold pieces. The idle weavers could not defray the passage-money, still less the agent's commission for smuggling them through.

"If I only had a few hundred roubles," Srul lamented to Leah, "I could get to a land where there is work without breaking the Sabbath, a land to which Biela could follow me when I waxed in substance."

Leah supported her household of three—for there was a younger sister, Tsirrélé, who, being only nine, did not count except at mealtimes—on the price of her piece-work at the Christian umbrella factory, where, by a considerate Russian law, she could work on Sunday, though the Christians might not. Thus she earned, by literal sweating in a torrid atmosphere, three roubles, all except a varying number of kopecks, every week. And when you live largely on black bread and coffee, you may, in the course of years, save a good deal, even if you have three mouths. Therefore, Leah had the sum that Srul mentioned so wistfully, put by for a rainy day (when there should be no umbrellas to make). And as the sum had kept increasing, the notion that it might form the nucleus of an establishment for Biela and Srul had grown clearer and clearer in her mind, which it tickled delightfully. But the idea that now came to her of staking all on a possible future was agitating.

"We might, perhaps, be able to get together the money," she said tentatively. "But—" She shook her head, and the Russian proverb came to her lips. "Before the sun rises the dew may destroy you."

Srul plunged into an eager recapitulation of the agent's assurances. And before the eyes of both the marriage-canopy reared itself splendid in the Land of Promise, and the figure of Biela flitted, crowned with the bridal wreath.

---

1 Cave-dwellers.
2 Also called a *tallit katan*, an undergarment containing the fringes prescribed in Numbers 15:38.

"But what will become of your mother?" Leah asked.

Srul's soap-bubbles collapsed. He had forgotten for the moment that he had a mother.

"She might come to live with us," Leah hastened to suggest, seeing his o'erclouded face.

"Ah, no, that would be too much of a burden. And Tsirrélé, too, is growing up."

"Tsirrélé eats quite as much now as she will in ten years' time," said Leah, laughing, as she thought fondly of her dear, beautiful little one, her gay whimsies and odd caprices.

"And my mother does not eat very much," said Srul, wavering.

In this way Srul became a "piece," and was dumped down in the Land of Promise.[1]

IV

To the four females left behind—odd fragments of two families thrown into an odder one—the movements of the particular piece, Srul, were the chief interest of existence. The life in the three-roomed wooden cottage soon fell into a routine, Leah going daily to the tropical factory, Biela doing the housework and dreaming of her lover, little Tsirrélé frisking about and chattering like the squirrel she was,[2] and Srul's mother dozing and criticising and yearning for her lost son and her unborn grandchildren. By the time Srul's first letter, with its exciting pictorial stamp, arrived from the Land of Promise, the household seemed to have been established on this basis from time immemorial.

"I had a lucky escape, God be thanked," Srul wrote. "For when I arrived in New York I had only fifty-one roubles in my pocket. Now it seems that these rich Americans are so afraid of being overloaded with paupers that they will not let you in, if you have less than fifty dollars, unless you can prove you are sure to prosper. And a dollar, my dear Biela, is a good deal more than a rouble. However, blessed be the Highest One, I learned of this ukase just the day before we arrived, and was able to borrow the difference from a fellow-passenger, who lent me the money to show the Commissioners. Of course, I had to give it back as soon as I was passed, and as I had to pay him five roubles for the use of it, I set foot on the soil of freedom with only forty-six. However, it was well worth it; for just think, beloved Biela, if I had been shipped back and all that money wasted! The interpreter also said to me, 'I suppose you have got some work to do here?' 'I wish

---

1 Like immigrants from many homelands throughout American history, the breadwinner often emigrated first, to earn passage for the rest of the family.

2 Tsirrélé, in Yiddish, connotes "little chirping one."

I had,' I said. No sooner had the truth slipped out than my heart seemed turned to ice, for I feared they would reject me after all as a poor wretch out of work. But quite the contrary; it seemed this was only a trap, a snare of the fowler. Poor Caminski fell into it—you remember the red-haired weaver who sold his looms to the Maggid's[1] brother-in-law. He said he had agreed to take a place in a glove factory. It is true, you know, that some Polish Jews have made a glove town in the north, so the poor man thought that would sound plausible. Hence you may expect to see Caminski's red hair back again, unless he takes ship again from Libau and tells the truth at the second attempt. I left him howling in a wooden pen, and declaring he would kill himself rather than face his friends at home with the brand on his head of not being good enough for America. He did not understand that contract-labourers are not let in. Protection is the word they call it. Hence, I thank God that my father—his memory for a blessing!—taught me to make Truth the law of my mouth, as it is written. Verily was the word of the Talmud (Tractate Sabbath) fulfilled at the landing-stage: 'False-hood cannot stay, but truth remains forever.' With God's help, I shall remain here all my life, for it is a land overflowing with milk and honey. I had almost forgotten to tell my dove that the voyage was hard and bitter as the Egyptian bondage; not because of the ocean, over which I passed as easily as our forefathers over the Red Sea, but by reason of the harshness of the overseers, who regarded not our com-plaints that the meat was not *kosher*, as promised by the agent. Also the butter and meat plates were mixed up. I and many with me lived on dry bread, nor could we always get hot water to make coffee. When my Biela comes across the great waters—God send her soon—she must take with her salt meat of her own."

From the first, Srul courageously assumed that the meat would soon have to be packed; nay, that Leah might almost set about salting it at once. Even the slow beginnings of his profits as a peddler did not daunt him. "A great country," he wrote on paper stamped with the Stars and Stripes, with an eagle screaming on the envelope. "No special taxes for the Jews, permission to travel where you please, the schools open freely to our children, no passports and papers at every step, above all, no conscription. No wonder the people call it God's own country. Truly, as it is written, this is none other but the House of God, this is the Gate of Heaven.[2] And when Biela comes, it will be Heaven." Letters like this enlarged the little cottage as with an Amer-ican room, brightened it as with a fresh wash of blue paint. Despite the

---

1 An itinerant preacher, skilled as a story-teller.
2 Genesis 28:17.

dreary grind of the week, Sabbaths and festivals found the household joyous enough. The wedding-canopy of Srul and Biela was a beacon of light for all four, which made life livable as they struggled toward it. Nevertheless, it came but slowly to meet them: nearly three years oozed by before Srul began to lift his eye toward a store. The hereditary weaver of business combinations had emerged tardily from beneath the logic-weaver and the cloth-weaver, but of late he had been finding himself. "If I could only get together five hundred dollars clear," he wrote to Leah. "For that is all I should have to pay down for a ladies' store near Broadway, and just at the foot of the stairs of the Elevated Railway. What a pity I have only four hundred and thirty-five dollars! Stock and goodwill, and only five hundred dollars cash! The other five hundred could stand over at five per cent. If I were once in the store I could gradually get some of the rooms above (there is already a parlour, in which I shall sleep), and then, as soon as I was making a regular profit, I could send Biela and mother their passage-money, and my wife could help 'the boss' behind the counter."

To hasten the rosy day Leah sent thirty-five roubles, and presently, sure enough, Srul was in possession, and a photograph of the store itself came over to gladden their weary eyes and dilate those of the neighbours. The photograph of Srul, which had come eighteen months before, was not so suited for display, since his peaked cap and his caftan had been replaced by a jacket and a bowler, and, but for the ear-locks which were still in the picture, he would have looked like a factory-owner. In return, Srul received a photograph of the four—taken together, for economy's sake—Leah with her arm around Biela's waist, and Tsirrélé sitting in his mother's lap.

V

But a long, wearying struggle was still before the new "boss," and two years crept along, with their turns of luck and ill-luck, of bargains and bad debts, ere the visionary marriage-canopy (that seemed to span the Atlantic) began to stand solidly on American soil. The third year was not half over ere Srul actually sent the money for Biela's passage, together with a handsome "waist"[1] from his stock, for her to wear. But Biela was too timid to embark alone without Srul's mother, whose fare Srul could not yet manage to withdraw from his capital. Leah, of course, offered to advance it, but Biela refused this vehemently, because a new hope had begun to spring up in her breast. Why should she be parted from her family at all? Since her marriage had been

---

1 Woman's shirt or blouse.

delayed these five and a half years, a few months more or less could make no difference. Let Leah's savings, then, be for Leah's passage (and Tsirrélé's) and to give her a start in the New World. "It rains, even in America, and there are umbrella factories there, too," she urged. "You will make twice the living. Look at Srul!"

And there was a new fear, too, which haunted Biela's aching heart, but which she dared not express to Leah. Leah's eyes were getting worse. The temperature of the factory was a daily hurt, and then, too, she had read so many vilely printed Yiddish books and papers by the light of the tallow candle. What if she were going blind? What if, while she, Biela, was happy with Srul, Leah should be starving with Tsirrélé? No, they must all remain together: and she clung to her sister, with tears.

To Leah the prospect of witnessing her sister's happiness was so seductive that she tried to take the lowest estimate of her own chances of finding work in New York. Her savings, almost eaten up by the journey, could not last long, and it would be terrible to have to come upon Srul for help, a man with a wife and (if God were good) children, to say nothing of his old mother. No, she could not risk Tsirrélé's bread.

But the increased trouble with her eyes turned her in favour of going, though, curiously enough, for a side reason quite unlike Biela's. Leah, too, was afraid of a serious breakdown, though she would not hint her fears to any one else. From her miscellaneous Yiddish reading she had gathered that miraculous eye-doctors lived in Königsberg.[1] Now a journey to Germany was not to be thought of; if she went to America, however, it could be taken en route. It would be a sort of saving, and few things appealed to Leah as much as economy. This was why, some four months later, the ancient furniture of the blue-washed cottage was sold off, and the quartette set their faces for America by way of Germany. The farewell to the home of their youth took place in the cemetery among the high-shouldered Hebrew-speaking stones. Leah and Biela passionately invoked the spirits of their dead parents and bade them watch over their children. The old woman scribbled Srul and Biela's interlinked names over the flat tomb of a holy scholar. "Take their names up to the Highest One," she pleaded. "Entreat that their quiver be full,[2] for the sake of thy righteousness."

More dead than alive, the four "pieces" with their bundles arrived at Hamburg. Days and nights of travelling, packed like "freight" in

---

1 A port city in Germany that was taken over by the Soviet Union in 1945, renamed Kaliningrad in 1946. Still part of Russia today, it lies between Poland and Lithuania.

2 That they have many children (from Psalms 127:4–5).

hard, dirty wooden carriages, the endless worry of passports, tickets, questions, hygienic inspections and processes, the illegal exactions of petty officials, the strange phantasmagoria of places and faces—all this had left them dazed. Only two things kept up their spirits—the image of Srul waiting on the Transatlantic wharf in hymeneal[1] attire, and the "pooh-pooh" of the miraculous Königsberg doctor, reassuring Leah as to her eyes. There was nothing radically the matter. Even the inflamed eyelids—though incurable, because hereditary—would improve with care. Peasant-like, Leah craved a lotion. "The sea voyage and the rest will do you more good than my medicines. And don't read so much." Not a groschen did Leah have to pay for the great specialist's services. It was the first time in her hard life anybody had done anything for her for nothing, and her involuntary weeping over this phenomenon tended to hurt the very eyelids under attention. They were still further taxed by the kindness of the Jewish committee at Hamburg, on the look-out to smooth the path of poor emigrants and overcome their dietary difficulties. But it was a crowded ship, and our party reverted again to "freight." With some of the other females, they were accommodated in hammocks swung over the very dining-tables, so that they must needs rise at dawn and be cleared away before breakfast. The hot, oily whiff of the cooking-engines came through the rocking doorway. Of the quartette, only Tsirrélé escaped sea-sickness, but "baby" was too accustomed to be petted and nursed to be able suddenly to pet and nurse, and she would spend hours on the slip of lower deck, peering into the fairy saloons which were vivified by bugle instead of bell, and in which beautiful people ate dishes fit for the saints in Heaven. By an effort of will, Leah soon returned to her rôle of factotum,[2] but the old woman and Biela remained limp to the end. Fortunately, there was only one day of heavy rolling and battened-down hatches. For the bulk of the voyage the great vessel brushed the pack of waves disdainfully aside. And one wonderful day, amid unspeakable joy, New York arrived, preceded by a tug and by a boat that conveyed inquiring officials. The great statue of Liberty, on Bedloe's Island,[3] upheld its torch to light the new-comers' path. Srul—there he is on the wharf, dear old Srul!—God bless him! despite his close-cropped hair and his shaven ear-locks. Ah! Heaven be praised! Don't you see him waving? Ah, but we, too, must be content with waving. For here only the *tschinovniks*[4] of the gilded saloon may land. The "freight" must be packed later into rigid gangs, according to

---

1 Wedding.
2 One who does all kinds of work.
3 Renamed Liberty Island in 1956.
4 Russian: officials.

the ship's manifest, transferred to a smaller steamer and discharged on Ellis Island,[1] a little beyond Bedloe's.

VI

And at Ellis Island a terrible thing happened, unforeseen—a shipwreck in the very harbour.

As the "freight" filed slowly along the corridor-cages in the great bare hall, like cattle inspected at ports by the veterinary surgeon, it came into the doctor's head that Leah's eye-trouble was infectious. "Granular lids—contagious," he diagnosed it on paper. And this diagnosis was a flaming sword that turned every way, guarding against Leah the Land of Promise.

"But it is not infectious," she protested in her best German. "It is only in the family."

"So I perceive," dryly replied America's Guardian Angel, who was now examining the obvious sister clinging to Leah's skirts. And in Biela, heavy-eyed with sickness and want of sleep, his suspicious vision easily discovered a reddish rim of eyelid that lent itself to the same fatal diagnosis, and sent her to join Leah in the dock of the rejected. The fresh-faced Tsirrélé and the wizen-faced mother of Srul passed unscrutinized, and even the dread clerk at the desk who asked questions was content with their oath that the wealthy Srul would support them. Srul was, indeed, sent for at once, as Tsirrélé was too pretty to be let out under the mere protection of a Polish[2] crone.

When the full truth that neither she nor Biela was to set foot in New York burst through the daze in Leah's brain, her protest grew frantic.

"But my sister has nothing the matter with her—nothing. O *gnädiger Herr*,[3] have pity. The Königsberg doctor—the great doctor—told me I had no disease, no disease at all. And even if I have, my sister's eyes are pure as the sunshine. Look, *mein Herr*, look again. See," and she held up Biela's eyelids and passionately kissed the wet bewildered eyes. "She is to be married, my lamb—her bridegroom awaits her on the wharf. Send *me* back, *gnädiger Herr*; I ought not to have come. But for God's sake, don't keep Biela out, don't." She wrung her hands. But the marriage card had been played too often in that hall of despairing

---

1 The US immigration inspection station at Ellis Island opened in 1892 and soon became the busiest immigration entry point in the United States. In 1956 it closed as an inspection station; in 1965, it became part of the Statue of Liberty National Monument; and in 1990 became home to a museum that seeks to re-create the immigrants' experience.

2 Parts of historical Poland were within the Russian Pale of Settlement.

3 German: My lord (literally, merciful lord).

dodges. "Oh, *Herr Doktor*," and she kissed the coat-tail of the ship's doctor, "plead for us; speak a word for her."

The ship's doctor spoke a word on his own behalf. It was he who had endorsed the two girls' health-certificates at Hamburg, and he would be blamed by the Steamship Company, which would have to ship the sisters back free, and even defray their expenses while in quarantine at the dépôt. He ridiculed the idea that the girls were suffering from anything contagious. But the native doctor frowned, immovable.

Leah grew hysteric. It was the first time in her life she had lost her sane standpoint. "Your own eye is affected," she shrieked, her dark pock-marked face almost black with desperate anger, "if you cannot see that it is only because my sister has been weeping, because she is ill from the voyage. But she carries no infection—she is healthy as an ox, and her eye is the eye of an eagle!" She was ordered to be silent, but she shrieked angrily, "The German doctors know, but the Americans have no *Bildung*."[1]

"Oh, don't, Leah," moaned Biela, throwing her arms round the panting breast. "What's the use?" But the irrepressible Leah got an S.I. ticket of Special Inquiry, forced a hearing in the Commissioners' Court.

"Let her in, kind gentlemen, and send back the other one. Tsirrélé will go back with me. It does not matter about the little one."

The kind gentlemen on the bench were really kind, but America must be protected.

"You can take the young one and the old one both back with you," the interpreter told her. "But they are the only ones we can let in."

Leah and Biela were driven back among the damned. The favoured twain stood helplessly in their happier compartment. Even Tsirrélé, the squirrel, was dazed. Presently the spruce Srul arrived—to find the expected raptures replaced by funereal misery. He wormed his way dizzily into the cage of the rejected. It was not the etiquette of the Pale to kiss one's betrothed bride, but Srul stared dully at Biela without even touching her hand, as if the Atlantic already rolled again between them. Here was a pretty climax to the dreams of years!

"My poor Srul, we must go back to Hamburg to be married," faltered Biela.

"And give up my store?" Srul wailed. "Here the dollar spins round. We have now what one names a boom. There is no land on earth like ours."

The forlornness of the others stung Leah to her senses.

"Listen, Srul," she said hurriedly. "It is all my fault, because I wanted to share in the happiness. I ought not to have come. If we had

---

1 German: education, enlightenment.

not been together they never would have suspected Biela's eyes—who would notice the little touch of inflammation which is the most she has ever suffered from? She shall come again in another ship, all alone—for she knows now how to travel. Is it not so, Biela, my lamb? I will see you on board, and Srul will meet you here, although not till you have passed the doctor, so that no one will have a chance of remembering you. It will cost a heap, alas! but I can get some work in Hamburg, and the Jews there have hearts of gold. Eh, Biela, my poor lamb?"

"Yes, yes, Leah, you can always give yourself a counsel," and Biela put her wet face to her sister's, and kissed the pock-marked cheek.

Srul acquiesced eagerly. No one remembered for the moment that Leah would be left alone in the Old World. The problem of effecting the bride's entry blocked all the horizon.

"Yes, yes," said Srul. "The mother will look after Tsirrélé, and in less than three weeks Biela will slip in."

"No, three weeks is too soon," said Leah. "We must wait a little longer till the doctor forgets."

"Oh, but I have already waited so long!" whimpered Srul.

Leah's eyes filled with sympathetic tears. "I ought not to have made so much fuss. Now she will stick in the doctor's mind. Forgive me, dear Srul, I will do my best and try to make amends."

Leah and Biela were taken away to the hospital, where they remained isolated from the world till the steamer sailed back to Hamburg. Herein, generously lodged, they had ample leisure to review the situation. Biela discovered that the new plan would leave Leah deserted, Leah remembered that she would be deserting little Tsirrélé. Both were agreed that Tsirrélé must go back with them, till they bethought themselves that her passage would have to be paid for, as she was not refused. And every kopeck was precious now. "Let the child stay till I get back," said Biela. "Then I will send her to you."

"Yes, it is best to let her stay awhile. I myself may be able to join you after all. I will go back to Königsberg, and the great doctor will write me out a certificate that my affliction is not contagious."

At the very worst—if even Biela could not get in—Srul should sell his store and come back to the Old World. It would put off the marriage again. But they had waited so long. "So let us cheer up after all, and thank the Lord for His mercies. We might all have been drowned on the voyage."

Thus the sisters' pious conclusion.

But though Srul and his mother and Tsirrélé got on board to see them off, and Tsirrélé gave graphic accounts of the wonders of the store and the rooms prepared for the bride, to say nothing of the great city itself, and Srul brought Biela and Leah splendid specimens of his stock for their adornment, yet it was a horrible thing for them to go back again without having once trodden the sidewalks of the Land of Promise. And when the others were tolled off, as by a funeral bell, and became specks in a swaying crowd; when the dock receded and the cheers and good-byes faded, and the waving handkerchiefs became a blur, and the Statue of Liberty dwindled, and the lone waste of waters faced them once more, Leah's optimism gave way, a chill sinister shadow fell across her new plan, some ominous intuition traversed her like a shudder, and she turned away lest Biela should see her tears.

VII

This despair did not last long. It was not in Leah's nature to despair. But her wildest hopes were exceeded when she set foot again in Hamburg and explained her hard case to the good committee, and a member gave her an informal hint which was like a flash of light from Heaven—its answer to her ceaseless prayer. Ellis Island was not the only way of approaching the Land of Promise. You could go round about through Canada, where they were not so particular, and you could slip in by rail from Montreal without attracting much attention. True, there was the extra expense.

Expense! Leah would have gladly parted with her last rouble to unite Biela with her bridegroom. There must be no delay. A steamer for Canada was waiting to sail. What a fool she had been not to think that out for herself! Yes, but there was Biela's timidity again to consider. Travel by herself through this unknown Canada! And then if they were not so particular, why could not Leah slip through likewise?

"Yes, but my eyes are more noticeable. I might again do you an injury."

"We will separate at the landing-stage and the frontier. We will pretend to be strangers." Biela's wits were sharpened by the crisis.

"Well, I can only lose the passage-money," said Leah, and resolved to take the risk. She wrote a letter to Srul explaining the daring invasion of New York overland which they were to attempt, and was about to post it, when Biela said:—

"Poor Srul! And if I shall not get in after all!" Leah's face fell.

"True," she pondered. "He will have a more heart-breaking disappointment than before."

"Let us not kindle their hopes. After all, if we get in, we shall only be a few days later than our letter. And then think of the joy of the surprise."

"You are right, Biela," and Leah's face glowed again with the anticipated joy of the surprise.

The journey to Canada was longer than to the States, and the "freight" was less companionable. There were fewer Jews and women, more stalwart shepherds, miners, and dock-labourers. When after eleven days, land came, it was not touched at, but only remained cheeringly on the horizon for the rest of the voyage. At last the sisters found themselves unmolested on one of the many wharves of Montreal. But they would not linger a day in this unhomely city. The next morning saw them, dazed and worn out but happy-hearted, dodging the monstrous catapults of the New York motor-cars, while a Polish porter helped them with their bundles and convoyed them toward Srul's store. Ah, what ecstasy to be unregarded units of this free chaotic crowd. Outside the store—what a wonderful store it was, larger than the largest in the weavers' colony!—the sisters paused a moment to roll the coming bliss under their tongues. They peeped in. Ah, there is Srul behind the counter, waiting for customers. Ah, ah, he little knows what customers are waiting for him! They turned and kissed each other for mere joy.

"Draw your shawl over your face," whispered Leah merrily. "Go in and ask him if he has a wedding-veil." Biela slipped in, brimming over with mischief and tears.

"Yes, Miss?" said Srul, with his smartest store manner.

"I want a wedding-veil of white lace," she said in Yiddish. At her voice Srul started. Biela could keep up the joke no longer. "Srul, my darling Srul!" she cried hysterically, her arms yearning to reach him across the counter.

He drew back, pale, gasping for breath.

"Ah, my dear ones!" blubbered Leah, rushing in. "God has been good to you, after all."

"But—but—how did you get in?" he cried, staring.

"Never mind how we got in," said Leah, every pock-mark glistening with smiles and tears. "And where is Tsirrélé—my dear little Tsirrélé?"

"She—she is out marketing, with the mother."

"And the mother?"

"She is well and happy."

"Thank God!" said Leah fervently, and beckoned the porter with the bundles.

"But—but I let the room," he said, flushing. "I did not know that— I could not afford—"[1]

"Never mind, we will find a room. The day is yet high." She settled with the porter.

Meantime Srul had begun playing nervously with a pair of scissors. He snipped a gorgeous piece of stuff to fragments.

"What are you doing?" said Biela at last.

---

1 It was common for Jewish immigrants to take in others as boarders.

"Oh—I—" he burst into a nervous laugh. "And so you ran the blockade after all. But—but I expect customers every minute—we can't talk now. Go inside and rest, Biela: you will find a sofa in the parlour. Leah, I want—I want to talk to you."

Leah flashed a swift glance at him as Biela, vaguely chilled, moved through the back door into the revivifying splendours of the parlour.

"Something is wrong, Srul," Leah said hoarsely. "Tsirrélé is not here. You feared to tell us."

He hung his head. "I did my best."

"She is ill—dead, perhaps! My beautiful angel!"

He opened his eyes. "Dead? No. Married!"

"What! To whom?"

He turned a sickly white. "To me."

In all that long quest of the canopy, Leah had never come so near fainting as now. The horror of Ellis Island was nothing to this. That scene resurged, and Tsirrélé's fresh beauty, unflecked by the voyage, came up luridly before her; the "baby," whom the unnoted years had made a young woman of fifteen, while they had been aging and staling Biela.

"But—but this will break Biela's heart," she whispered, heartbroken.

"How was I to know Biela would *ever* get in?" he said, trying to be angry. "Was I to remain a bachelor all my life, breaking the Almighty's ordinance?[1] Did I not wait and wait faithfully for Biela all those years?"

"You could have migrated elsewhere," she said faintly.

"And ruin my connection—and starve?" His anger was real by now. "Besides I have married into the family—it is almost the same thing. And the old mother is just as pleased."

"Oh, she!" and all the endured bitterness of the long years was in the exclamation. "All she wants is grandchildren."

"No, it isn't," he retorted. "Grandchildren with good eyes."

"God forgive you," was all the lump in Leah's throat allowed her to reply. She steadied herself with a hand on the counter, striving to repossess her soul for Biela's sake.

A customer came in, and the tragic universe dwindled to a prosaic place in which ribbons existed in unsatisfactory shades.

"Of course we must go this minute," Leah said, as Srul clanked the coins into the till. "Biela cannot ever live here with you now."

"Yes, it is better so," he assented sulkily. "Besides, you may as well know at once. I keep open on the Sabbath, and that would not have

---

1 Genesis 1:28: Be fruitful and multiply.

pleased Biela. That is another reason why it was best not to marry Biela. Tsirrélé doesn't seem to mind."

The very ruins of her world seemed toppling now. But this new revelation of Tsirrélé's and his own wickedness seemed only of a piece with the first—indeed, went far to account for it.

"You break the Sabbath, after all!"

He shrugged his shoulders. "We are not in Poland any longer. No dead flies here. Everybody does it. Shut the store two days a week! I should get left."

"And you bring your mother's gray hairs down with sorrow to the grave."

"My mother's gray hairs are no longer hidden by a stupid black *Shaitel*.[1] That is all. I have explained to her that America is the land of enlightenment and freedom. Her eyes are opened."

"I trust to God, your father's—peace be upon him!—are still shut!" said Leah as she walked with slow steady steps into the parlour, to bear off her wounded lamb.

---

1 A wig that observant married women and widows wear to cover their hair.

Appendix E: The Settlement House

[A settlement house plays a significant role in *The Melting-Pot* as the place where Vera Revendal meets David Quixano and where his American Symphony is first performed. As an institution, the settlement helped immigrants acclimate to American life with educational and cultural programs as well as training workshops and programs on health and hygiene. The Introduction to this edition discusses the movement's history and the role of educated young people such as Vera in its work (see pp. 27–31).]

1. From Jane Addams, "Chapter VI: Subjective Necessity for Social Settlements," *Twenty Years at Hull-House* (New York: Macmillan, 1910), 113–27

[Addams (1860–1935) originally gave this talk in 1892, at a gathering of Ethical Culture Societies, organizations that promoted humanistic beliefs as a foundation for social action. Her speech reflects both her upper-class perspective on social responsibility and her impassioned feminism as she explains the need for activist outlets for well-to-do young women.]

This paper is an attempt to analyze the motives which underlie a movement based, not only upon conviction, but upon genuine emotion, wherever educated young people are seeking an outlet for that sentiment for universal brotherhood, which the best spirit of our times is forcing from an emotion into a motive. These young people accomplish little toward the solution of this social problem, and bear the brunt of being cultivated into unnourished, oversensitive lives. They have been shut off from the common labor by which they live which is a great source of moral and physical health. They feel a fatal want of harmony between their theory and their lives, a lack of coördination between thought and action. I think it is hard for us to realize how seriously many of them are taking to the notion of human brotherhood, how eagerly they long to give tangible expression to the democratic ideal. [...] There is something primordial about these motives, but I am perhaps overbold in designating them as a great desire to share the race life.[1] We all bear traces of the starvation struggle which for so long made up the life of the race. [...] To shut one's self away from that half of the race life is to shut one's self away from the most

---

1   The life of the human race, as further discussion makes clear.

vital part of it; it is to live out but half the humanity to which we have been born heir and to use but half our faculties. We have all had longings for a fuller life which should include the use of these faculties. [...]

You may remember the forlorn feeling which occasionally seizes you when you arrive early in the morning a stranger in a great city: the stream of laboring people goes past you as you gaze through the plate-glass window of your hotel; you see hard working men lifting great burdens; you hear the driving and jostling of huge carts and your heart sinks with a sudden sense of futility. The door opens behind you and you turn to the man who brings you in your breakfast with a quick sense of human fellowship. You find yourself praying that you may never lose your hold on it all. A more poetic prayer would be that the great mother breasts of our common humanity, with its labor and suffering and its homely comforts, may never be withheld from you. You turn helplessly to the waiter and feel that it would be almost grotesque to claim from him the sympathy you crave because civilization has placed you apart, but you resent your position with a sudden sense of snobbery. Literature is full of portrayals of these glimpses [...].

"It is true that there is nothing after disease, indigence and a sense of guilt, so fatal to health and to life itself as the want of a proper outlet for active faculties."[1] I have seen young girls suffer and grow sensibly lowered in vitality in the first years after they leave school. In our attempt then to give a girl pleasure and freedom from care we succeed, for the most part, in making her pitifully miserable. She finds "life" so different from what she expected it to be. She is besotted with innocent little ambitions, and does not understand this apparent waste of herself, this elaborate preparation, if no work is provided for her. There is a heritage of noble obligation[2] which young people accept and long to perpetuate. The desire for action, the wish to right wrong and alleviate suffering haunts them daily. Society smiles at it indulgently instead of making it of value to itself. The wrong to them begins even farther back, when we restrain the first childish desires for "doing good," and tell them that they must wait until they are older and better fitted. We intimate that social obligation begins at a fixed date, forgetting that it begins with birth itself. [...] Parents are often inconsistent: they deliberately expose their daughters to knowledge of the distress in the world; they send them to hear missionary addresses on famines in India and China; they accompany them to lectures on the suffering in Siberia; they agitate together over the forgotten region of East London. In addition to this, from babyhood the altruistic tendencies

---

1   Addams here quotes John Stuart Mill (1806–73) in *The Subjection of Women* (1869).

2   Often referred to by the French term *noblesse oblige*. See p. 98, n. 2.

of these daughters are persistently cultivated. They are taught to be self-forgetting and self-sacrificing, to consider the good of the whole before the good of the ego. But when all this information and culture show results, when the daughter comes back from college and begins to recognize her social claim to the "submerged tenth,"[1] and to evince a disposition to fulfill it, the family claim is strenuously asserted; she is told that she is unjustified, ill-advised in her efforts. If she persists, the family too often are injured and unhappy unless the efforts are called missionary and the religious zeal of the family carry them over their sense of abuse. [...] The girl loses something vital out of her life to which she is entitled. She is restricted and unhappy; her elders meanwhile, are unconscious of the situation and we have all the elements of a tragedy. [...]

The Settlement then, is an experimental effort to aid in the solution of the social and industrial problems which are engendered by the modern conditions of life in a great city. It insists that these problems are not confined to any one portion of a city. It is an attempt to relieve, at the same time, the overaccumulation at one end of society and the destitution at the other; but it assumes that this overaccumulation and destitution is most sorely felt in the things that pertain to social and educational privileges. From its very nature it can stand for no political or social propaganda. It must, in a sense, give the warm welcome of an inn to all such propaganda, if perchance one of them be found an angel.[2] The only thing to be dreaded in the Settlement is that it lose its flexibility, its power of quick adaptation, its readiness to change its methods as its environment may demand. It must be open to conviction and must have a deep and abiding sense of tolerance. It must be hospitable and ready for experiment. It should demand from its residents[3] a scientific patience in the accumulation of facts[4] and the steady holding of their sympathies as one of the best instruments for that accumulation. It must be grounded in a philosophy whose foundation is on the solidarity of the human race, a philosophy which will not waver when the race happens to be represented by a drunken woman or an idiot boy. Its residents must be emptied of all conceit of opinion and all self-assertion, and ready to arouse and interpret the public opinion of their neighborhood. They must be content to live

---

1   The supposed percentage of the English population living permanently in poverty, according to William Booth in *In Darkest England and the Way Out* (1890). Booth (1829–1912) founded the Salvation Army.
2   See Genesis 18:1–10; also Luke 2:7.
3   The upper-middle-class workers who live in the settlement house.
4   Reformers in the Progressive Era believed that scientific study could help bring about reform.

quietly side by side with their neighbors, until they grow into a sense of relationship and mutual interests. Their neighbors are held apart by differences of race[1] and language which the residents can more easily overcome. They are bound to see the needs of their neighborhood as a whole, to furnish data for legislation, and to use their influence to secure it. In short, residents are pledged to devote themselves to the duties of good citizenship and to the arousing of the social energies which too largely lie dormant in every neighborhood given over to industrialism. They are bound to regard the entire life of their city as organic, to make an effort to unify it, and to protest against its over-differentiation.

2. From Jane Addams, "Chapter XI: Immigrants and Their Children," *Twenty Years at Hull-House* (New York: Macmillan, 1910), 231–58

[In this chapter, from which a small extract is presented, Addams considers the kinds of generational conflict among various groups that Zangwill illustrates in *The Melting-Pot*.]

From our very first months at Hull-House we found it much easier to deal with the first generation of crowded city life than with the second or third, because it is more natural and cast in a simpler mold. The Italian and Bohemian[2] peasants who live in Chicago still put on their bright holiday clothes on a Sunday and go to visit their cousins. They tramp along with at least a suggestion of having once walked over plowed fields and breathed country air. The second generation of city poor too often have no holiday clothes and consider their relations a "bad lot." I have heard a drunken man in a maudlin stage babble of his good country mother and imagine he was driving the cows home, and I knew that his little son who laughed loud at him would be drunk earlier in life and would have no pastoral interlude to his ravings. Hospitality still survives among foreigners, although it is buried under false pride among the poorest Americans. One thing seemed clear in regard to entertaining immigrants; to preserve and keep whatever of value their past life contained and to bring them in contact with a better type of Americans. For several years, every Saturday evening the entire families of our Italian neighbors were our guests. These evenings were very popular during our first winters at Hull-House. Many educated Italians helped us, and the house became known as a place

1 Nationality or ethnicity.
2 From the westernmost part of what is now the Czech Republic. Many Bohemians were ethnic Germans and spoke German.

where Italians were welcome and where national holidays were observed. They come to us with their petty lawsuits, sad relics of the *vendetta*, with their incorrigible boys, with their hospital cases, with their aspirations for American clothes, and with their needs for an interpreter. [...]

An evening similar in purpose to the one devoted to the Italians was organized for the Germans, in our first year. Owing to the superior education of our Teutonic[1] guests and the clever leading of a cultivated German woman, these evenings reflected something of that cozy social intercourse which is found in its perfection in the fatherland. Our guests sang a great deal in the tender minor of the German folksong or in the rousing spirit of the Rhine, and they slowly but persistently pursued a course in German history and literature, recovering something of that poetry and romance which they had long since resigned with other good things. We found strong family affection between them and their English-speaking children, but their pleasures were not in common, and they seldom went out together. Perhaps the greatest value of the Settlement to them was in placing large and pleasant rooms with musical facilities at their disposal, and in reviving their almost forgotten enthusiasms. I have seen sons and daughters stand in complete surprise as their mother's knitting needles softly beat time to the song she was singing, or her worn face turned rosy under the hand-clapping as she made an old-fashioned courtsey at the end of a German poem. It was easy to fancy a growing touch of respect in her children's manner to her, and a rising enthusiasm for German literature and reminiscence on the part of all the family, an effort to bring together the old life and the new, a respect for the older cultivation, and not quite so much assurance that the new was the best.

3. The Settlement House Pledge to the Flag

[This section presents excerpts from articles in the *New York Times* and the *Times* of London, and from H.G. Wells's *The Future in America* (1906), all of which depict scenes similar to the patriotic settlement house event that David Quixano describes early in Act II. Wells records the complete pledge to the flag exactly as it appears in Zangwill's play, although all three accounts quote a version of the pledge; the *New York Times* describes a more enthusiastic and widespread celebration than does its London counterpart. Zangwill may have based his description on any or all of these accounts.]

---

1   Germanic.

a. [From Our Correspondent,] "New York Municipal Celebration," *Times* [London] (27 May 1903): 7

New York to-day is celebrating the 250th anniversary of the foundation of civic government here. Flags are flying everywhere in the business section, some of the important buildings are elaborately decorated, and the City Hall and the City Hall Park are lavishly adorned with flags and bunting. As far as the public are concerned, however, the celebration seems to be of a somewhat perfunctory character. It has often been remarked that there is less civic pride in New York than in many a mushroom town[1] of the West, and though among the more thoughtful section of the community there is to-day a full appreciation of the significance of the celebration, it is doubtful whether the great majority of New Yorkers are aware even that the celebration is going on. Perhaps the most interesting of all the many events of the day was the celebration at the Educational Alliance in the east-side tenement section, where 500 children who arrived here less than a month ago from Russia took part in patriotic exercises. Some of the parents of these children were compelled to flee from Russia, and in view of the recent horrors in Bessarabia[2] peculiar significance attached to the words in which the children pledged allegiance to the star-spangled banner:—"We, the natives of distant lands who find rest under thy folds, do pledge our hearts, our lives, and our sacred honour to love and protect thee, our country, and the liberty of the American people for ever." General Greene,[3] the Police Commissioner, addressed the children in Russian, making a particularly happy speech, which added one more to the laurels he has gained since he took charge of the police force five months ago.

Mr. Low,[4] the Mayor, received many telegrams of congratulation to-day, including messages from the London county Council, the Corporation of York,[5] and the Municipal and County Club of Great Britain.

---

1 A town that develops quickly, like a mushroom.
2 Where Kishinev is located; the pogrom had taken place less than two months earlier.
3 Francis Vinton Greene (1850–1921), New York City Police Commissioner, 1903–04.
4 Seth Low (1850–1916), educator and political figure who served as president of Columbia University from 1890 to 1901, when he became mayor of New York. He lost re-election in 1903.
5 A major city in the north of England; New York was named for the Duke of York at the time of English settlement.

b. From "Father Knickerbocker Celebrates Birthday," *New York Times* (27 May 1903): 1

[This was a much longer article than the one in the London *Times*, with several subsections giving accounts of celebrations throughout the city and at many schools. This extract deals specifically with immigrants.]

Police Commissioner Greene addressed about 500 boys and girls at the Educational Alliance in the forenoon. The children were members of the classes in English for immigrants at the Baron de Hirsch School.[1] [...]

It was an inspiring sight to witness the youngsters, whose parents were compelled recently to fly[2] from Russia to escape religious persecution, publicly pledging their allegiance to the American flag[3] [...].

Commissioner Greene saluted the children in Russian and asked them as to their health and happiness in their native language. Then in English he told how, twenty-five years ago, he served with the Russian Army at the gates of Constantinople, fighting against the Turks.[4] [...]

[L]ast night [New York] twinkled with electric lights at every skyscraper window, so that to the surrounding communities it looked as if Manhattan were ablaze.

There were other and very small rays on the east side,[5] where patriotic newcomers lit up their windows with candles or petroleum lights, and on the west side, where people as poor as the east siders and as recently arrived in New York loyally tried to observe the Mayor's request for a general illumination of the households. The rest of the city was not given to illumination, with the exception of the great department stores, which were elaborately decorated with strings of electric lights.

---

1 One of the Educational Alliance programs.
2 I.e., flee.
3 Here the words to the pledge are repeated.
4 In the Russo-Turkish war of 1877–78, one of a series of wars between the Russian and Ottoman Empires. Constantinople is now Istanbul.
5 The Lower East Side.

c. From H.G. Wells, Chapter IX, "The Immigrant," *The Future in America: A Search After Realities* (New York: Harper & Brothers, 1906), 148–49

[Herbert George Wells (1866–1946) was a British writer later best known for his futuristic works of science fiction, such as *The Time Machine* (1895), *The Island of Doctor Moreau* (1896), *The Invisible Man* (1897), and *The War of the Worlds* (1898). In the spring of 1906 Wells travelled in the United States for two months and recorded his impressions in *The Future in America*. His discussion of immigrants reflects some of the fears about immigration common at the time, as one sees in his final summary: "I have tried to make the note of immigration grow slowly to a dominating significance in this panorama [of America], and with that, to make more and more evident my sense of the need of a creative assimilation, the cry for synthetic effort,[1] lest all this great being, this splendid promise of a new world, should decay into a vast unprogressive stagnation of unhappiness and disorder" (202). His chapter on "The Immigrant," however, includes an admiring scene of children at the Educational Alliance.]

I told these doubts of mine [about the effects of mass immigration] to a pleasant young lady of New York, who seems to find much health and a sustaining happiness in settlement work on the East Side. She scorned my doubts. "Children make better citizens than the old Americans," she said, like one who quotes a classic, and took me with her forthwith to see the central school of the Educational Alliance, that fine imposing building in East Broadway.

It's a thing I'm glad not to have missed. I recall a large cool room with a sloping floor, tier rising above tier of seats and desks, and a big class of bright-eyed Jewish children, boys and girls, each waving two little American flags to the measure of the song they sang, singing to the accompaniment of the piano on the platform beside us.

"God bless our native land," they sang with a considerable variety of accent and distinctness, but with a very real emotion.

Some of them had been in America a month, some much longer, but here they were under the auspices of the wealthy Hebrews of New York and Mr. Blaustein's[2] enthusiastic direction being Americanized. They sang of America "sweet land of liberty"; they stood up and

---

1 Effort to unite (or synthesize) immigrants into the American whole.
2 David Blaustein was appointed Superintendent of the Educational Alliance in 1898.

drilled with the little bright pretty flags; swish they crossed and swish they waved back, a waving froth of flags and flushed children's faces; and they stood up and repeated the oath of allegiance, and at the end filed tramping by me and out of the hall. The oath they take is finely worded. It runs:

"Flag [of] our great Republic, inspirer in battle, guardian of our homes, whose stars and stripes stand for bravery, purity, truth, and union, we salute thee! We, the natives of distant lands, who find rest under thy folds, do pledge our hearts, our lives, and our sacred honor to love and protect thee, our country, and the liberty of the American people forever." [...]

"It *is* touching!" whispered my guide, and I saw she had caught a faint reflection of that glow that lit the children. I told her it was the most touching thing I had seen in America.

And so it remains.

4. Documents of Various Programs at the Educational Alliance, from the Archives of the YIVO Institute for Jewish Research, New York

E D U C A T I O N A L   A L L I A N C E

197 EAST BROADWAY, NEW YORK

THE EDUCATIONAL ALLIANCE offers a free course of popular lectures and discussions on American history, government, customs and general conditions.

The lectures will be given in simple English so that persons having a slight command of the language can understand them.

While the course is open to all, it is especially designed to meet the needs of those who have attended the Public Evening Schools for Immigrants during the past season.

The course will be open on SATURDAY EVENING, APRIL 2nd, 1910, in rooms 20 and 21. Lectures begin promptly at 8.30 p. m.

PLEASE KEEP FOR REFERENCE

Card advertising a lecture series on history and government.

A Public Mass-Meeting

will be held on

Wednesday Evening, April 27th, 1910, at 8 o'clock

The following speakers will address the meeting

ON THE

cause, prevention and cure of

TUBERCULOSIS

Hon. Samuel Greenbaum, Chairman

Mr. Jacob H. Schiff

Mr. Cyrus L. Sulzberger
President of the United Hebrew Charities

Dr. J. E. Lederle
President, Board of Health

Dr. L. Rosenberg
Superintendent of Bedford Sanitarium

Dr. Maurice Fishberg

Stereopticon views will be shown describing the work of the Board of Health, the Montefiore Home, the Committee on Prevention of Tuberculosis and other organizations.

MUSIC BY MR. MAURICE NITKE

Admission free.   All Welcome.   Doors open at 7.30

NO CHILDREN WILL BE ADMITTED AT NIGHT

א פּאבליק מאסס-מיטינג

וועט אבגעהאלטען ווערען אין אוידיטאריום פון עדיוקיישאנאל אלליענס

מיטוואך אבענד, דען 27טען אפריל, 1910, 8 אוהר

פאלגענדע רעדנער וועלען אדרעסירען דעם מיטינג וועגען
דיא אורזאכע, פערמיידונג און קורירונג פון

שווינדזוכט

האנ. סעמועל גרינבאום, טשערמאן. מר. דזשייקאב ה. שיף, מר. סיירוס ל. סולצבערגער, סיקרעטאר פון דיא יוניטעד היברו טשאריטיעס, דר. י. ע. לעדערלע, פרעזידענט פון באארד אוו העלטה, דר. ל. ראזענבערג, סופעראינטענדענט פון בעדפאארד סאנאטאריום, און דר. מאריס פישבערג.

סטערעאפטישע בילדער וועלען געצייגט ווערען, בעשרייבענדיג דיא ארבייט פון באארד אוו העלטה, מאנטעפיארע האום, דיא קאמיטע צו פער-מיידען שווינדזוכט, און אנדערע ארגאניזאציאנען.

מוזיק ביי מר. מאריס ניטקע

איינטריט פריי.   אלע ווילקאמען.   דיא טיהרען עפנען זיך אום 7.30

קינדער וועלען ניט אריינגעלאזען ווערען אם אבענד.

Flyer advertising a lecture on tuberculosis.

IN THE AUDITORIUM

OF THE

EDUCATIONAL ALLIANCE

East Broadway and Jefferson Street

Concert

given by the

PUPILS OF PUBLIC SCHOOL No. 62

Grammar Intermediate Department

Mr. John S. Roberts, Principal

for the

PUPILS OF THE

Educational Alliance School of Religious Instruction

AND THEIR PARENTS

Sunday Afternoon, May 8th, 1910, at 2.30 o'clock

Program

1. a) Tannhauser March — — — *Wagner*
   b) Berceuse — — — *Godard*
   W. R. JOHNSON ORCHESTRA CLUB

2. Song: "May Morning"
   MISS BELLE BRAND

3. Blue Danube Waltz — — — *Strauss*
   ORCHESTRA CLUB

4. Violin Solos
   a) Medisation from "Thais" — — *Massenet*
   b) Gavotte — — *Gossec*
   MASTER HYMAN STARK

5. a) Old Folks at Home — — *Foster*
   b) O let us all go maying — — *Old English*
   GLEE CLUB

6. Prelude to "Traviata" — — *Verdi*
   ORCHESTRA CLUB

7. Piano Solo: Sonata Pathetique — — *Beethoven*
   MR. BENJAMIN EDISON, of the Institute of Musical Art

8. Song: "The Year's at the Spring" — *Mrs. Beach*
   MASTER ISIDOR GOLDSTEIN

9. Stars and Stripes Forever — — *Sousa*
   ORCHESTRA CLUB

Program of a concert featuring patriotic music and popular classics.

5. From Israel J. Zevin, "Melting Pot Square, 'Most Efficiently Populated Spot in World,' Welds Individuals of Many Races and Creeds to Make Real Americans," *New York Herald* (5 March 1916): 10

[Israel J. Zevin (1872–1926) wrote and compiled Yiddish folklore, in Yiddish, under the pseudonym Tashrak. "Melting Pot Square"— Seward Park in lower Manhattan—was surrounded by the Educational Alliance, the Seward Park Library, and Public School 62. Until 1903, when it became part of the New York Public Library system, the Seward Park Library was the Aguilar Free Library, a constituent member of the Educational Alliance named after Grace Aguilar (1816–47), a prominent Anglo-Jewish writer. Seward Park still looks much as Zevin describes it, although the children playing and going in and out of the library are now mostly not Jewish but of many different ethnicities. The "labor exchange" may no longer take place there, but it is common to other immigrant communities today.]

In size the park is not larger than an ordinary city block, but what it lacks in space it makes up by its wonderful compactness. In fact, the east side[1] in all is—in spite of figures[2]—merely compact, not congested. Compactness, or the efficiency of space, is utilized in the east side to its utmost. You cannot find another spot in the world of the size of this park serving so many purposes. In the first place, it is a park with real trees—a breathing spot for the people of the neighborhood and their little ones. [...]

But the most interesting feature of the park is its open air labor exchange.

At all hours of the day you will find here groups of men of various ages posed near the north side of the park, as if they were persons of leisure out for an airing. Basking in the sunshine, they stand here every clear day waiting for some one to call them to work. Among them are tailors, shirtmakers, carpenters, with their boxes of tools; painters, paper-hangers, men of all jobs and glaziers, who walk around looking wistfully at the boys in the enclosure of the gymnasium, who weeks ago abandoned baseball for football. The former game means so much to the poor glazier.

A man of prosperous appearance appears on the scene. There is a slight commotion among the jobless group. "He is a shirt manufacturer," some one comments in a whisper. The prosperous looking man hails a friend, "Come, Binem, I want you." [...]

---

1 The area is now known as the Lower East Side (of Manhattan).
2 Statistics.

Two walk away with the man, glad to find employment. The third remains with the crowd. Until Monday there are still four working days, and he may get something else by then. [...]

Coming home from school [the] children bring their English with them, and the parents have learned to understand it, even if they cannot speak it themselves. Therefore it is a very usual thing to hear a child talking to father or mother in English and the parent replying in Yiddish. [...]

The Educational Alliance is a fair example of the rule of compactness prevailing on the east side. This institution, which is of the size of an ordinary metropolitan school building,[1] has thirty-two classes in domestic arts and sciences, in which 1,489[2] scholars receive instruction, four day classes in English for adults and immigrants, in which 588 are taught, one citizens' "quiz" class, nine classes in physical training, with an attendance of 990 pupils, a reading room with an average daily attendance of 859, 100 lectures in English and Yiddish, with an average attendance of 450.

The Alliance building has under its roof 31 clubs for women and girls, a social room for girls, 35 clubs for boys, a social room for junior boys, a social room for middle aged and senior boys, a social room for adults, 25 free concerts (average attendance of 700), 204 motion picture concerts (700 being the average attendance), 424 entertainments (total attendance 274,862), and a roof garden whose average daily attendance during the hot summer months is 5,711.

---

1   As when Zevin mentions an "ordinary city block," one must keep in mind that in New York City both blocks and schools were and are quite large. In a part of the article I have not reprinted, Zevin mentions that the two public schools near Seward Park together educate 5,000 students.

2   In the microform printout that I produced at Columbia University's Butler Library, the numbers are difficult to read, and so these may be slightly in error. However, that this one is at least 1,400 is quite clear. Zevin does not list the sources of his information, but we may assume that the numbers are approximately correct and probably represent the figures for one year.

The Educational Alliance, June 2016. Photograph: Meri-Jane Rochelson.

Seward Park Library, June 2016. Photograph: Meri-Jane Rochelson.

Appendix F: Anti-Immigrant Images and Texts

1. Political Cartoons

[The first image, from an 1889 American humour magazine, shows that the metaphor of the melting pot was current considerably before it was popularized by Zangwill's play. The simian-faced "one element that won't mix" represents the Irish. The second cartoon, published in 1919, reflects growing fears that immigrants from "the world's melting pot" would bring undesirable political views and activities to the United States. Jews, for example, were often associated with Russian revolutionary activities.]

THE MORTAR OF ASSIMILATION — AND THE ONE ELEMENT THAT WON'T MIX.

C.J. Taylor, "The Mortar of Assimilation—And the One Element that Won't Mix," *Puck* (1889), n.p.

Billy Ireland, "We Can't Digest the Scum," *Columbus Dispatch* (4 March 1919), n.p. The Ohio State University Billy Ireland Cartoon Library & Museum.

2. From Edward Alsworth Ross, Chapter XII, "American Blood and Immigrant Blood," *The Old World in the New: The Significance of Past and Present Immigration to the American People* (New York: Century, 1914), 282–304

[Edward A. Ross (1866–1951) was a sociologist and eugenicist who compared the "new" immigration from southern and eastern Europe unfavourably with the "old" from northern Europe. He approved the melting-pot ideal only with lip service, to the extent that assimilation into an American type, where possible, would maintain the character of the white Anglo-Saxon founders, despite higher immigrant birthrates. In this extract, however, Ross emphasizes the eugenic (or "race"-based) arguments against increased immigration, calling upon pernicious stereotypes of the time.]

[T]he conditions of settlement of this country caused those of uncommon energy and venturesomeness to outmultiply the rest of the population. Thus came into existence the pioneering breed; and this breed increased until it is safe to estimate that fully half of white Americans with native grandparents have one or more pioneers among their ancestors. Whatever valuable race traits distinguish the American people from the parent European stocks are due to the efflorescence of this breed. Without it there would have been little in the performance of our people to arrest the attention of the world. Now we confront the melancholy spectacle of this pioneer breed being swamped and submerged by an overwhelming tide of latecomers from the old-world hive. [...] *Certainly never since the colonial era have the foreign-born and their children formed so large a proportion of the American people as at the present moment.*[1] I scanned 368 persons as they passed me in Union Square, New York, at a time when the garment-workers of the Fifth Avenue lofts were returning to their homes. Only thirty-eight of these passers-by had the type of face one would find at a county fair in the West or South. [...] [I]t is fair to say that the blood now being injected into the veins of our people is "sub-common." To one accustomed to the aspect of the normal American population, the Caliban[2] type shows up with a frequency that is startling. Observe immigrants not as they come travel-wan up the gang-plank, nor as they issue toil-begrimed from pit's mouth or mill gate, but in their gatherings, washed, combed, and in their Sunday best. You are struck by the fact that from ten to twenty per cent. are hirsute,[3] low-browed, big-faced

---

1 Italics in original, here and elsewhere in the extract.

2 The monstrous son of the witch Sycorax in Shakespeare's *The Tempest* (c. 1611).

3 Hairy.

persons of obviously low mentality. Not that they suggest evil. They simply look out of place in black clothes and stiff collar, since clearly they belong in skins, in wattled huts at the close of the Great Ice Age. These oxlike men are descendants of those *who always stayed behind.* Those in whom the soul burns with the dull, smoky flame of the pine-knot stuck to the soil, and are now thick in the sluiceways of immigration. Those in whom it burns with a clear, luminous flame have been attracted to the cities of the home land and, having prospects, have no motive to submit themselves to the hardships of the steerage. [...]

On the physical side the Hebrews are the polar opposite of our pioneer breed. Not only are they undersized and weak-muscled, but they shun bodily activity and are exceedingly sensitive to pain. Says a settlement worker: "You can't make boy scouts out of the Jews. There's not a troop of them in all New York." Another remarks: "They are absolute babies about pain. Their young fellows will scream with a hard lick." [...]

That the Mediterranean peoples are morally below the races of northern Europe is as certain as any social fact. Even when they were dirty, ferocious barbarians, these blonds[1] were truth-tellers. Be it pride or awkwardness or lack of imagination or fair-play sense, something has held them back from the nimble lying of the southern races. Immigration officials find that the different peoples are as day and night in point of veracity, and report vast trouble in extracting the truth from certain brunet[2] nationalities. [...]

Nothing less than verminous is the readiness of the Southern Europeans to prey upon their fellows. Never were British or Scandinavian immigrants so bled by fellow-countrymen as are South Italian, Greek and Semitic immigrants. Their spirit of mutual helpfulness saved them from *padrone*, "banker," and Black Hand.[3] Among our South Italians this spirit shines out only when it is a question of shielding from American justice some cut-throat of their own race. The Greek is full of tricks to skin the greenhorn.[4] A grocer will warn fellow-countrymen who have just established themselves in his town that he will have the

---

1 Immigrants from northern Europe.

2 Dark-haired.

3 Unsavoury figures among Italian immigrants: the *padrone*, often a Mafia boss, would supply Italian workers to (usually exploitative) employers; the "banker" would supply bail and other loans at extortionate rates; and the "Black Hand" was a secret criminal organization, often involved in blackmail.

4 Newly arrived immigrant. The term derives from the usage of "green" as new, young, or inexperienced, and evokes the green of new grass and the horns of young animals.

police on them for violating municipal ordinances unless they buy groceries from him. The Greek mill-hand sells the greenhorn a job, and takes his chances on the foreman giving the man work. A Greek who knows a little English will get a Greek peddler arrested in order that he may get the interpreter's fee. The Greek boot-black who has freed himself from his serfdom, instead of showing up the system, starts a place of his own, and exploits his help as mercilessly as ever he was exploited. [...]

The fewer brains they have to contribute, the lower the place immigrants take among us, and the lower the place they take, the faster they multiply. [...][1]

When a more-developed element is obliged to compete on the same economic plane with a less-developed element, the standards of cleanliness or decency or education cherished by the advanced element act on it like a slow poison. William does not leave as many children as 'Tonio, because he will not huddle his family into one room, eat macaroni off a bare board, work his wife barefoot in the field, and keep his children weeding onions instead of at school. Even moral standards may act as poison. Once the women raisin-packers at Fresno, California, were American-born. Now the American women are leaving because of the low moral tone that prevails in the working force by reason of the coming in of foreigners with lax notions of propriety. The coarseness of speech and behavior among the packers is giving raisin-packing a bad name, so that American women are quitting the work and taking the next best job. Thus the very decency of the native is a handicap to success and to fecundity. [...]

Very truly says a distinguished economist, in praise of immigration: "The cost of rearing children in the United States is rapidly rising. In many, perhaps in most cases, it is simpler, speedier, and cheaper to import labor than to breed it."[2] In like vein it is said that "a healthy immigrant lad of eighteen is a clear $1000 added to the national wealth of the United States."

Just so. "The Roman world was laughing when it died."[3] Any couple or any people that does not feel it has anything to transmit to its children may well reason in such fashion. A couple may reflect, "It is simpler, speedier, and cheaper for us to adopt orphans than to produce children of our own." A nation may reason, "Why burden

---

1 This sentence starts a section of the chapter titled "Race Suicide."

2 W.F. Willcox (1861–1964), *Papers and Proceedings of the Twenty-Fourth Annual Meeting of the American Economic Association*, Supplement to *The American Economic Review* 2.1 (March 1912): 71. I have been unable to locate the source of the quotation that follows.

3 Attributed to Salvian, a fifth-century monk.

ourselves with the rearing of children! Let them perish unborn in the womb of time. The immigrants will keep up the population." A people that has no more respect for its ancestors and no more pride of race than this deserves the extinction that surely awaits it.

3. From [William Jennings Bryan,] "The Yellow Peril," *Commoner* (6 December 1901): 1

[Chinese immigrants came to the United States, mostly through California, to work on the railroad and do other low-wage labour in the middle years of the 1800s. As labour competition increased, however, opposition to these migrants also increased, resulting in the Chinese Exclusion Act of 1882 that prohibited all immigration by Chinese labourers. The law was made permanent in 1902 and repealed only in 1943. One of its strongest proponents was William Jennings Bryan (1860–1925) a Democratic populist who ran unsuccessfully for president in 1908. He argued strenuously for the continuation of the exclusionary law, as in this page-one editorial of his Nebraska paper, *The Commoner*. In September 1908, the *Los Angeles Herald* summarized Bryan's points in its own editorial, showing the endurance of anti-Asian feeling in the 1908 campaign.]

The Chinese question is one that effects [sic] the entire country, not the Pacific Coast alone or the laboring men alone. It is true that the Pacific Coast would feel the evil effects of Chinese emigration first, and it is also true that the laboring men would come into immediate contact with oriental labor, but in its ultimate influence the subject touches all parts of the country and reaches all classes. The question is whether we are going to build up a strong, independent, upright and patriotic people and develop a civilization that will exert a helpful influence on all the world, or whether we are going to be a greedy, grasping nation, forgetful of high ideals and concerned only in the making of money.

Chinese emigration is defended by two classes of people. First, by those, comparatively few in number, who believe that universal brotherhood requires us to welcome to our shores all people of all lands. This is the sentimental argument advanced in favor of Chinese emigration. There is no more reason why we should construe brotherhood to require the admission of all people to our country than there is that we should construe brotherhood to require the dissolution of family ties. The family is a unit; it is the place where character and virtue and usefulness are developed, and from the family a good or evil influence emanates. It is not necessary nor even wise that the family environment should be broken up or that all who desire entrance should be admitted to the family circle. In a larger sense a nation is a family. It is the center for the cultivation of national character, national virtue and national usefulness. A nation is under no obligation to the outside world to admit any body or anything that would injuriously effect [sic] the national family; in fact it is under obligation to itself not to do so. The influence of the United States will be much more potent for good if we remain a homogeneous nation with all citizens in full sympathy with all other citizens. No distinct race like the Chinese can come into this country without exciting a friction and a race prejudice which will make it more difficult for us to exercise a wholesome influence upon the Chinese in China, not to speak of our influence on other nations. [...]

The second, and by far the larger class, embraces those who advocate Chinese emigration on the ground that it will furnish cheap labor for household and factory work. There is no force in the argument that is made by some that it is difficult to secure girls to do housework. If domestic service is not popular as compared with other work, it is because the pay is not sufficient to make it attractive and the remedy lies in better wages. Labor can be secured for any and every honorable position when the price is sufficient to attract it, and the demand for Chinese servants comes with poor grace from those who often spend on a single social entertainment as much as a servant's wages would amount to in an entire year. At this time when skilled and intelligent American labor is able to compete in foreign markets with the cheapest labor of the world, it is absurd to talk about the necessity for cheap factory hands. [Bryan goes on to suggest restrictions on immigration from Japan and the Philippines, as well as China.]

Appendix G: Alternatives to the Melting-Pot Model

1. From Mary Antin, *The Promised Land* (Boston: Houghton Mifflin, 1912), 206–08

[Mary Antin (1881–1949) is often taken to exemplify the immigrant who readily and eagerly assimilated to the Anglo-Saxon type. She emigrated to Boston from the Russian Empire with her family as a child, and early on began writing and publishing. The passage below, from the beginning of Chapter 10 of *The Promised Land*, "Initiation," shows how readily Antin became an American. However, she did not entirely abandon her Jewish roots; the title of her autobiography is taken from Jewish culture and religion, although in this case America is her promised land.]

It is not worth while to refer to voluminous school statistics to see just how many "green" pupils entered school last September, not knowing the days of the week in English, who next February will be declaiming patriotic verses in honor of George Washington and Abraham Lincoln, with a foreign accent, indeed, but with plenty of enthusiasm. It is enough to know that this hundred-fold miracle is common to the schools in every part of the United States where immigrants are received. [...]

I shall never have a better opportunity to make public declaration of my love for the English language. I am glad that American history runs, chapter for chapter, the way it does; for thus America came to be the country I love so dearly. I am glad, most of all, that the Americans began by being Englishmen, for thus did I come to inherit this beautiful language in which I think. It seems to me that in any other language happiness is not so sweet, logic is not so clear. I am not sure that I could believe in my neighbors as I do if I thought about them in un-English words. I could almost say that my conviction of immortality is bound up with the English of its promise. And as I am attached to my prejudices, I must love the English language!

2. From Horace M. Kallen, "Democracy Versus the Melting-Pot: A Study of American Nationality," *The Nation* (18 February 1915): 190–94; (25 February 1915): 217–20

[From the 1960s to recent times, many Americans have opposed the assimilationism in the "melting pot" metaphor, proposing instead images of a salad bowl or a mosaic to represent the cultural distinctiveness of ethnic groups in the United States. These views were anticipated, however, in the era of Zangwill's play by the American Jewish writer and philosopher Horace Meyer Kallen (1882–1974), who coined the term "cultural pluralism." His influential 1915 essay "Democracy Versus the Melting Pot" reviewed *The Old World in the New*, by Edward Alsworth Ross, an American sociologist and eugenicist who feared "race suicide" (see Appendix F2).

[From] Part I

Today the descendants of the colonists are reformulating a declaration of independence. Again, as in 1776, Americans of British ancestry find that certain possessions of theirs, which may be lumped under the word "Americanism," are in jeopardy. This is the situation which Mr. Ross's book, in common with many others, describes. The danger comes, once more, from a force across the water, but the force is this time regarded not as superior, but as inferior. The relationships of 1776 are, consequently, reversed. To conserve the inalienable rights of the colonists of 1776, it was necessary to declare all men equal; to conserve the inalienable rights of their descendants in 1914, it becomes necessary to declare all men unequal. In 1776 all men were as good as their betters; in 1914 men are permanently worse than their betters. "A nation may reason," writes Mr. Ross, "why burden ourselves with the rearing of children? Let them perish unborn in the womb of time. The immigrants will keep up the population. A people that has no more respect for its ancestors and no more pride of race than this deserves the extinction that surely awaits it."[1]

Respect for ancestors, pride of race! Time was when these would have been repudiated as the enemies of democracy, as the antithesis of the fundamentals of our republic, with its belief that "a man's a man for a' that."[2] And now they are being invoked in defence of democracy, against the "melting pot," by a sociological protagonist of the "democratic idea"! How conscious their invocation is cannot be said. But

---

1 See Appendix F.
2 From the poem with that title by Scots poet Robert Burns (1759–96); it urges that all people recognize human equality.

that they have unconsciously colored much of the social and political thinking of this country from the days of the Cincinnati[1] on, seems to me unquestionable, and even more unquestionable that this apparently sudden and explicit conscious expression of them is the effect of an actual, felt menace. Mr. Ross, in a word, is no voice crying in a wilderness. He simply utters aloud and in his own peculiar manner what is felt and spoken wherever Americans of British ancestry congregate thoughtfully [...]

In 1776 the mass of white men in the colonies were actually, with respect to one another, rather free and rather equal. I refer, not so much to the absence of great differences in wealth, as to the fact that the whites were *like-minded*. They were possessed of ethnic and cultural unity; they were homogeneous with respect to ancestry and ideals. Their century-and-a-half-old tradition as Americans was continuous with their immemorially older tradition as Britons. They did not, until the economic-political quarrel with the mother country arose, regard themselves as other than Englishmen, sharing England's dangers and England's glories [...]

Now, it happens that the preservation and development of any given type of civilization rests upon these two conditions—like-mindedness and self-consciousness. Without them art, literature—culture in any of its nobler forms—is impossible: and colonial America had a culture—chiefly of New England—but representative enough of the whole British-American life of the period. Within the area of what we now call the United States this life was not, however, the only life. Similarly animated groups of Frenchmen and Germans, in Louisiana and Pennsylvania, regarded themselves as the cultural peers of the British, and because of their own common ancestry, their like-mindedness and self-consciousness, they have retained a large measure of their individuality and spiritual autonomy to this day, after generations of unrestricted and mobile contact and a century of political union with the dominant British populations.

In the course of time the state, which began to be with the Declaration of Independence, became possessed of all the United States. French and Germans in Louisiana and Pennsylvania remained at home; but the descendants of the British colonists trekked across the continent, leaving tiny self-conscious nuclei of population in their wake, and so established ethnic and cultural standards for the whole country. Had the increase of these settlements borne the same proportion to the unit of population that it bore between 1810 and 1820, the Americans of British stock

---

1   A patriotic organization founded by French and American officers of the American Revolution.

would have numbered today over 100,000,000. The inhabitants of the country do number over 100,000,000; but they are not the children of the colonists and the pioneers; they are immigrants and the children of immigrants, and they are not British, but of all the other European stocks.

First came the Irish, integral to the polity of Great Britain, but ethnically different, Catholic in religion, fleeing from economic and political oppression, and—self-conscious and rebellious. They came seeking food and freedom, and revenge against the oppressors on the other side. Their area of settlement is chiefly the East. There they were not met with open arms. [...]

Behind the Irish came the great mass of the Germans, quite diverse in speech and customs, culturally and economically far better off than the Irish, and self-conscious, as well through oppression and political aspiration as for these other reasons. They settled inland, over a stretch of relatively continuous territory extending from western New York to the Mississippi, from Buffalo to Minneapolis, and from Minneapolis to St. Louis. Spiritually, these Germans were more akin to the American settlers than the Irish, and, indeed, although social misprision pursued them also, they were less coldly received and with less difficulty tolerated. As they made their way, greater and greater numbers of the peasant stock joined them in the Western nuclei of population, so that between the Great Lakes and the Mississippi Valley they constitute the dominant ethnic type.

Beyond them, in Minnesota, their near neighbors, the Scandinavians, prevail, and beyond these, in the mountain and mining regions, the central and eastern and southern Europeans—Slavs of various stocks, Magyars, Finns, Italians. Beyond the Rockies, cut off from the rest of the country by this natural barrier, a stratum of Americans of British ancestry balances the thinnish stratum on the Atlantic sea coast; flanked on the south by Latins and scattering groups of Asiatics, and on the north by Scandinavians. The distribution of the population upon the two coasts is not dissimilar; that upon the Atlantic littoral[1] is only less homogenous. There French-Canadians, Irish, Italians, Slavs, and Jews alternate with the American population and each other, while in the West the Americans lie between and surround the Italians, Asiatics, Germans, and Scandinavians. [...]

South of Mason and Dixon's line[2] the cities exhibit a greater homogeneity. Outside of certain regions in Texas the descendants of the native white stock, often degenerate and backward, prevail among the

---

1 Shore.

2 A line that resolved a border dispute between Pennsylvania, Maryland, and Delaware in colonial America, traditionally considered a boundary between north and south.

whites, but the whites as a whole constitute a relatively weaker proportion of the population. They live among nine million negroes, whose own mode of living tends, by its mere massiveness, to standardize the "mind" of the proletarian South in speech, manner, and the other values of social organization. [...]

The fact is that similarity of class rests upon no inevitable external condition, while similarity of nationality is inevitably intrinsic. Hence the poor of two different peoples tend to be less like-minded than the poor and the rich of the same peoples. At his core no human being, even in a "state of nature," is a mere mathematical unit of action like the "economic man." Behind him in time and tremendously in him in quality are his ancestors; around him in space are his relatives and kin, looking back with him to a remoter common ancestry. In all these he lives and moves and has his being.[1] They constitute his, literally, *natio*,[2] and in Europe every inch of his non-human environment wears the effects of their action upon it and breathes their spirit. The America he comes to, beside Europe, is nature virgin and inviolate; it does not guide him with ancestral blazings; externally he is cut off from the past. Not so internally: whatever else he changes, he cannot change his grandfather. Moreover, he comes rarely alone; he comes companioned with his fellow-nationals; and he comes to no strangers, but to kin and friend who have gone before. If he is able to excel, he soon achieves a local habitation. There he encounters the native American to whom he is a Dutchman, a Frenchy, a Mick, a wop, a dago, a hunky, or a sheeny,[3] and he encounters these others who are unlike him, dealing with him as a lower and outlandish creature. Then, be he even the rudest and most primeval peasant, heretofore totally unconscious of his nationality, of his categorical difference from other men, he must inevitably become conscious of it. Thus, in our industrial and congested towns where there are real and large contacts between immigrant nationalities the first effect appears to be an intensification of spiritual dissimilarities, always to the disadvantage of the dissimilarities.

The second generation, consequently, devotes itself feverishly to the attainment of similarity. The older social tradition is lost by attrition or thrown off for advantage. The merest externals of the new one are acquired—via the public school. But as the public school imparts

---

1 See Acts 17:28, often quoted in other contexts.

2 Latin: nation.

3 A series of ethnic slurs for various immigrant groups, fortunately now so rare that some require a note. The slurs from "Mick" to "sheeny" were derogatory terms for, respectively, people from Ireland, Italy, Spain and Portugal, central Europe and Slavic countries, and Jews. These terms are considered racist and should not be used.

it, or as the settlement imparts it, it is not really a *life*, it is an abstraction, an arrangement of words: as an historic fact, a democratic ideal of life, it is not realized at all. [...]

He remains still the Slav, the Jew, the German, or the Irish citizen of the American commonwealth. Again, in the mass, neither he nor his children nor his children's children lose their ethnic individuality. For marriage is determined by sexual selection and by propinquity, and the larger the town, the lesser the likelihood of mixed marriage. Although the gross number of such marriages is greater than it was fifty years ago, the relative proportions, in terms of variant units of population, tends, I think, to be significantly less. As the stratification of the towns echoes and stresses the stratification of the country as a whole, the likelihood of a new "American" race is remote enough, and the fear of it unnecessary. But equally remote also is the possibility of a universalization of the inwardness of the old American life. Only the externals succeed in passing over.

[From] Part II

At the present time there is no dominant American mind. Our spirit is inarticulate, not a voice, but a chorus of many voices each singing a rather different tune. How to get order out of this cacophony is the question for all those who are concerned about those things which alone justify wealth and power, concerned about justice, the arts, literature, philosophy, science. What must, what *shall* this cacophony become—a unison or a harmony? [...]

[T]he great ethnic groups of proletarians, thrown upon themselves in a new environment, generate from among themselves the other social classes which Mr. Ross misses so sadly among them: their shopkeepers, their physicians, their attorneys, their journalists, and their national and political leaders, who form the links between them and the greater American society. They develop their own literature, or become conscious of that of the mother-country. As they grow more prosperous and "Americanized," as they become free from the stigma of "foreigner," they develop group self-respect: the "wop" changes into a proud Italian, the "hunky" into an intensely nationalist Slav. They learn, or they recall, the spiritual heritage of their nationality. Their cultural abjectness gives way to cultural pride and the public schools, the libraries, and the clubs become beset with demands for texts in the national language and literature. [...]

What is the cultural outcome likely to be, under these conditions? Surely not the melting pot. [...]

The eastern neighbor of Minnesota is Wisconsin, a region of great concentration of Germans. Is it merely a political accident that the centralization of State authority and control has been possible there to a degree heretofore unknown in this country? [...] That German is the overwhelmingly predominant "foreign language" in the public schools and in the university? [...] The earliest German immigrants to America were group conscious to a high degree. They brought with them a cultural tradition and political aspiration. They wanted to found a State. If a State is to be regarded as a mode of life of the mind, they have succeeded. Their language is the predominant "foreign" one throughout the Middle West. The teaching of it is required by law in many places, southern Ohio and Indianapolis, for example.

Similar are the Irish, living in strength in Massachusetts and New York. [...]

And, finally, the Jews. [...] They come from lands of sojourn, where they have been for ages treated as foreigners, at most as semi-citizens, subject to disabilities and persecutions. [...] They come with the intention to be completely incorporated into the body-politic of the state. [...] Yet of all self-conscious peoples they are the most self-conscious. [...] [O]nce the wolf is driven from the door and the Jewish immigrant takes his place in our society a free man and an American, he tends to become all the more a Jew. The cultural unity of his race, history and background is only continued by the new life under the new conditions. [...]

Immigrants appear to pass through four phases in the course of being Americanized. In the first phase they exhibit economic eagerness, the greed of the unfed. Since external differences are a handicap in the economic struggle, they "assimilate," seeking thus to facilitate the attainment of economic independence. Once the proletarian level of such independence is reached, the process of assimilation slows down and tends to come to a stop. The immigrant group is still a national group, modified, sometimes improved, by environmental influences, but otherwise a solitary spiritual unit, which is seeking to find its way out on its own social level. This search brings to light permanent group distinctions, and the immigrant, like the Anglo-Saxon American, is thrown back upon himself and his ancestry. Then a process of dissimilation begins. The arts, life, and ideals of the nationality become central and paramount; ethnic and national differences change in status from disadvantages to distinctions. All the while the immigrant has been using the English language and behaving like an American in matters economic and political, and continues to do so. The institutions of the Republic have become the liberating cause and the background for the rise of the cultural consciousness and social autonomy of the immigrant Irishman, German, Scandinavian, Jew, Pole, or Bohemian. On the whole, Americanization has not repressed nationality. Americanization has liberated nationality.

Hence, what troubles Mr. Ross and so many other Anglo-Saxon Americans is not really inequality; what troubles them is *difference*. [...] Democratism and the Federal principle have worked together with economic greed and ethnic snobbishness to people the land with all the nationalities of Europe, and to convert the early American nation into the present American state. For in effect we are in the process of becoming a true federal state, such a state as men hope for as the outcome of the European war,[1] a great republic consisting of a federation or commonwealth of nationalities. [...]

The notion that the program [of creating a "unison"] might be realized by radical and even enforced miscegenation,[2] by the creation of the melting-pot by law, and thus the development of the new "American race," is, as Mr. Ross points out, as mystically optimistic as it is ignorant. In historic times, so far as we know, no new ethnic types have originated, and what we know of breeding gives us no assurance of the disappearance of the old types in favor of the new, only the addition of a new type, if it succeeds in surviving, to the already existing older ones. Biologically, life does not unify; biologically, life diversifies; and it is sheer ignorance to apply social analogies to biological processes. [...] The unison to be achieved cannot be a unison of ethnic types. It must be, if it is to be at all, a unison of social and historic interests, established by the complete cutting-off of the ancestral memories of our populations, the enforced, exclusive use of the English language and English and American history in the schools and in the daily life.

The attainment of the other alternative, a harmony, also requires concerted public action. But the action would do no violence to our fundamental law and the spirit of our institutions, nor to the qualities of men. It would seek simply to eliminate the waste and the stupidity of our social organization, by way of freeing and strengthening the strong forces already in operation. Starting with our existing ethnic and cultural groups, it would seek to provide conditions under which each may attain the perfection that is proper to its kind. The provision of such conditions is the primary intent of our fundamental law and the function of our institutions. And the various nationalities which compose our commonwealth must first of all learn this fact, which is perhaps, to most minds, the outstanding ideal content of "Americanism"—that democracy means self-realization through self-control, self-government, and that one is impossible without the other. [...]

What is inalienable in the life of mankind is its intrinsic positive quality—its psychophysical inheritance. Men may change their clothes, their politics, their wives, their religions, their philosophies, to a greater

---

1 World War I, which was being fought as this essay was published.
2 Intermarriage.

or lesser extent: they cannot change their grandfathers. Jews or Poles or Anglo-Saxons, would have to cease to be. The selfhood which is inalienable in them, and for the realization of which they require "inalienable" liberty, is ancestrally determined, and the happiness which they pursue has its form implied in ancestral endowment. This is what, actually, democracy in operation assumes. There are human capacities which it is the function of the state to liberate and to protect; and the failure of the state as a government means its abolition. [...]

Thus "American civilization" may come to mean the perfection of the cooperative harmonies of "European civilization," the waste, the squalor, and the distress of Europe being eliminated—a multiplicity in a unity, an orchestration of mankind. As in an orchestra, every type of instrument has its specific timbre and tonality, founded in its substance and form; as every type has its appropriate theme and melody in the whole symphony, so in society each ethnic group is the natural instrument, its spirit and culture are its theme and melody, and the harmony and dissonances and discords of them all make the symphony of civilization, with this difference: a musical symphony is written before it is played; in the symphony of civilization the playing is the writing, so that there is nothing so fixed and inevitable about its progressions as in music, so that within the limits set by nature they may vary at will, and the range and variety of the harmonies may become wider and richer and more beautiful.

But the question is, do the dominant classes in America want such a society? [Here Kallen's essay ends.]

3. From W.E.B. Du Bois, "The Economic Revolution in the South," *The Negro in the South: His Economic Progress in Relation to His Moral and Religious Development*, by Booker T. Washington and W.E. Burghardt Du Bois (Philadelphia: George W. Jacobs, 1907), 113–21

[In different ways, both opponents and proponents of immigration left African Americans out of their discussions. However, W.E.B. Du Bois (1868–1963), a sociologist, historian, and leading theorist and practitioner of black empowerment, discussed immigration in relation to his own people in one of the lectures that he and Booker T. Washington—usually his ideological opponent—presented and compiled in *The Negro in the South*. Here Du Bois examines the arrival of immigrants into a situation in which African Americans have been denied the right to vote yet are maintained as a labour force in the American South.]

[T]he South itself faced a puzzling paradox. The industrial revolution was demanding labor; it was demanding intelligent labor, while the

supposed political and social exigences of the situation called for ignorance and subserviency. It was an impossible contradiction and the
South to-day knows it.

What is it that makes a successful laboring force? It is laborers of
education and natural intelligence, reasonably satisfied with their conditions, inspired with certain ideals of life, and with a growing sense of
self-respect and self-reliance. How is the caste system of the South
influencing the Negro laborer? It is systematically restricting his development; it is restricting his education so that the public common
schools of the South except in a few cities are worse this moment than
they were twenty years ago; it is seeking to kill self-respect by putting
upon the accident of color every mark of humiliation that it can
invent; it is discouraging self-reliance by treating a class of men as
wards and children; it is killing ambition by drawing a color line
instead of a line of desert[1] and accomplishment; and finally, through
these things, it is encouraging crime, and by the unintelligent and
brutal treatment of criminals, it is developing more crime. [...]

The voice that calls foreign immigrants southward to-day is not
single but double. First, the exploiter of common labor wishes to
exploit this new labor just as formerly he exploited Negro labor. On
the other hand the far-sighted ones know that the present freedom of
labor exploitation must pass—that some time or other the industrial
system of the South must be made to conform more and more to the
growing sense of industrial justice in the North and in the civilized
world. Consequently the second object of the immigration philosopher is to make sure that, when the rights of the laborer come to be
recognized in the South, that laborer will be white, and just so far as
possible the black laborer will still be forced down below the white
laborer until he becomes thoroughly demoralized or extinct.

The query is therefore: If immigration turns toward the South as it
undoubtedly will in time, what will become of the Negro? The view of
the white world is usually that there are two possibilities. First, that the
immigrants will crush the Negro utterly; or secondly, that by competition there will come a sifting which will lead to the survival of the
best in both groups of laborers.

Let us consider these possibilities. First it is certain that so far as
the Negroes are land holders, and so far as they belong to a self-
employing, self-supplying group economy, no possible competition
from without can disturb them. I have shown already how rapidly this
system is growing. Further than that, there is a large group of Negroes
who have already gained an assured place in the national economy as

---

1 What is deserved.

artisans, servants, and laborers. The worst of these may be supplanted, but the best could not be unless there came a sudden unprecedented and improbable influx of skilled foreign labor. A slow infiltration of foreigners cannot displace the better class of Negro workers; simply because the growing labor demand of the South cannot spare them. If then it is to be merely a matter of ability to work, the result of immigration will on the whole be beneficial and will differentiate the good Negro workman from the careless and indifferent.

But one element remains to be considered, and this is political power. If the black workman is to remain disfranchised[1] while the white native and immigrant not only has the economic defense of the ballot, but the power to use it so as to hem in the Negro competitor, cow and humiliate him and force him to a lower plane, then the Negro will suffer from immigration.

It is becoming distinctly obvious to Negroes that to-day, in modern economic organization, the one thing that is giving the workman a chance is intelligence and political power, and that it is utterly impossible for a moment to suppose that the Negro in the South is going to hold his own in the new competition with immigrants if, on the one hand, the immigrant has access to the best schools of the community and has equal political power with other men to defend his rights and to assert his wishes, while, on the other hand, his black competitor is not only weighed down by past degradation, but has few or no schools and is disfranchised.

The question then as to what will happen in the South when immigration comes, is a very simple question. If the Negro is kept disfranchised and ignorant and if the new foreign immigrants are allowed access to the schools and given votes as they undoubtedly will be, then there can ensue only accentuated race hatred, the spread of poverty and disease among Negroes, the increase of crime, and the gradual murder of the eight millions of black men who live in the South except in so far as they escape North and bring their problems there as thousands will.

If on the contrary, with the coming of the immigrants to the South, there is given to the Negro equal educational opportunity and the chance to cast his vote like a man and be counted as a man in the councils of the county, city, state and nation, then there will ensue that competition between men in the industrial world which, if it is not altogether just, is at least better than slavery and serfdom.

There of course could be strong argument that the nation owes the Negro something better than harsh industrial competition just after

---

1 Deprived of the right to vote, disenfranchised.

slavery, but the Negro does not ask the payment of debts that are dead. He is perfectly willing to come into competition with immigrants from any part of the world, to welcome them as human beings and as fellows in the struggle for life, to struggle with them and for them and for a greater South and a better nation. But the black man certainly has a right to ask, when he starts into this race, that he be allowed to start with hands untied and brain unclouded.

Select Bibliography

Selected Books and Articles on Israel Zangwill and on *The Melting-Pot*

Adams, Elsie Bonita. *Israel Zangwill*. New York: Twayne, 1971.

Biale, David. "The Melting Pot and Beyond: Jews and the Politics of American Identity." *Insider/Outsider: American Jews and Multiculturalism*. Ed. David Biale, Michael Galchinsky, and Susannah Heschel. Berkeley: U of California P, 1998. 17–33.

Cheyette, Bryan. "Englishness and Extraterritoriality: British-Jewish Writing and Diaspora Culture." The Avraham Harman Institute of Contemporary Jewry, Hebrew University of Jerusalem. *Studies in Contemporary Jewry, An Annual* 12 (1996): 21–39.

——. "The Other Self: Anglo-Jewish Fiction and the Representation of Jews in England, 1875–1905." *The Making of Modern Anglo-Jewry*. Ed. David Cesarani. London: Basil Blackwell, 1990. 97–111.

Glover, David. "Liberalism, Anglo-Jewry and the Diasporic Imagination: Herbert Samuel via Israel Zangwill, 1890–1914." *The Image of the Jew in European Liberal Culture, 1789–1914*. Ed. Bryan Cheyette and Nadia Valman. London: Vallentine Mitchell, 2004. 186–216.

Harrison-Kahan, Lori. "'A Grave Experiment': Emma Wolf's Marriage Plots and the Deghettoization of American Jewish Fiction." *American Jewish History* 101.1 (2017): 5–34.

Kraus, Joe. "How *The Melting Pot* Stirred America: The Reception of Zangwill's Play and Theater's Role in the American Assimilation Experience." *MELUS* 24.3 (1999): 3–19.

Leftwich, Joseph. *Israel Zangwill*. London: James Clarke, 1957.

Nahshon, Edna, ed. *From the Ghetto to the Melting Pot: Israel Zangwill's Jewish Plays*. Detroit: Wayne State UP, 2006.

Penkower, Monty Noam. "The Kishinev Pogrom of 1903: A Turning Point in Jewish History." *Modern Judaism* 24.3 (October 2004): 187–225.

Rochelson, Meri-Jane. "Introduction." *Children of the Ghetto*. By Israel Zangwill. Detroit: Wayne State UP, 1998.

——. *A Jew in the Public Arena: The Career of Israel Zangwill*. Detroit: Wayne State UP, 2008.

——. "Language, Gender, and Ethnic Anxiety in Zangwill's *Children of the Ghetto*." *ELT: English Literature in Transition 1880–1920* 31 (1988): 399–412.

———. "'A Religion of Pots and Pans': Jewish Materialism and Spiritual Materiality in Israel Zangwill's *Children of the Ghetto*." *Victorian Vulgarity*. Ed. Susan David Bernstein and Elsie Michie. Surrey, UK; Burlington, VT: Ashgate, 2009: 119–35.

Shumsky, Neil Larry. "Zangwill's *The Melting Pot*: Ethnic Tensions on Stage." *American Quarterly* 27 (1975): 29–40.

Szuberla, Guy. "Zangwill's 'The Melting Pot' Plays Chicago." *MELUS* 20.3 (1995): 3–20.

Taubenfeld, Aviva F. *Rough Writing: Ethnic Authorship in Theodore Roosevelt's America*. New York: New York UP, 2008.

Udelson, Joseph H. *Dreamer of the Ghetto: The Life and Works of Israel Zangwill*. Tuscaloosa: U of Alabama P, 1990.

Valdez, Jessica R. "How to Write Yiddish in English, or Israel Zangwill and Multilingualism in Children of the Ghetto." *Studies in the Novel* 46.3 (2014): 315–34.

Valman, Nadia. "Little Jew Boys Made Good: Immigration, the South African War, and Anglo-Jewish Fiction." *"The Jew" in Late-Victorian and Edwardian Culture*. Ed. Eitan Bar-Yosef and Nadia Valman. Basingstoke: Palgrave Macmillan, 2009.

Winehouse, Bernard. "The Literary Career of Israel Zangwill from its Beginning Until 1898." Doctoral Dissertation, University of London, 1970.

Wohlgelernter, Maurice. *Israel Zangwill: A Study*. New York: Columbia UP, 1964.

Zatlin, Linda Gertner. *The Nineteenth-Century Anglo-Jewish Novel*. Boston: Twayne, 1981.

Selected Primary and Secondary Sources on Immigration, Ethnicity, and Assimilation from the Progressive Era to the Twenty-First Century

Addams, Jane. *Twenty Years at Hull-House with Autobiographical Notes*. New York: Macmillan, 1910.

Antin, Mary. *From Plotzk to Boston*. 1899. New York: Markus Wiener, 1986.

———. *The Promised Land*. 1912. New York: Modern Library, 2001.

Biale, David, Michael Galchinsky, and Susannah Heschel, eds. *Insider/Outsider: American Jews and Multiculturalism*. Berkeley: U of California P, 1998.

Breitzer, Susan Roth. "Uneasy Alliances: Hull House, the Garment Workers Strikes, and the Jews of Chicago." *Indiana Magazine of History* 106.1 (March 2010): 40–70.

Cadle, Nathaniel. *The Mediating Nation: Late American Realism, Globalization, and the Progressive State*. Chapel Hill: U of North Carolina P, 2014.

Cahan, Abraham. *The Rise of David Levinsky*. 1917. Ed. Jules Chametzky. New York: Penguin, 1993.

——. *Yekl and The Imported Bridegroom and Other Stories of Yiddish New York*. New York: Dover, 1970.

Deaux, Kay. *To Be an Immigrant*. New York: Russell Sage Foundation, 2006.

Diner, Hasia R. *Lower East Side Memories: A Jewish Place in America*. Princeton, NJ: Princeton UP, 2000.

Du Bois, W.E.B. *The Souls of Black Folk*. 1903. Ed. Henry Louis Gates Jr. and Terri Hume Oliver. New York: Norton, 1999.

Eiselein, Gregory, ed. *Emma Lazarus: Selected Poems and Other Writings*. Peterborough, ON: Broadview P, 2002.

Freedman, Jonathan. *Klezmer America: Jewishness, Ethnicity, Modernity*. New York: Columbia UP, 2008.

Gartner, Lloyd P. *American and British Jews in the Age of the Great Migration*. London: Vallentine Mitchell, 2009.

Gilman, Sander L. "Are Jews Musical? Historical Notes on the Question of Jewish Musical Modernism and Nationalism." *Modern Judaism* 28.3 (October 2008): 239–56.

Gleason, Philip. "The Melting Pot: Symbol of Fusion or Confusion?" *American Quarterly* 16.1 (1964): 20–46.

Gordon, Milton M. *Assimilation in American Life: The Role of Race, Religion, and National Origins*. New York: Oxford UP, 1964.

Greene, Daniel. *The Jewish Origins of Cultural Pluralism: The Menorah Association and American Diversity*. Bloomington: Indiana UP, 2011.

Haskin, Frederic J. *The Immigrant: An Asset and a Liability*. New York: Fleming H. Revell, 1913.

Higham, John. *Strangers in the Land: Patterns of American Nativism 1860–1925*. 1955. New Brunswick, NJ: Rutgers UP, 1988.

Kazal, Russell A. "Revisiting Assimilation: The Rise, Fall, and Reappraisal of a Concept in American Ethnic History." *The American Historical Review* 100.2 (April 1995): 437–71.

Lazarus, Emma. *"The New Colossus," by Emma Lazarus. An Interactive Poem Annotated by Esther Schor*. http://nextbookpress.com/new-colossus/.

Lissak, Rivka Shpak. *Pluralism & Progressives: Hull House and the New Immigrants, 1890–1919*. Chicago: U of Chicago P, 1989.

Sollors, Werner. *Beyond Ethnicity: Consent and Descent in American Culture*. New York: Oxford UP, 1986.

———, ed. *Theories of Ethnicity: A Classical Reader*. New York: New York UP, 1996.

Taubenfeld, Aviva F. *Rough Writing: Ethnic Authorship in Theodore Roosevelt's America*. New York: New York UP, 2008.

Yezierska, Anzia. *Bread Givers*. 1925. New York: Persea Books, 1999.

From the Publisher

A name never says it all, but the word "Broadview" expresses a good deal of the philosophy behind our company. We are open to a broad range of academic approaches and political viewpoints. We pay attention to the broad impact book publishing and book printing has in the wider world; for some years now we have used 100% recycled paper for most titles. Our publishing program is internationally oriented and broad-ranging. Our individual titles often appeal to a broad readership too; many are of interest as much to general readers as to academics and students.

Founded in 1985, Broadview remains a fully independent company owned by its shareholders—not an imprint or subsidiary of a larger multinational.

For the most accurate information on our books (including information on pricing, editions, and formats) please visit our website at www.broadviewpress.com. Our print books and ebooks are also available for sale on our site.

broadview press
www.broadviewpress.com

The interior of this book is printed on 100% recycled paper.